The King's Highway

and Some Detours

by Dr. Lee R. Minton

KINGSLEY BOOKS
NASHVILLE, TENNESSEE

This copy is number _____

of a limited edition of 1,000 books.

Published by Kingsley Book, P.O. Box 121584, Nashville, Tennessee 37212.

Back cover photo of Dr. Lee Minton is when he was Grand Marshall of the Fourth of July parade on Pawleys Island, 2001.

Map on page 18 courtesy of Melissa Lang.

Typography and design by Geoffrey D. Stone, Nashville, Tennessee.

ISBN: 0-9713499-0-8

Printed in the United States of America
1 2 3 4 5   05 04 03 02 01

CONTENTS

PART THREE: GOING PLACES

Biting my truant pen
Beating myself for spite.
"Fool," said my muse to me,
"Look in thy heart and write."
                    Sir Phillip Sidney
                    "Sonnet" 1591

FOREWORD

$\mathcal{L}$ee Minton is one of the most generous men I know. He spent a quarter of a century serving people of middle Tennessee as an ophthalmologist in Nashville. When he retired from practicing medicine at age fifty, his life of service did not end; it simply went in new directions. Those new directions have enriched the lives of nearly everyone with whom he has come into contact. For fourteen years he divided his residence between London and Pawleys Island, South Carolina, before making the latter his full-time home. I have been the beneficiary of his friendship and hospitality at Pawleys for more than a decade.

Lee Minton's generous spirit has revealed itself in many ways, some private and some public. The most public expression was his founding of the Pawleys Island Festival of Music and Art in 1991. Financed by the Minton Foundation, the festival began as a trans-Atlantic affair, featuring operatic, choral, and instrumental performances by American and British artists. Continuing an earlier tradition, he included an evening called "Eine Kleine Nachtmusik" that combined classical and some popular music forms. From the start, he included in the festival the great African-American spiritual and gospel music that flourishes locally; it was performed by traditional artists from up and down the coast—the roots of the spiritual. Later, he added an evening of vernacular music from the Anglo-American tradition—Bluegrass on the Beach. Over the years the roster of the performers at this festival has included such distinguished artists as the noted English choral conductor John Hoban, the Metropolitan Opera conductor John Nelson, sopranos Jennifer Welch and Martina Arroyo, and baritone Tom Fox. Lee has organized the Miracles of Zion, a combination of singing groups from two local African-American churches, as well as the young Waccamaw Strings, providing the local elementary school with their violins. He has also organized the Pawleys Island Chamber Orchestra and a pops orchestra, both conducted by the young Russian-American maestro, Mikhail Agrest.

Quieter and more anonymous expressions of Lee Minton's generous spirit have been his physical and financial role in rebuilding the African-American community of McClellanville after the devastating effects of Hurricane Hugo in 1989. Closely related was his subsequent leading role in organizing a successful Boy Scout program, a community center, and soccer teams in McClellanville.

Now, in this book, we all become his friends and the beneficiaries of his memories of his life in London and Pawleys Island and of his travels to such varied destinations as Nepal, Turkey, Egypt, Italy, Burma, British Columbia, Alaska, East Germany, and the Galapagos Islands. He has even included several archaeological ventures in the Mediterranean area. What a life it has been! Minton's stories of his life and the places he has lived are unforgettable.

I knew that Lee was the author of professional articles in medical journals and related publications. And I already knew that he was a great conversationalist—on rare occasions a deft raconteur but more often a gifted listener, the kind that elicits more stories than he tells. But I was unprepared for what I found in the pages of Minton's manuscript. The stories in this volume are the work of a skilled literary artist, a master of the short story. He wears his sophistication lightly, and his stories can be read for light entertainment. But they are more than that. He structures his stories with great skill, subtly foreshadowing here and adding a delightful surprise there. His pacing is superb—sometimes brisk, some-times leisurely, sometimes playing with time to build suspense. Perhaps it is too much to praise the author's true stories for their ability to create great plots or memorable characters. But we all have read history books full of people and events that were real but that the author was unable to render believable. Lee Minton characterizes the real people in his true stories with great perception yet deceptive simplicity, and they are so believable they almost step from the pages. While he does not "create" his plots in the sense that a writer of fiction does, Lee is himself an influential actor in most of them. To say that when he writes his stories he does not invent his plots is not to say that he had no role in making them turn out as they did, either in life or on the page. The manuscript is filled with local history and nature woven masterfully into his stories.

It is not easy to transform real events that actually happened to real people into believable and enjoyable stories without falsifying them in the process. But Lee Minton has done just that in this book, which is his great artistic achievement.

Dr. Charles Joyner

ACKNOWLEDGMENTS

Many people have helped in the creation of this book. Melissa Lang deserves significant credit for her encouragement. She was also helpful in editing and typing the manuscript. I also thank Heather Steere for tolerating my indecisions in completing the typing of this work. I am also grateful for the opinions and suggestions of the many people who read the manuscript, including Dr. Philip Nichol, Charles Swenson, and Mayor Bill Otis. A tribute also goes to my late friend, Dick Crayton, who taught me much about Pawleys Island and the Waccamaw Neck. A special thanks goes to my friends from around the world, who by their being, have contributed to this book.

INTRODUCTION

$\mathcal{T}$hese are all true stories of my life here in South Carolina near the coastal highway—Route 17—which runs very close to sections of the old road known for two hundred years as The King's Highway, and about adventures and experiences in many other parts of the world.

Life moved at a different and faster pace after I retired from my ophthalmology practice in Nashville, Tennessee. I was fifty and far too young to retire, but this was something I had promised myself after coronary artery bypass surgery four years earlier. My self esteem did not hinge on doing more eye surgery.

I broke the Nashville umbilical cord by buying a home on Pawleys Island, South Carolina—the same house I had vacationed in for five years. As I was settling into life on this island, I was accepted into Christie's Fine Arts School in London for an academic year. During that time, a second floor was added to the Duck's Nest, as my island home was called.

The stories in the first section of this book tell of my experiences while living on Pawleys Island and the interactions with locals. Although I have lived here for twenty-five years, the locals still don't consider me to be "native," as my roots here are not deep enough. On Pawleys, nature has become a part of my life and I write about what is around me, whether it be the Sanderlings, the Wood Storks, or my two Dalmatians, Tom Jones and John Brown.

The next group of stories concerns my years in London. Soon after arriving, there I was invited to lunch by Sir John Miller at the Crown Equerry House of the Royal Mews. The visit with Sir John lasted for four years. I resided on the top floor of this John Nash house until this proper gentleman and highly decorated military officer finally retired after twenty-five years service to Her Majesty and moved to the family home, Shotover House, near Oxford. During this period, my calling card read on the left, "The Crown Equerry House, The Royal Mews, Buckingham Palace," and on the right, "The Duck's Nest, General Delivery, Pawleys Island, South Carolina."

Before leaving the Crown Equerry House, I bought a residence at No. 6 Eaton Square two blocks away. Sean Connery, my neighbor upstairs, declared that I was the first person ever to move "down" to Eaton Square. During the next ten years I divided my time between London and South Carolina and also, during a two-year period, spent time in Georgetown, Washington, DC, where I had another home.

The contrast between Pawleys Island and London could not have been more pronounced. National Geographic Traveler has called Pawleys Island "a laid-back spit of land that still looks and feels like a 1950s family getaway—it never changes." A northern newspaper has written of Pawleys: "The look of Pawleys Island is striking for what is absent. Travelers will find no high-rise hotels, no neon signs, no concession stands, no amusement parks, no shops of any kind. A vacation on this history-rich island refreshes the spirit and restores the soul." I didn't want to change this image but felt comfortable starting a music and arts festival over on the mainland, which is now in its eleventh year. I have recently formed a chamber orchestra, a pops orchestra, and have joined two African-American church singing groups into the Pawleys Island Miracles of Zion. But our image is still the same. They call us "arrogantly shabby."

Enough has been written about London and I would not attempt to add to it, but life at the Crown Equerry House of the Royal Mews added another dimension to my life. Living at this address, I attended, and was expected to attend, the Queen's birthday celebration, "Trooping the Colour," the Queen's Garden Party and other notable annual events such as Royal Ascot and the Derby, for which I was privileged to be included in the Royal Enclosure. I am not particularly interested in the racing of horses, and I must confess that I attended these events because of the champagne picnics before and after.

I took advantage of the London arts scene and frequently attended sales at Christie's, Sotheby's, and Phillip's auction houses. And my interest in music did not suffer. After hosting ten years of "Eine Kleine Nachtmusik" in Nashville, I revived this tradition across the Atlantic, utilizing young musicians from the Royal Academy of Music, Guildhall School of Music, and Purcell School of Music. These events took place in progressively larger venues from the Warwick Arts Trust, to Leighton House in Holland Park, to Lambeth Palace, and finally to St. James's Palace, always raising funds for charities. These concerts culminated in Florence, Italy, where I organized and sponsored two concerts to commemorate the bicentennial of Rossini at the American Consulate and at the Palazzo Perugi.

I think my restless nature will be rather apparent from the "Going Places" section of this book. In none of my narrations do I mention five "children"— not biologically mine—who have been under my wing since they were teenagers or before. These now-grown "children" include an ophthalmic assistant, an orthopedic surgeon, a corporate lawyer, an ex-professional baseball player turned businessman, and a foremost sports attorney, who died in a tragic airplane accident two months after helping to celebrate my seventieth birthday. These "children" have been on my mind at many bends of rivers across the world, from the Tatshenshini in Alaska to the Irrawaddy in Burma, to the frozen Elba in East Germany.

I have kept diaries over the years, and through reading them I have enjoyed reliving all these experiences. But the first five decades await me and some day I will try to recall those formative years.

PART ONE

Around Pawleys Island

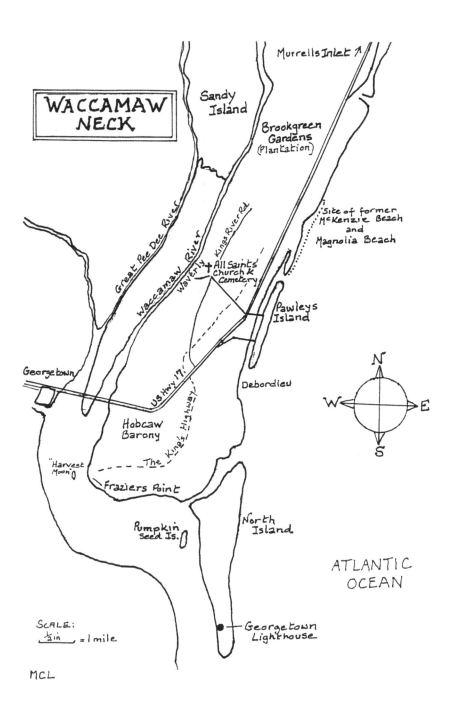

WACCAMAW NECK

Murrells Inlet ↗

Sandy Island

Brookgreen Gardens (Plantation)

Great Pee Dee River

Waccamaw River

Kings River Rd.

Waverly

Site of former McKenzie Beach and Magnolia Beach

† All Saints' Church & Cemetery

Pawleys Island

Georgetown

US Hwy 17

Debordieu

Hobcaw Barony

The Kings' Highway

"Harvest Moon" ⸰

Fraziers Point

Pumpkin Seed Is.

North Island

N
W   E
S

ATLANTIC OCEAN

SCALE:
½ in = 1 mile

● — Georgetown Lighthouse

MCL

OUR STAGE AND OUR PLAY

"All the world's a stage and all the men and women merely players. They have their exits and their entrances."

—Shakespeare, "As You Like It"

Our stage is a little island one house wide and three miles long and part of what some call the "Grand Strand" on the coast of South Carolina. Some advertisements say Pawleys Island is the oldest vacation spot on the Atlantic coast. We doubt that but go along with it.

This stage has two entrances and two exits—a north and a south causeway, each crossing the creek and marsh leading over to the mainland and to Route 17, a road they used to call the King's Highway. The sets on this stage have been kept simple: some old, shabby, wind-blown houses along with a few new ones. Here and there we have things called "Historical Houses," like Governor Robert F. W. Allston's place and old Col. Joshua Ward's house, Pawleys House, Liberty Lodge, and Pelican Inn, which they say was built by Renty Tucker, a nineteenth century African-American carpenter. There are about seven or eight of these places, most dating from the mid 1800s. They have important-looking signs out front telling visitors about who lived there.

Over on the creek there's a church building that looks like an asbestos covered box with a little cross sticking up on it. This is where folks get married, and only volunteers can preach on Sunday to church-goers who don't wear neckties. It has an out-of-tune piano, but it works for us as we sing hymns like "Holy, Holy, Holy" and "Faith of our Fathers."

Visitors notice the crabbing docks running out into the creek and ask about them. We tell them that they are for crabbing when actually it is where we go to sit and think or to watch the sunset or to watch the stars on a clear night. To outsiders they're not for anything much, but to us, they're a source of inspiration. But the ocean out there is the backdrop lit up by the sun, and the moon when it is bright enough.

Our stage is rickety and old. It has been here for millennia, but used by people like us for only three hundred years. It shakes with little tremors sometimes, but I suppose it always has. This shaking makes visitors nervous when they're trying to go to sleep, but we don't pay much attention. When they mention it the next day, we change the subject.

For our day to day entertainment, we have a deputy sheriff named Claude Roundtree to keep order, a weekly newspaper to keep us informed, and a United States Post Office on the mainland. The post office visit is a big event of the day. This is not just where we get mail, but it is also where we get our "How you doins" from friends and neighbors, even from people we don't know.

Over the years this old stage has been used by its share of characters like the Gray Man, whom some say still walks the beach before great storms. We have impressive special effects like hurricane Hazel of 1954, and hurricane Hugo that nearly blew us away in 1989.

Instead of Percival and George Pawley, today our main characters are Dick Crayton, Uncle Zachary Allston, Page Oberlin (the lady innkeeper), and Sumwalt Sawdo, who runs the filling station. Then there's the usual supporting cast. We have Doc Luckenchuk who moved here several years ago from Biloxi, retiring so that he could run a boarding house up on the north end of the island. There is talk that he'll run for mayor next year. There's Able Calhoun, our dependable garbage collector who says that he's related to Washington Allston, the painter who came from Brookgreen Plantation two hundred years ago. And there's Yum Yum Young who runs the barbecue place on Route 17.

Besides all these people, ghosts, and storms, we have many extras in the wildlife. There are a lot of willets living along our shore and they're here the year round as are the rare little sand doves and the wood storks who visit the mud faults on the creek. The cardinals add a touch of red to the stage. Some of these extras are only transient visitors, like the tiny sanderlings who stop off in the spring and fall as they come and go from the Arctic. The purple martin have a longer role in our play. Each spring they fly up here from the Amazon River basin and live in the houses and gourds we put up. They catch the mosquitoes, lay eggs, and hatch chicks that they drag back to the Amazon in early July.

Bigger decoration comes from the tracks of loggerhead turtles who visit during the middle of the night to dig holes in the edge of the dune where they lay eggs. Some of our local folk mark these nests and at the proper time, get up in the dark to help their babies find their way to the ocean. Hopefully, one or two might survive to return from we-don't-know-where in twenty five years to make more tracks across our stage. We remind ourselves that the wildlife have a certain priority here because they had roles in this play long before we came along. Since the main characters have arrived, let's take a closer look.

Sumwalt Sawdo has run a filling station across the causeway on Route 17 for over forty years, six or seven days a week. Short, bald, and fat, Sumwalt hasn't changed since I've known him. Dick Crayton declares that he hasn't changed since he was a tattletale, snotty-nosed boy growing up in Georgetown. We buy gas from Sumwalt because he keeps a spare set of our house keys and is always accommodating. He tells us when the air is low in our tires and warns us about the weather. When the law isn't looking, Sumwalt will sell us Waccamaw River caviar, but he looks to the right and the left before he does this because sturgeon fishing is banned on our rivers. His wife, Eileen, runs the cash register, ringing things up so we know that we've bought something. They say she can adjust the volume of the cash register's ring by pressing a button under her foot. Sumwalt stands there with a stubby unlit King Edward cigar clutched between his teeth, occasionally taking it out to lick his lips and smile. He gives a big grin when the register rings louder. We'd be lost without Sumwalt and Eileen.

Dick Crayton was born around here about eighty years ago, and he's been here ever since, except for a tour of duty in the U.S. Navy during World War II. He went out to the Pacific as a boiler mechanic. Dick says that he's been over to Columbia twice: once in 1939 to see Evelyn play her magic violin with the All-Girl Orchestra when somebody by the name of Fitz Towny directed the orchestra and a second time after the war, but he can't remember why.

Dick's physical appearance is unforgettable. He is salty, craggy, and a good bit weatherworn. The lines on his face look like watered ready-to-plant sweet potato roots. His hands tell a story. They're rough, callused, and covered with broad freckles, frog like. His fingernails are gray and bruised because he's apt to hammer them while building joggling boards, crabbing docks, and boats, and when repairing our houses. Dick also tends a mulberry tree and a vegetable garden over on the old Waverly Plantation. He gives away most of what he grows, leaving things like turnip greens on your porch. He's as easy to spot as our white chapel on the creek, driving a 1981 blue Ford pick-up truck. He always wears a well-ventilated straw hat, clean khaki trousers, a khaki shirt, and worn white tennis shoes. Dick smokes, or pretends to smoke, a pipe which he lights frequently, particularly when he's orating or tale telling. His companion is Homelite, a flea-encrusted mongrel he found over on Shell Road. Homelite, who does balloon tricks, used to growl at and bite anybody who came near Dick, but he's getting old and is not as vicious now. Sometimes he brings his wife's dog Titus, named for Rembrandt's son. Dick claims that Titus gives him more status, but we pay no attention to such comments because we know that Dick already has more status than Uncle Zachary Allston has sturgeon eggs.

Page Oberlin, who has a brown Labrador retriever named Macha and an opera-singing parrot called Gomez, is another of our main characters. Page is the lady who runs the Sea View Inn next door to the Duck's Nest where I live. Page came from somewhere in North Carolina as a little girl to vacation at this inn. Now she owns the place and has raised two or three girls and a boy or so there. She not only runs the inn, she's also on the town council and aims to keep the island as civilized as it's always been. Page is the one the *New York Times* reporter interviewed when he visited here. But she doesn't stop with innkeeping and politicking; she's also a writer and is now working on a novel about the natives she lived with in Guatemala. She is interested in nature and knows the difference between a spotted sandpiper and a willet and knows that a cloudless sulfur moth is not an ordinary butterfly. In the kitchen, by just looking, she can tell that a pinch of sugar has been left out of the turnip greens. When Page goes down to Charleston to the Spoleto Festival, she knows if the violinist hits a wrong note in the coda of a Bartok Quartet. She's our Renaissance woman. And, oh yes, she's a tennis player who has no interest in Tuesday morning ladies' doubles at the country club. She plays singles and doesn't run around her back-hands. Page Oberlin doesn't run around anything!

It would take too long to describe all the supporting cast, such as the people who are summer visitors. There were the folks who used to come here with their families and slaves to escape the "summer fever" on their inland plantations years ago. Now people come here from places like Atlanta, Nashville, and Spartanburg. Instead of Summer Fever, they're escaping T.M.P. (Too Many People), concrete, and their com-puters. Here on the island they have important supporting roles to play, like crabbing over on the creek, kite flying, and fishing for flounder from the causeways. Just as Shakespeare wrote, "They have their exits and their entrances." The characters on this little island stage have come and gone for three hundred years and no doubt others will do so for the next three hundred, unless a hurricane blows the island away.

THE KING'S HIGHWAY

While driving down to Yum Yum Young's barbecue place on Route 17, I thought about how important this highway is to us. This road was an Indian trail four hundred years ago. Now, it is simply

Route 17, and it takes a prominent position in our lives. It is the road we use when going to Yum Yum's, to Sumwalt's Filling Station and to the U.S. Post Office. It is also the road we use when going to more distant places like Georgetown, Awandaw, and over to Shulerville in the Francis Marion Forest.

I think that a highway this important deserves a more noble name than Route 17, which is altogether too sterile and mundane. When Britain colonized the land, it had the name "King's Highway," which is much more becoming to its status. The route has experienced important moments during its history, moments any highway would be proud of and that not many highways can boast. According to historical record, the Marquis de Lafayette journeyed northward on this highway in 1777 after landing at North Island just south of Pawleys Island. The ship had been blown off course on its way from France to Philadelphia. The Marquis wrote in his diary of the beauty and wildness along the King's Highway. He thought it so special that he came back down it in 1824 when visiting the South after his return from France.

Perhaps after 1791 the King's Highway should have become the President's Highway, since no king had ever set foot on it, and, more significantly, it was the year that President George Washington used the route to visit the South.

President Washington was not the only president to use the King's Highway. In 1819, President James Monroe traveled it on his way to visit Mary Allston and her new husband, Benjamin Huger, at Prospect Hill Plantation. This property, just south of Pawleys Island, had become a showplace with its gardens and an English gardener. Mary married her cousin Thomas Allston, but he died shortly after "The Big House" was completed. When she heard that President Monroe was going to visit, she married one of the Huger boys so that she would have something to show along with the house.

Twenty-five years later, in 1842, a year after he left office, the eighth president, Martin Van Buren, came down the King's Highway. He visited some old political cronies in Georgetown, trying to gather support for another nomination. He was still licking his wounds from his defeat in 1840. Halfheartedly, he was wined and dined in Georgetown.

In 1894, the King's Highway was graced by yet another president, Grover Cleveland, who rode down it towards the end of his second term. He came here under the pretense of going duck hunting, but some say that he came down to escape Washington after the Panic of 1893. Others say he came here to see political friends, the Republic "mugwumps" of Georgetown who had helped him to get elected. One of them, Edward Alexander, took him duck hunting, but he fell out of the boat. It took four of Alexander's ex-slaves to pull him out of the mire. He weighed 289 pounds.

Prime Minister Winston Churchill and his daughter, Diana, visited Bernard Baruch at Hobcaw, just south of Pawleys. They came over from Bermuda in the early forties but never set foot on our highway. They came by boat, anchored at Hobcaw's landing, and stayed only three days, so we cannot count them as Highway visitors.

President Franklin Roosevelt's visit is another story. In 1944, he came here by train, ending up south of Florence. Then, he drove by car down to Hobcaw Barony to visit Bernard Baruch for three weeks. Eleanor had other fish to fry during this period. She never graced the King's Highway with her presence.

But it was President George Washington's visit that was talked about around here for years and years. When things had settled down after the Revolution, President Washington decided it was time to come to the South to get some sun and visit the folks who had helped vanquish the British. He made the trip in a stage coach, setting out in early April 1791 from Mt. Vernon southward through Wilmington. He had been on the road for nearly two weeks and fatigue was eating on him, especially after coming through Myrtle Beach, which was called Wither's Swashes at the time. He had breakfast at the Vereens' place, and then he stopped and had a late lunch with some of the Pawleys who were scattered around Murrell's Inlet.

Dr. Henry Collins Flagg, who lived on down King's Highway at Brookgreen Plantation, somehow found out that the Father of Our Country was in the vicinity. He had finished house calls early that afternoon and announced to his wife, Rachel, that he would go up to the King's Highway, "flagg" down the president, and ask him to spend the night. One can imagine their conversation and how the visit played out: "Lordy, Henry, you can't do that. We don't have much around the house to feed him. You're always dragging people in here."

"Now Rachel, don't get hot under the collar. They say he's not particular about what he eats. We'll show him some southern hospitality and he can eat whatever you were going to fix tonight. You can freshen up a bit, and I'll go up to the highway and wait for him." Before getting on his horse, Dr. Flagg added, "I may be from Rhode Island, but I'll show him what hospitality is about."

Rachel leaned against the front door, still complaining, as Dr. Flagg rode off. She said one word, "Mercy," before going back in to start straightening up the living room. She moved things about, gathered up some toys strewn about, and then went to the yard to get the children, Polly and Benjamin. She took a damp cloth and rubbed hard at their faces. "What is it, Mamma?" Polly asked as Rachel put out some clean clothes.

"Don't ask questions, but if you have to know, your Daddy's gone up to the highway. He may bring back the Father of Our Country. Hurry and get into this clean dress."

Her brother stood there looking confused. "Ben, get into some clean overalls."

Before Rachel could do much more than smooth her hair, President Washington and her husband stood in the doorway grinning from ear to ear. She didn't mean for it to be heard, but she said again, "Mercy," and then stuck out her hand welcome the visitor.

Dr. Flagg carried President Washington's satchel upstairs and showed the guest to the bedroom where he would wash up. Rachel motioned for her husband to come back down. She took him by the elbow and said, "Now look here, Henry. You've got to occupy him while I make supper." They went into the living room, and she pointed towards the best chair. "Sit him down right there. Ask him about Martha's migraines. Ask him how the distillery is doing at Mt. Vernon. Inquire about Ben Franklin's kite flying. Take him outside and show him the early cherry tomato plant." She had more instructions, but the president was coming down, so she whispered to her husband, "Tell him about Little Washington. Tell him that we've got an eleven-year-old boy in school in Rhode Island who's named after him."

Rachel pushed the peeping kids out of the way and went into the kitchen. She yelled for Uncle Jeremiah, "Go kill a chicken!"

The president was pleased with this visit and got up early the next morning. Rachel put out a big breakfast, and he ate all of it: sausage with milk gravy, grits, hoecakes, scrambled eggs, and ham. He gathered up his things and gave Rachel a big hug. Before getting into his carriage, he stopped and reached into his pocket for a penny for Polly and Benjamin. They all stood at the doorway and waved as his carriage drove off down the driveway.

President Washington's carriage turned right onto the King's Highway. Driving southward, he passed by where Yum Yum's barbecue place is now. Late that morning, he turned into Clifton Plantation where Colonel William and Mary Allston awaited him for lunch. There was some pleasing conversation, particularly with the Colonel's son, Joseph, who by then was courting Theodosia Burr, the daughter of Aaron Burr. Washington did not linger at Clifton because he was expected in Georgetown late in the afternoon.

Colonel Allston accompanied the president back to the King's Highway, and they went on to what is now Frazier's Point on the Waccamaw. Some say that he got into a boat rowed by the captains of vessels in Georgetown Harbor. Some say they were dressed in round hats trimmed with gold lace, blue coats, and white jackets. But President Washington doesn't mention such things. He simply wrote in his diary, "We crossed the Waggamaw [sic] to Georgetown by descending the river three miles." They arrived at the foot of Broad Street in Georgetown where another Allston met him. He spent the night with Benjamin and Charlotte Allston. Before supper, they took him to the Masons' Lodge No. 16, where there was a great fanfare. By this time, the president was exhausted, but he managed to hold up a glass as they toasted the Federal Government, the United States of America, France, Lafayette, *and* Greece. Then Colonel Allston proposed a toast to their august visitor.

President Washington got up at daybreak the following day and made his way southward on the highway to Hampton Plantation. It would be a long day because there were three more rivers to cross. Almost before he vanished into the cloud of dust, Charlotte Allston was painting a sign to be put on her porch, "President George Washington slept here."

With all this attention, the King's Highway certainly had it over the other roads of South Carolina. It's too bad that numbers came along. I'd feel much more noble going to Yum Yum's on the King's Highway rather than on Route 17. But numbers are progress, and although we're shabby and arrogant, we wouldn't want to be left behind. Yum Yum would agree to this and, no doubt, so would President George Washington.

A GEOGRAPHY LESSON

*D*ick Crayton comes over to the island on Wednesdays to work around the house. I like to work with him because he's knowledgeable about almost everything from hurricanes and storms to bird habits and local geography.

Yesterday Dick came over and was in one of his talkative moods. I assigned him the job of taking down the purple martin house so that it might be cleaned from this year's nesting. He cussed the rusty bolt that holds up the four-by-four, then asked me to go and fetch the WD 40. While he sprayed the bolt there were several uncomplimentary comments about the golf course developers and how they were cutting too many of our trees and how all these golf courses added to the traffic on Route 17. He complained about the Yankee golfers and how they cluttered all the restaurants and talked too much. He was certainly in one of his complaining moods, so once we had cleaned the old nest from the martin house, I tried to change the subject. I brought our conversation around to geography, saying that I was still relatively new to this area and didn't fully understand the difference between Waccamaw Neck and Low Country or between Long Bay and Grand Strand. We were near the beach, so Dick asked me to come with him and he would give me a geography lesson. He took a screwdriver from his tool case and started explaining by drawing lines in the sand. He drew Pawleys Island, the mainland down to Winyah Bay, and then made at attempt to draw the Waccamaw River running roughly north and south. Pointing the screwdriver, he explained that the Waccamaw Neck is the narrow strip of land that extends from Winyah Bay near Georgetown in the south, northward about thirty-five miles to include the land between the Waccamaw River, and eastward over to the Atlantic Ocean. He explained that "the neck" is no wider than four miles at any point, its highest elevation is twenty feet, and it is bounded on the east by salt water and marshes and on the west by the river with its old ricefields and forests. When I asked him what *Waccamaw* meant, he said, "Damned if I know, and nobody else knows either. But there's an Indian word like this that means 'coming and going,' and it also means 'milky water.' You take your pick and you'll probably still be wrong. Maybe it means 'land between the waters' That would be logical, if logic still exists."

Then I asked him what is meant by the "Low Country." He drew more lines with the screwdriver explaining that Waccamaw Neck is the epicenter of a much larger area: the so-called Low Country, which is the coastal plain of South Carolina, extending sixty miles inland from east to west. He pointed northward and said, "It goes from Horry County all the way down southward to the Savannah River." He paused and added, "A few thousand years ago all of this was covered by the ocean, and if that ice cap keeps melting, she'll go under again. Even the frogs will be strangled." Just as I was trying to imagine a strangled frog, Dick pointed to the sand again, to the coast line he had drawn, and explained that Long Bay is not much of a bay at all. Rather it is an inward depression of the coast line reaching from Little River, north of Myrtle Beach, and south to Winyah Bay. "You're having to search for a bay to call this one a bay," he commented. I asked him about The Grand Strand. He was quick to say that most if it isn't so grand and that it is mainly a big golf course that extends from North Carolina southward to include the islands and inlets down to Charleston County. In typical Dick Crayton fashion he added, "All that grand stuff is to attract the tourists and golfers. It's about as grand as my old pick-up."

With the tide coming up, Dick's beach map was about to be erased and I was saturated with geography. I left Dick to repair the cypress boardwalk and drove to the post office. I was thinking about how ungrand the strand is.

BLESSINGS AT PAWLEYS ISLAND

*O*nly the Goodness of the Lord has blessed me with a view from the back upper porch of both the marsh and the wide sandy beach of the ocean. He has doubly blessed me as I can see the marsh and the beach with one gaze as I look southward. But he has blessed me once more with the recollection of lines written by the poet, Sidney Lanier—lines written not far south of here, on the coast of Brunswick, Georgia. Each time I look at the marsh and the ocean from the back porch I recall these lines.

Sidney Lanier wrote:

Sinuous southwards and sinuous northward
  the shimmering band
Of the sand beach as it fastens the fringe
  of the marsh to the folds of the land.
Inward and outward, to northward and southward
  the beach lines linger and curl,
As a silver-wrought garment that clings to and
  follows the firm sweet limbs of a girl.
Vanishing, swerving, evermore curving again
  into sight,
Softly the sand beach wavers away into a dim
  gray looping of light.

Then in the evenings when I come back to the porch to look at the stars, the "flowers without stems," I think of the lines written in a diary of an unknown turn-of-the-century six-year-old girl. She wrote about these "flowers without stems:"

> *I did have knowings of star songs.*
> *I have kept watch in the fields at night.*
> *And I have seen stars.*
> *I have seen flowers without stems.*
> *They look down on me kindly at night.*

Three blessings during the day. One at night. This is enough to keep me going . . . for another day.

A BOAT AND A TRAIN TO PAWLEYS ISLAND

Yesterday, on Sunday afternoon, I took my usual jog on the road down to the south end of the island. Down around the south causeway there was an unusual amount of traffic coming and going. Frequently, I had to get off the pavement and run by the side of the island road.

I put my mind on automatic pilot while running and do a lot of thinking during these times. As I was jogging by the south causeway I thought of an old photograph that had been given to me for an archival book I made concerning the history of the island. From this 1901 photograph it was obvious that traffic was not a problem on the island then. Depicted were elegant ladies in hats and long skirts mingling with rather formally dressed gentlemen as they alighted from the Georgetown–Pawleys Island train, which terminated at the south causeway. They had come up from Georgetown on the riverboat *Comanche*, leaving at mid-morning from Dover, the terminal at Georgetown, arriving at the Waverly Plantation boat landing where the train awaited them for the three-mile trip over to Pawleys Island.

According to an old preserved *Comanche* menu, they did not eat hot dogs on the way up, for the *Comanche* was known for its cuisine. They would have been aboard for three and a half hours, just enough time for a lavish noon meal. The lunch started with oyster stew, followed by a choice of roast choate, wild duck, or shrimp pie. The main course was served with Guinea squash, Irish potatoes, turnips, and Sewee beans. Dessert included pumpkin pie, custard, coconut cake, and fresh fruit. Indeed, by the time they reached Pawleys Island they needed a walk!

After alighting from the train, these strollers walked across a path in the dune by the ex-Governor Robert F. W. Allston House. On the beach, they probably took off their shoes and gently tipped their feet into the surf while holding up their long dresses and trouser legs, then walked barefooted up and down the beach.

Their stay was not for long as the train had to make a connection with the *Elizabeth Ann* to take them back to Georgetown; the *Comanche* was still on its way northward to Conway. They boarded for the voyage back, then sat and drank lemonade or tea, listening to the engine of the *Elizabeth Ann*. It sang "Hootenanny cha-cha, Hootenanny cha-cha," at Clifton Plantation and then Calais near Frazier's Point on Winyah Bay. Their day's outing ended across the bay at Georgetown's Dover.

The Georgetown–Pawleys Island Railroad and its train might still be in operation and our traffic problem partially solved except for a hurricane that visited the island in 1906 and blew the tracks away. Now, our Georgetown visitors zoom out of Georgetown in their red Chrysler Sebring convertibles and stop by the drive-by window of Taco Bell for a burrito, perhaps to be eaten on their ten minute drive up the island.

Back on the porch of the Duck's Nest I sat and rested after the jog, thinking again of all this gentle commotion. I concluded that I was born a century too late. It would have been more pleasurable to glide up or down the Waccamaw and dine on roast pig and Guinea squash than to speed into town eating a thrown-together Mexican burrito or chalupa. It would have been more pleasurable to prop my feet up and listen to the engines singing "Hootenanny cha-cha" than to ride on Route 17 being deafened by the roar of an eighteen wheeler.

I also realize that customs continue to change, and we no longer merely dip our toes into the ocean. Sometimes we even wear our baseball caps backwards. Sometimes we watch TV. We watch *Survivor* and eat burritos from Taco Bell. We do this with our feet propped up on a coffee table. We do this in our dens.

PAWLEYS ISLAND INCORPORATED

I remember it well. I remember the sweltering day. I can recall the conversations in detail. I can still see the signs that islanders were holding. I remember Mae, Hazel, and sweat-drenched Myrtle. I can recall exactly how John Rutledge was dressed. I have distinct visions of the crowded voting place—our chapel on the creek.

On August 27, 1985, one hundred and eighteen island residents came in the late summer heat to that little white, asbestos-shingled building on Pawleys to vote "yes" or "no" on whether or not to make Pawleys Island a town. Proposed a year earlier, the Pawleys Island Incorporation Referendum was finally taking place. Officials expected a heavy turnout. They expected a hundred percent to vote and their expectations were met. Even Columbia natives, who owned island property, changed their legal residence, so that they might have a chance to vote on this issue. There was an air of excitement, and they talked about it at the post office on the mainland. It was like an old-time county fair. Heated arguments between opponents and supporters would finally come to rest.

About noon I walked the few yards down to the island road toward the chapel and could feel the political convention-like atmosphere long before reaching the voting place. Mae Young left her place in front of the chapel and walked hurriedly towards me carrying a sign with red lettering. The three lines read: "GO TO GARDEN CITY . . . LOOK . . . THEN PUKE." Mae urged me to vote "yes" saying, "We've got to become a town or go high-rise. We don't want con-damn-eniums. We don't want that." She pointed northward toward Pawleys Pier, whose foundation hadn't yet dried. "Just look at that five-story carbuncle. It looks like a German war prison. The Georgetown County jail looks like the Garden of Eden as compared to that. Our daddies didn't want that." We walked on towards the chapel, slowing down as she mopped sweat from her face, then fanned with the wet handkerchief. She took me by the elbow, tugged at it, and said, "Now get yourself in there and vote right!"

John Rutledge stood outside by the chapel steps, dressed as usual in golfing attire—a green sweat-stained Izod shirt, reddish-pink trousers, and a Clemson-orange cap. John, concerned about his pocket book, nervously warned the approaching voters about taxes. "Don't vote for that city stuff. Our taxes will go out of sight with the paying of a police force, mayors, and things like that. No to police forces," he yelled. As I passed by I said, "Give 'em hell, John."

Mae had followed me to the chapel's entrance and I whispered to her. "Mae, I think I prefer taxes to carbuncles." Two little green lizards shaded themselves on the steps near Hazel Swearengen's feet. Hazel lived down the island in the Bird's Nest section on the south end. She made her feelings known with a primitive sign: "BIRD'S NEST SAYS YES." Avoiding the lizards, I nodded to Hazel, then went inside to the crowded voting place, where there was a sweet-tinged church aroma, like an old church in the country. Pauline Vereen handed me a simple ballot, and it didn't take long to mark it.

Myrtle Grant, acting as a poll watcher, stood by the ballot box trying to cool herself with a Mayer Funeral Home fan, switching Da Vinci's "Last Supper" back and forth in front of her face. "How you doin'?" she inquired, then added before I could answer, "I've drunk two diet Dr. Peppers, and I'm still thirsty. Bout wore out this fan." Pauline got up from her table and brought Myrtle another diet Dr. Pepper, and a Lily cup of ice. I took the ballot, folded it, and stuffed it into the slit of the upside-down Mason fruit jar box as Myrtle watched like a hawk. For a moment I stood gazing westward through the all-glass back wall of the one-room chapel building. A great blue heron flew lazily by and landed on the Morris' crabbing dock next door. I turned and thanked Myrtle and Pauline, making my way out of the crowded doorway.

A long line of brown pelicans glided by, barely scraping the rooftops as I walked back down the island road to my home. Later in the afternoon I went next door to Sea View Inn just before they served supper. Page Oberlin, the inn's owner, was coming to the long porch for a rest, so we sat in old faded rockers while the warm breeze ruffled her straight blonde hair. Page's sun-mellowed face bore an expression of calm confidence. She was sure that residents would vote in the best interest of the island. She looked out towards the surf whipping against the groin, sat silently for a moment, then brushed back the hair that had blown across her face.

As we talked about the issue and the voting, an inn guest from the North joined us and asked why we were so concerned that we would not become incorporated. Page became philosophical, "A lot of people have their roots so firmly in the soil of this little island; there's a lot of trust, and there's a lot of vulnerability here. We don't want to lose the island. We just want to stem the tide of development." She sipped iced tea and continued, "Scheduled over on the mainland there are thousands of units of housing to be built. It's my gut feeling that here on this island if anything goes, it all goes." She paused, looked at me and then the lady from the North. "Garden City looked a lot like Pawleys Island only a few years ago. Look at it now. High rises, neon signs, pink buildings, hamburger joints, those awful beach shops like Waves, and people, people, people; it's crawling with people up there."

The polls had closed and we could hear the radio from the inn's kitchen. We listened closely to Georgetown's WGTN news broadcast. Claude Whitworth, the folksy announcer, tried to keep us in suspense as he read an advertisement for the Piggly Wiggly grocery store and then one about a used car sale on Highmarket Street. He talked about Georgetown's asthma epidemic, supposedly caused by fumes from the International Paper Company.

Finally Claude got around to us and announced, "By a vote of 71 for and 47 against, Pawleys Island has become an incorporated town."

Page had Maude turn the radio off and asked her to bring each of us another glass of iced tea for a celebration. We toasted the victory. The lady from the North joined us.

Eventually, Jim Prince was elected the first mayor and served four years. He was succeeded by Jack Bland, who died three years after taking office. Dr. Julian Kelly, previous owner and operator of the island's Tip Top Inn and a retired Atlanta dentist, became the third mayor. Dr. Kelly's efforts to make improvements—or what he thought were improvements—concerning the island became controversial during the next six years he served. A prime concern of Mayor Kelly, and many islanders, was the dredging of Pawleys Creek and the dispensing of the dredged material. Mayor Kelly and his council found a cohort in the Prince George Development Company, which owned 2000 acres of land just south of Pawleys Island, a stretch of land going from the Atlantic to the Waccamaw River, previously owned by the George Vanderbilt family. This organization wanted to develop the land but did not want to be under the dictates of Georgetown County. They offered Mayor Kelly and his Town Council incentives for annexing the property to Pawleys Island. The mayor and council considered this offer, then met at 5:00 P.M. one day, notifying only a few residents of the pending action of annexation, which would make the Pawleys Island domain 200 percent larger. The final annexation vote took place two weeks later at a second reading, without as many claimed, any public input. Once islanders became aware of this move, there were lawsuits and counter suits, and finally a de-annexation vote was forced. Opponents of the annexation won handily. This unfortunate period in history of Pawleys Island caused discord and strained relationships that still exist among those on opposite sides of the Prince George issue.

Bill Otis was elected the new mayor, at the same time islanders voted to change the form of government from a mayor-council form to a council type of government, with elected officials serving only two-year terms.

But for some people, all was not calm after the incorporation vote. One former high official of Pawleys Island, during an interview with a regional newspaper reporter, made a comment that he regretted. In a state of aggravated emotion, he told the reporter jokingly that if she wrote any more derogatory articles about him, he would put out a contract on her life. She took this comment seriously, or perhaps wanted to create more controversy to sell more newspapers, and brought a lawsuit against him. The case dragged on and on, selling more newspapers and advertisements. Attorneys ended up the winners, as the case was eventually settled out of court.

I was aware of incorporation facts that islanders didn't know about or had forgotten. This incorporation issue had come up before, in 1954, thirty years ago, long before most voters of today had lived on the island.

Two island residents, Joe Havell and L. Vivette had organized a night meeting in a Pawleys Island home in September 1954 for island residents to vote on this issue. Havell and Vivette indicated that they desired better fire and police protection, but a rumor circulated that they wanted to establish a liquor store at Pawleys, an issue they denied. They also wanted to include a two-mile stretch westward from each end of the island—from the Atlantic to the Waccamaw River, which would include a large section of the African-American community and would make the town many times longer than the island. The forty to fifty islanders who attended the meeting that night voted unanimously against the idea.

Ten years passed and the issue came up again but this time in the state legislature. In March 1964, Georgetown Sen. C. Clymon Grimes, Jr. had a second reading of a bill authorizing the incorporation of the island. Senator Grimes indicated that the town would be limited to the island, and its major intent was to "provide island residents protection against boisterous sightseers and for a satisfactory arrangement for garbage collection." Senator Grimes held up the hearing for another opinion by the public. The legislation never came to a vote. (During this session of the legislature, Senator Grimes also introduced a bill which required that persons dealing in sturgeon and caviar be licensed!)

THE TINGLESCALE HOUSE

*T*here was a stifling haze over the island that morning. It was hot. There wasn't much to do that had to be done except that it was time to scrub and clean the garbage can lids, which reside on the boardwalk and serve as watering places for the birds. Before undertaking this task, I sat down on the old church bench, which was brought over to the island from an abandoned Pentecostal church building I had bought. It was not particularly comfortable, but it did for resting.

A tall, angular lady in a print dress appeared at the end of the board-walk. "I'm Hattie Carrington." she said. "You look right busy there, but I have a question, if you don't mind too much."

From my seat on the pew I answered, "No, I don't mind, I suppose. I'm just resting here, thinking about cleaning these garbage can tops. The birds have messed and messed in them, and I've got to make them civilized again. Do it every so often."

"Well, Horace and I retired here to the Bird's Nest end of the island from Spartanburg. We live in that house down by the Johnsons that Horace calls Hattie's Haven." She pointed southward. "I come up here shelling most mornings." She reached out and showed me a handful of shells. "I've become curious about you." Then, quickly, "No, no, not about you. I mean, I'm curious about your house with all those strange-looking columns and spindles and things that don't match. You know, we southern women like for things to match. They're not matching any-thing, at least as far as I can see." Hattie placed both hands above her eyes as if to shade them and to get a better view as she gazed up at my house.

"I guess I'm not much of a matcher, Mrs. Carrington."

Before I could go on, she pointed to my house and said, "I'm also curious about the old house that used to be right there. Horace and I used to vacation in a house right there beside Sea View Inn. We rented it from that precious Nell Foster, who lived down the street from us in

Spartanburg. She told me she'd inherited it from her daddy. It had a strange name, as I remember." She paused for a moment. "The Tinglescale House, that's it. But gracious me, that *can't* be the Tinglescale House!"

I stood up and interrupted, "No, no, Mrs. Carrington, it *wasn't* the Tinglescale House. It was the Clinkscale House. Clink. Clinkscale, a perfectly good and respectable South Carolina family name."

I took a breath and continued, "Since you are curious about my house and since you vacationed here, you just have a seat on this Pentecostal church pew here. Have a seat and swat those biting sand flies off your feet, and I'll explain."

Hattie was looking a little impatient, but she sat down. "Well, I've got to get back down to Horace and make him some breakfast." She swatted a fly, looked up again at my house and said, "I've got a minute, I guess." She placed her handful of shells on the pew beside her and folded her arms.

With this captive audience of one, I started in on the story of how my dwelling got to be the way it is. "Once upon a time there was a Converse College professor. You know, Converse there in Spartanburg? Well, this old Professor Clinkscale could not only teach arithmetic, he could do carpentry, he could do plumbing, and he was proficient at electrical wiring too. Years ago, he bought this lot and during his summer vacation constructed a rooming house hotel right here. These days we'd call it an inn, maybe. The place thrived I am told, but then almost fifty years ago, a big hurricane, Hazel they called it, blew that hotel clear across the creek and left him with nothing much over here. Two or three days later, the professor came back, took a look around, and then went all over the neighborhood and the beach gathering up everything he could find—bits and pieces of everybody's homes: a commode from here, a sink from there. And the old professor put together that house you and Horace vacationed in. I guess you could say that the house just happened. Just happened more than it was planned."

I paused to give Hattie a chance to catch up in her own mind. She swatted another sand fly and pretended to fan herself. "Well, mercy, I didn't know all that."

I wondered how confused and possibly distorted my story would be once it reached the south end of the island. But I continued, "Like you and Mr. Carrington, I used to rent that Clinkscale House from Nell Foster. Then, sometime a while back, I got fed up with that eye practice I had in Nashville. I was burned out and tired of skimming eyes, dry contact lenses, headaches, and Medicare forms. About that same time, Nell and Julian got fed up with trying to keep this house nailed together and its walls straight while dodging hurricanes, so they up and sold the place to me. I lived in it in the spring and fall each year. I was here when I wasn't in London. But then I got concerned about its shaking when the wind blew, so I had her jacked up and a new foundation put under it. I'll bet you and Mr. Carrington remember how it used to shake and tremble when the wind blew."

Hattie put her hand up and exclaimed, "Oh Lordy, yes! Yes, I remember the shaking. It was hard to keep Horace in bed some nights."

Hattie looked down at her watch, so I went on quickly, "We stopped most of the shaking with the new foundation, but then I got cramped for space with so many visitors, people from here, people from there. I could see that the island would become incorporated into a real town with rules and regulations and inspectors snooping around, so I decided to add a second floor before that happened. I drove to Georgetown and got a building permit on the spur of the moment. Peter Porcher and his crew were over before I knew it to start adding a floor to this Clinkscale House. I told Pete I'd be pleased to have some blue prints drawn, but Pete just said, "Shoot. J. R. and that bunch can't read blue prints." So I took a pencil and drew some pictures as best I could. Drew them on a left-over prescription pad. They built pretty much as best they could, except for their triflingness." I pointed up at the second floor. "That upstairs just more or less happened, like the rest of the house."

Hattie was obviously trying to take it all in, but she was getting fidgety on that pew. "But Hattie, I haven't answered your question about the columns and spindles. Those things that don't match." I sat down again and went on, "Well, from the look of the drawings on the prescription pad, it appeared that the house didn't have any personality, no character. Looked like everything else around here. Pete and I agreed that the porches had to be held up with something, so he let me borrow his pick-up. I drove down to Coastal Wrecking Company in Charleston and bought a truck-load of old columns and spindles, some of them up to two hundred years old. I remember that day. They cost me over three hundred dollars, and the old pick-up blew a tire on the way home. Got two tickets that day—for speeding."

Hattie was backing down the boardwalk. I followed her and kept talking because I wanted the record straight for the south end of the island.

"Anyhow, we finally got the columns and spindles put up. J. R. and Porcher's crew laughed at me, saying that I was silly for not using new ones from the Pelican Lumber Company. I just let them laugh. I liked the way both porches looked." Then I pointed, "You see, Mrs. Carrington, look. There are only four styles of columns and six or seven different patterns of spindles! With all these things sticking up around the porches, I decided to rename the place the Duck's Nest. And some people have said that that was silly too. 'A silly name,' they said."

Hattie had reached the end of the boardwalk, and the haze of the morning was clearing. She had a lot to tell Horace and a lot to discuss: hotels, storms, spindles, skimming eyes, London, ducks, and prescription pads.

"Mercy, I've got to get home and scramble Horace some Egg Beaters." She started off down the beach, then stopped and stood with her hands on her hips facing my house. By this time I was back on the porch. Hattie yelled, "Horace'll be surprised to know what happened to the Tinklescale House."

"Clink! Clink, Mrs. Carrington!" I yelled back. "Clinkscale. Clinkscale!

J. R., CONSTRUCTION BOSS

J. R. Plunkett, Lonnie Snellgrove, and Harvey Ray Figgins were the trio of Philistines who were making halting attempts at constructing a second floor onto my house. They were assisted periodically by Phyllis Mayberry, a youngish and rather pretty girl who said that she came down to the Low Country to escape her job as a short order cook at the Greyhound Bus Station in Beaver Falls, Pennsylvania. Over on Route 17 at Jake Young's Happy Day Lounge, she met Peter Porcher, the owner and president of Pete's Construction Company, the company I was paying to add the second floor. "Mr. Peter put me to work," she said. Never mind that she was a girl because Phyllis was the best of his crew. Phyllis was on time, she didn't cuss, she didn't spit, and she called me "Mister." Phyllis Mayberry nailed her nails straight.

Little Sammy Ray was a later addition to the crew. He was an African-American who lived over on Shell Road with his mother and seven brothers and sisters. He carried on in an almost soprano voice. He was terrified by crawling things and things with more than four legs. In particular, he was terrified by things with <u>no</u> legs. Sammy Ray was just plain terrified.

Another important part-time person in this entourage was Lurleen Snellgrove, Lonnie's wife. Lurleen was tall and angular. She stood straight like some African princess and went about the day singing and humming spirituals, sometimes making up her own words. Lurleen, when she was present, was good help.

J. R. and Harvery Ray drove to the island from Little River up near the North Carolina line. Lonnie would look down at the untied laces of his yellow tennis shoes, then up at J. R. on the ladder, and would apologize for being late.

"J. R., I couldn't get the damned pick-up to start this morning, and then when I got a push, it was slow and a pure mess on Route 17. Too much traffic. I'm sorry, and I'll tell that to Mr. Peter, too, if he comes to check up on us. Lurleen didn't come in today. She got up, got the spirit, shoutin' and everything. Said she was goin' to stay home and keep the spirit all day. She'll be here tomorrow, I promise."

Lonnie addressed his orations to J. R. because he was the boss . . . this J. R., the boss of Peter Porcher's Construction Company. J. R., who owns a parakeet named Alfred, was not only bossy, he was ornery, characteristics that interfered with neither his slight physical build nor his near desiccation. J. R. would tell you that he weighed in at 125 pounds, but nobody knew where those pounds were. His little buttocks looked like two navy beans stuck together, his arms and legs looked about as sturdy as the sea oats out on the dune, and his muscles would have been envious of north Georgia shriveled pecan nuts. He appeared to be mostly head, which was covered with long, straight hair and topped by a yellow and purple baseball cap. His face had a fair helping of undernourished, blond hair, something he referred to as his beard. This face was punctuated by a little sharp nose and a thin upper lip canopied by his "mushtask," as he called it. His few developed muscles seemed to be centered around his mouth because J. R. could talk. He could cuss, he could yell, and he could spit. J. R. could spit when there was no need to spit. And he could spit far. J. R. could spit as far as a Missouri toad frog can jump. He was a spitter's spitter. This J. R. was a bird!

I would think to myself, "I'm paying Peter Porcher for this J. R.'s supervising; this bossing; this spitting." I couldn't seem to escape listening to his supervising, particularly of Lonnie.

"I can't do nothing, Lonnie, if you don't nail them two-by-fours straight. Right here you've got one aiming toward Myrtle Beach and the one next to it is aiming up toward Conway. And the next one, too. Hell's fire, Lonnie!"

He would command Phyllis as if she was still a short order cook doing French fries or scrambling eggs. "Damn it, we're out of them ten-penny nails again. Lonnie must be eatin' them. Phyllis, you swish your ass into my pick-up and go over to Buz's Roost Hardware and get enough this time. And don't stop at Jake Young's place on the way back, 'cause Mr. Porcher has seen enough of you there."

With Phyllis gone, he was after his favorite target, Lonnie. "Get your black ass down off that ladder and stop lookin' into Sea View's bedrooms. That girl from Charlotte who talked to you through the window yesterday don't want nothin' like you. Save it for Lurleen, 'cause you've got a good woman there. A good woman."

Harvey Ray was given to being "not well today" and took frequent naps. J. R. had no sympathy. "Harvey Ray, you ain't done nothin' today 'cept sleep, and when you wake up you're always watchin' Phyllis carry shingles up to the roof. Lord A'mighty, Harvey Ray!"

To Little Sammy Ray, there were only two words, "You're pitiful."

In South Carolina on Friday afternoons everything stops at 2:30, as did the building of this addition to my house. The crew drove off in the stream of pick-ups, heading northward and southward.

J. R. sometimes stayed behind and would sit down, take his cap off, and give me some indication of his plans for the weekend. One Friday, I remember, he announced, "Damn, I'm glad today is a Friday 'cause this old J. R. is aleavin' in the mornin'—maybe at 5:30—and drivin' to Atlanta. I'm goin' to see the Braves eat the ass off that New York Yankee bunch." There was a silence, then he added, "Well, Ralph and I are goin' if Betty Sue will look after Alfred." He looked at me inquiringly, "You know Alfred, don't you? Alfred's my parakeet. Alfred's been sick with the runs. The runs." I nodded and said I hoped that Alfred got better. J. R. said nothing more, got up, and drove off in his pick-up.

That afternoon, with the Philistines gone, I sat in the swing on the lower porch, half asleep, dozing, while I thought of this idea of an additional floor, of hiring the Porcher Construction Company, and of J. R., its supervisor. I decided that distractions were the problem. Distractions!

Half asleep and half dreaming, I could hear J. R. pretending to complain about distractions. But then, of course, J. R. knew that distractions were welcome. They were flirted with and encouraged. J. R. supervised over distractions, not the construction on my house. Wonderful distractions, such as an encouraged dog-fight between Homelite and the neighbor's yellow Lab. A fight for which they could all stop work to enjoy watching. Then the UPS driver might come along and ask for directions, and they could take their time helping him out. A work stoppage was called to debate the ownership of any shrimp boat which happened to be out beyond the dune. There was an hour-long destruction of a wasp's nest down under the house. The flight of the next north-flying cormorants would be predicted. J. R. counted them several times when they eventually flew over. Then there were interludes for cold R.C. Colas brought over from Swado's filling station—extended interludes.

Well, I grew accustomed to J. R.'s face, his spitting, his bossing, and even the distractions. As I spent my days picking up loose nails, I expected distractions and even dreamed about them. And I also dreamed that perhaps one day the house would be finished. Some day.

A VIPER UNDER THE HOUSE

*P*ete's Construction Company workers, if they deserve to be called that, killed a rather imposing snake down under the house yesterday afternoon. Sammy Ray came running up the steps yelling and interrupting my afternoon nap in the hammock. "Doc, Doc, come and look what we done! We killed a big poison snake." He went running back down the steps and yelled, "It's dead."

I slowly got out of the hammock and followed him down the steps. There were the construction workers standing in a circle around the snake, with J. R. taking a prominent place inside the group. Sammy Ray seemed to be their excited spokesman.

"Old J. R. had to chop over five times to get through its old tough skin. And we was watchin' it all go on after I saw it a-crawlin' that-a-way," pointing towards the creek.

By now I was awake and joined this group of Low Country rednecks all standing with hands on hips, except, of course, J. R. their leader, who leaned on an old rusty hoe. He leaned as if exhausted, not from his escapades of last night nor from work this morning, but from the exertion of chopping at an evil viper. He turned his head towards the creek, pretended to spit, adjusted a red and yellow baseball cap, and rubbed at his sparse beard. He rolled the headless snake over with his worn jogging shoe and pronounced with a convincing growl, "Yeah, it's a tough old copperhead, boys. Betcha it's five or six years old. Maybe some more. Been around here for a while." He looked at Sammy Ray. "Could 'a killed somebody the size of you."

"Lordy!" exclaimed Sammy Ray, "Don't want no snake a-killin' me. Watched Uncle Zachary suffer after he got bit in our garden. The 'mergency room in Georgetown just saved him. Lordy, don't want that!"

I looked down at this headless "evil snake" with its thick maroon blood seeping into the sand. Then I raised my arms and said, "Praise be to the workers of Pete's Construction Company for what you've done." Walking round the inside of this Philistine circle, I shook all their hands: Lonnie's, Harvey Ray's, Phyllis's, Lurleen's, and then Little Sammy Ray's. I stopped in front of J. R., patted him on the shoulder, squeezed his hand, and said, "Little Sammy Ray and I won't forget this day and your deed." To show my gratitude, I went up the steps to the kitchen. I prepared five tall plastic glasses of sweet iced tea for the crew and brought them down on a tray with a cold Dr. Pepper for J. R.

They all left the job early.

The convoy of old pick-ups drove away from the house headed for Swado's filling station over on the corner of Route 17. I walked to the end of the driveway and waved until they were out of sight. As I walked back, it dawned on me that snakes don't really die until the sun sets. Thinking of the doom that might have come to Little Sammy Ray—or to me—I grabbed the hoe and drew it into an attacking position. Then, feeling a bit sheepish, I realized that the snake had been separated from its head and was really dead, sunset or no sunset.

As I stood there with my hoe, Dick Crayton drove up with his dog, Homelite, in his familiar blue truck. He parked in the driveway and was nearly knocked over by the dog rushing out of the truck. It was obvious that news of the construction workers' deed had reached Swado's place. Dick, dressed in sun-bleached khakis and his usual straw hat, said nothing but hurried towards me and the evil viper, which Homelite was busy sniffing. Dick glanced at the copperish-brown snake, took his hat off and slammed it against his trousers.

"Lordy, they shouldn't have killed that snake!" Rolling it over with the tip of his shoe, he added, "It's a corn snake. The best damned snake on the Waccamaw Neck. Just look how pretty. It's beautiful!"

Dick and his dog walked back towards his truck. He stopped, looked at me and said, "Now you'll be eaten by all the rats and mice on this island." Disgusted, they got back into the truck and drove off.

I just stood there not knowing what to think. I felt downgraded and unworthy. I felt humiliated by this dead snake. I yelled, "Dick, it won't happen again. I promise you!" But I knew he didn't hear me. I could imagine Homelite peering at me disapprovingly through the truck's back window. I just stood there with my hoe. The Labrador from Sea View Inn came by. She sniffed and then stood back and growled at the dead snake. I dropped the hoe and retreated into the house. The sun had set. I began searching for the K-Mart rat trap.

THE MEDICIS OF THE WACCAMAW

I looked for the telephone number of the Allstate Insurance Company in the Georgetown County directory. Below the insurance company there was the listing for Mary Allston, and following her name there were thirty-three Alstons with the one 'L' spelling. I looked in the Horry County section of the directory, and there were twenty-seven Alstons but no Allstons. That's a ratio of fifty Alstons to one Allston.

Nobody seems to know why the name of Allston is vanishing. The family name Alston was unheard of here until the early 1800s when Capt. William Allston of Clifton Plantation legally changed his name to Alston because of the confusion between him and another Capt. William Allston, his cousin. During the American Revolution they were both officers in "Swamp Fox" Francis Marion's command. People couldn't refer to "Mary's husband, Captain William," because both had a wife named Mary. Thus the Alston family evolved.

But this was not the first name change for this prominent South Carolina family. Their ancestors in England were called the Alstanes. By the time William's grandfather, John, arrived in Charles Town in the 1600s, his name was changed to Allston, and from this John Allston sprang all the Allstons and Alstons.

For over two hundred years the Allstons and Alstons were the most prominent families of the Waccamaw Neck. These families owned nearly all of the fifty plantations up and down The Neck at one time or another. The Allstons and Alstons gathered plantations and slaves like we gather coupons at the Piggly Wiggly grocery store. As an example, Gov. R. F. W. Allston, at one time, owned properties scattered from Sandy Island to Georgetown on both sides of the Waccamaw River and the Pee Dee River. His holdings included Chicora Wood, Exchange, Guendalos, Nightingale Hill Plantations, and Pipe Dream on Sandy Island. His sons inherited most of these. Other Allstons owned Brookgreen, The Oaks, Springfield, Arundel, Rosemont, Waterford, and Clifton Plantations. The list is endless. The Waccamaw Neck should have been called "The Kingdom of the Allstons."

In Florence, Italy, while a student at The British Institute, I heard lectures on the influence of the Medici family in the fifteenth and sixteenth centuries—they controlled the finances and social structure of Tuscany. I was reminded of the similarities between these two families, the Medicis of Tuscany and the Allstons and Alstons of the Waccamaw Neck. Tuscany was geographically larger, but the populations were somewhat comparable. The rampant slavery of South Carolina was in contrast to the servitude of Tuscany. The Florentine Medicis were the first to organize and own banks. The Allstons were the first to become plantation owners in Georgetown County. The Medicis collected and commissioned art—paintings and sculpture. The Allstons and Alstons collected slaves. In South Carolina it was easier to own a thousand slaves than to be a bank director.

Here are some specific examples comparing the Medicis of Florence and the Allstons and Alstons of the Waccamaw Neck:

In around 1400, Cosimo de Medici became Florence's first great banker. He started Florence's public library system and collected art. Three hundred fifty years later, William Allston became the first great landowner in Georgetown County, and here he collected slaves and plantations.

Lorenzo de Medici married Madeline de la Tour. This wealthy merchant of Florence commissioned and collected art. Another William Allston came up to the Waccamaw Neck, married one of the Pawleys girls and proceeded to buy plantations and collected slaves.

Minovanni de Medici, a military officer, married Maria Salvioti from a prominent Siena family. He died of gangrene after a battlefield amputation. Capt. Henry Allston, a Revolution officer who came home to Brookgreen Plantation after being wounded at the battle of Cowpens, also died shortly after being wounded. He left a beautiful widow, Rachel Moore of Charleston. He was the father of the American painter, Washington Allston.

Cosimo I de Medici married Eleanor de Toledo, the daughter of a wealthy Viceroy of Naples. Eleanor and their three children died of the plague. This Florentine family might be compared to Joseph Allston and his family. Joseph went off to upstate New York and married the daughter of Vice President Aaron Burr, Theodosia. Joseph brought her back to Brookgreen Plantation where they had a son. The little boy died of malaria. Broken hearted, Theodosia vanished at sea going back to New York.

The women fared no better. Maria de Medici, daughter of the Grand Duke of Tuscany, married King Henry IV of France. Soon afterwards, he was murdered. Sara Alston was as unfortunate when she married a close relative of a signer of the Declaration of Independence. Three years later he died of malaria.

Concerning church matters, the Medicis outdid the Alstons and Allstons. The Medicis provided three popes: Pope Leo X, Clement VII, and Leo XI. The Allstons and Alstons were too busy with plantations and slaves to even produce an Episcopal bishop. The best they could do was a notable Episcopal minister, Rev. Benjamin Allston.

The Medicis produced two Grand Dukes of Tuscany. Three hundred years later, the Allstons and Alstons produced three South Carolina governors.

However, the Allstons of the Waccamaw produced something the Medicis of Florence did not, a painter. Washington Allston is sometimes referred to as the "American Titian." He was born at Brookgreen Plantation in 1779, at a time when the Florentine Medicis were seeing their last days of glory. His artistic sensibilities were recognized early, and at age eleven he was sent off to Rhode Island for proper schooling. He went on to Harvard College and at the age of twenty-one arrived in London. By the time he was twenty-five, he was an established landscape and portrait painter in Rome, where German painters compared him to Titian. He returned to America and became recognized as this country's first Romantic painter, a celebrated portrait painter, and man of letters. Like all the other Allstons and Alstons he married into a significant family, twice. Both wives were granddaughters of Declaration signers.

Washington Allston was also a plantation owner. He inherited Springfield Plantation, a one-thousand-acre plot of land just north of Brookgreen that reached from the Atlantic Ocean to the Waccamaw River. He sold this tract of land to obtain funds for his studies in Europe; however, he kept the slaves and sold them much later.

The Allstons and Alstons might be called the Medicis of Wacca-maw Neck. They were the nobility of South Carolina, but instead of banking and art, the Allstons and Alstons collected plantations and slaves.

PAWLEYS ISLAND LOT SALE

I felt good about the investment in my home here on Pawleys Island until yesterday. I received a letter from the lady from whom I bought my house, Nell Foster. Nell wrote from Spartanburg, telling about the history of the house, then added, "Daddy bought the lot for about $800 in 1938."

Perhaps Professor Clinkscale, her father, would have had second thoughts about that $800 had he seen this advertisement in the August 26, 1914, issue of the *Georgetown Times*. In 1914, the same lot could have been purchased for two hundred dollars—quadruple appreciation in twenty-five years, from 1914 to 1938. Today these fifty-foot lots will cost you half a million dollars—if there is one left.

August 26, 1914

LOTS FOR SALE

I have for quick sale 28 lots on Pawleys Island near the very center of the island.

Pawlyes Island is destined soon to become one of the most popular resorts on the South Atlantic coast. Last season, the beach was crowded with visitors. This season it is overcrowded. All the island houses for sale have been bought up. Demands for larger accommo-dations are urgent.

Buy a lot now for building or spectacultion. These lots are each 50 feet in width and extend from the ocean across to the salt marshes. Located on the best part of the island. Price only $200. See me today.

--Hugh L. Oliver

DEPUTY ROUNDTREE

$\mathcal{D}$eputy Sheriff Claude Roundtree had worked for the sheriff's office in Georgetown for seventeen years. A stout African American, he was generally a kind soul, but had a tendency to be naïve. Many times the sheriff had offered Roundtree the day shift, but he preferred evenings and nights, when there was more action around Pawleys Island and the mainland where he was usually assigned.

Deputy Roundtree's exploits were frequently written up in the weekly newspaper, in a column the locals refer to as the "Crime Column." Here are some excerpts from December issues of that newspaper:

December 10, 5:10 p.m.

A Pawleys Island woman called the Sheriff's Office from the Food Lion grocery store, stating that she had spotted her gold and diamond ring on the finger of another customer at the deli counter. She told the sheriff's office that the ring had been missing for a month. According to the report, the complainant stated that while she was working — flouring chicken at the Shell Stop — she had taken the ring off and put it behind the counter. Later that evening, she discovered it missing.

Deputy Sheriff Roundtree was on the scene in six minutes, but the culprit had fled in a blue Ford Maverick station wagon. He chased her northward on Route 17, and at a distance could see the station wagon turn left and disappear on Sandy Island Road. Roundtree had to discontinue the chase when he was called to Old King's Highway by the Sheriff's Office. But Deputy Sheriff Roundtree announced that he would like to receive information on a woman driving a blue station wagon and wearing a gold and diamond ring. Roundtree says that the culprit may be on Sandy Island or anywhere north of Pawleys. He said she might be spotted in Conway or Myrtle Beach.

December 10, 6:05 p.m.

The sheriff's office was called from Old King's Highway by a fourteen-year-old girl stating that she had received a cut on her forehead during a spat with her grandmother over using the telephone and not doing her homework. The girl told the sheriff's office that her grandmother's arm was also cut in the fight, which, according to the young girl, lasted thirty minutes. She said that alarmed neighbors couldn't stop the fight.

When Deputy Sheriff Roundtree arrived on the scene ten minutes later, all the neighbors were in the yard. The girl and her grandmother told him that it was all an accident. In his report, Roundtree stated that they both looked tired and neither had the energy to place charges. He urged all the neighbors' children to go home. Roundtree urged the children to not use the telephone and to do their homework.

December 11, 7:50 p.m.

The sheriff's office notified Deputy Sheriff Roundtree to go to the Anchor Inn and Lounge because of a fight between a couple from the Hagley section of Pawleys on the dock behind the lounge. According to several witnesses, the couple had been standing there watching a shrimp boat when the man grabbed the woman by her hair. She managed to struggle and get loose, and then she lunged at him, shoving him into a bed of oyster shells, where he lay when Roundtree arrived. He was bleeding from cuts on his forehead and left hand. Roundtree helped the woman pull the injured man from the oyster bed. Witnesses say that the man and woman hugged each other. The lounge's owner immediately filed charges for disorderly conduct and disturbing the peace. They were placed in the deputy's patrol car and taken to Georgetown County Jail where they were booked. They paid the bail and hugged again as they were released. They told Roundtree that they were going back to the Anchor Inn to have supper.

December 12, 5:50 p.m.

The Sheriff's Office radioed Deputy Sheriff Roundtree to go to Old Pond Road to talk to an 83-year old woman who had taken out a warrant against a former roomer, complaining that this woman took items worth $2,548 when she left her house three days prior. This roomer had worked as a waitress at the Hi Tide Diner. According to the complainant, during the roomer's nine-week stay, she had been an undue nuisance, yelling at night about water bugs in her room. The complainant said that the roomer, who she thought had moved to Moncks Corner, took four table lamps, a bed, a picnic table, a refrigerator, a religious picture of Jesus, and the family Bible. The complainant stated that the roomer had left during the wee hours.

December 13, 7:08 p.m.

The Pantry at Litchfield was robbed of $37 by a man described as having a "peculiar nose." Deputy Roundtree, who went to the scene, asks that anyone seeing such a person call the Sheriff's Office.

December 14, 8:08 p.m.

Deputy Roundtree was called to the Shell Road in Pawleys Island where a man was found to be carrying a concealed weapon and charged with criminal domestic violence in connection with an incident involving his wife or girlfriend. The woman had suffered a bump on her head when the man hit her with a conch shell and then threw her to the floor. The man, a local construction worker, declared that she had hit him first, and he was only acting in self-defense. Deputy Roundtree didn't believe him, handcuffed him, and drove him to Georgetown County jail where he awaits bail.

December 17, 8:21 p.m.

Deputy Roundtree was radioed to go to the Rising Sun Restaurant in Litchfield when some diners got into a fracas. In his report, Roundtree said that one party of diners had been loud and vulgar, and had called the complainant's wife a whore. The complainant began fighting the alleged offender, causing a minor burn on his arm when he was pinned to the tableside grill. Roundtree arrived and observed some of this as he approached the diner's tables. He unpinned the complainant and comforted his wife, according to the report. Deputy Roundtree refused to arrest anyone, as the alleged offender had calmed down and was eating his shrimp and noodles.

December 18, 5:27 p.m.

A Pawleys Island youth called the Sheriff's Office to ask for help in stopping a fight between his parents in their front yard. Deputy Sheriff Roundtree responded to the call on Parkersville Road. When he arrived at the scene, the father told him that he had been napping in the hammock when his wife came onto the porch and began cursing and slapping him. The man declared that his wife had been drinking. He tried to get away from her and retreated to his pick-up truck when she threw a running power drill through the window. The man then yelled to his son to call the Sheriff's Office, according to the deputy's report. When Roundtree arrived, the wife had gone back inside and was smashing things while the victim was crouched in his pick-up. Their son, being afraid, had fled the scene but returned when Roundtree arrived. Roundtree calmed everybody down, but there were no charges placed since the culprit had since gone to the bedroom and was sleeping. Her husband refused to place charges.

December 22, 5:20 p.m.

Deputy Claude Roundtree responded to a call from Pawleys Island by a seventy-three-year-old housewife who was visiting her home from Aiken, S.C. When Roundtree arrived on the scene he found the housewife "near hysterical," saying that when she came in from a walk on the beach, she had observed a young man jumping into his car "with a sack of things." According to the report filed, the young man jumped out of the car and snatched up more things from under a live oak in her garden. The victim said that the culprit had just fled across the south causeway. Roundtree jumped into his patrol car and over took the culprit down Route 17 near Pawleys Plantation, pulling the VW over. As the culprit stood with his arms in the air, Roundtree searched his car where he found Volumes II, V, and IX of the 1938 American People's Encyclopedia, a half empty box of Roach Motels, a small statue of St. Francis of Assisi, statues of two ducks and a pelican, and a sack of warm chocolate brownies. The nineteen-year old Coastal Carolina University student was taken to the Georgetown County Jail where he was finally turned over to his parents and a Coastal Carolina University official. They were last seen driving toward Conway.

December 24, 5:10 p.m.

Deputy Roundtree investigated an altercation on Wesley Road reported by an eighteen year old. The victim heard his car alarm go off at about 5:00 p.m. while changing out of his Hardee's uniform after a long day at work. He rushed onto the porch, dressed only in his underwear, while the door slammed behind and locked him out. According to Roundtree's report, the young man was greeted by a blast from his own shotgun, which had been left in his car. The young man told Deputy Roundtree that he had observed the culprit returning to the car where he snatched two large white teddy bears and a sack of oranges intended for the victim's girlfriend. The culprit then raced with these items toward a waiting get-away vehicle, described as a large red Chevrolet with silver mud flaps. Deputy Roundtree stated that the victim stood on the porch, chilled "to the bone," but unhurt after he had run to the safe haven of a neighbor's home down Wesley Road. He returned home when the deputy arrived. Deputy Roundtree jumped into his patrol car and started searching for the silver mud-flapped Chevrolet.

December 24, 6:03 p.m.

After investigating a shooting on Wesley Road, Deputy Roundtree was radioed to go to nearby Dump Road to investigate an altercation at the Coastal Breeze Trailer Park.

According to the deputy's report, an elderly lady resident alleged that a neighbor's seventy-three-year-old boyfriend had deliberately driven over several large plastic bags of used Christmas wrapping paper and two bags of trash which had been scattered about, and caused $54.42 of other damage. This included a crushed Styrofoam snowman and three strings of outside Christmas lighting. In Deputy Roundtree's report, the complainant said the subject blamed her because the trailer park's owner came and ordered the subject and his girlfriend to cut down the loud and continual playing of Bing Crosby's "White Christmas."

While Deputy Roundtree was taking the report, he was rudely interrupted by a neighbor of the complainant who stormed into the trailer, "ranting, and raving loudly and cussing to high heaven" at Roundtree, who's patrol car radio was causing static on his CB radio. According to the report, the deputy told the intruder several times to calm down, to take it easy and go home, but when the thirty-four-year-old shrimper refused, he was arrested for breach of the peace. He was handcuffed and placed in the waiting patrol car.

Deputy Roundtree then returned to the trailer where he managed to obtain the surrender of the "White Christmas" record. The complainant appeared at the scene but refused to press charges when the alleged offender offered her homemade eggnog.

On Route 17, while driving the offending shrimper toward the Georgetown County jail, Deputy Roundtree's patrol car was passed near Yum Yum's Bar-B-Q place by a large red Chevrolet with prominent silver mud flaps. Roundtree became suspicious when he spotted two white teddy bears in the rear window and orange peelings being thrown from the car's window. According to Roundtree's report, he set in after the suspected culprit, whose vehicle quickly turned left into the Debordieu Colony. A chase in the colony ensued, but the culprit's track was lost. Deputy Roundtree gave up the chase and headed to the Georgetown County jail to deposit the shrimper, who appeared tired and confused. The shrimper was booked, but his wife arrived from Pawleys to give bond before he was locked up. They were last seen driving northward.

December 24, 7:10 p.m.

An elderly Wesley Road couple telephoned the Sheriff's Office, reporting that they had heard someone out on the road in front of their house, and when they looked out the window, a young man in his late teens was seen running down the road wearing only his underwear. The sheriff's office telephone line was too jammed so the clerk told the couple to turn off their Christmas lights, go to the edge of the road and wave down the next deputy sheriff's vehicle.

RUBY THROATED HUMMINGBIRD

$\mathcal{D}$ick Crayton came to the island on Monday, and before finding him a job we sat on the porch talking. Just then a ruby throated hummingbird visited the feeder which dangled from the eaves of the porch. We watched this minute bird as it quickly probed in and out of the feeder, only a few feet from where we sat. Then it flew directly toward a live oak, which is in a sheltered place between my house and the inn next door. Talking about this bird, I told Dick that I had never seen a hummingbird's nest. Between drawing on his pipe and thinking, he proceeded to give me a dissertation on hummingbirds and their lifestyle. A knowledgeable and astute observer of nature, he told me that the hummingbird's nest is constructed by the female and is no larger than a golf ball shell. Dick said that he could probably find a nest, and when he did he could guarantee that it would be woven together with Spanish moss.

In seconds, the bird returned to the feeder, and then as suddenly it darted away, but it didn't escape Dick's sharp eye. He got up and asked me to follow closely behind to a cluster of live oaks, and sure enough, just above his head there was a nest dangling from two twigs. It was a work of art, as if sculpted from Spanish moss. Dick asked me to get the step ladder, which he positioned for a later view when the female bird was away.

We went back to the porch where he told me more about this intriguing little bird. He rambled on about its migration pattern of thousands of miles, flying between Pawleys Island and Central America and South America. He said, like other birds, it is apt to fly directly across the Gulf of Mexico in a single flight. Dick even covered the aerodynamics of the bird's flight, and the fact that its wings beat nearly a hundred times a second. He offered some explanation, which I didn't understand, about how it flies backwards. Trying to explain more clearly, he got up and flapped his arms as if he were a hummingbird. He also explained that surprisingly it's main diet is insects.

We went back to the live oak and Dick climbed the step ladder. The bird was away, so he invited me to take a turn. There were two little eggs only millimeters in diameter. When the female returned, she buzzed about very irritated by our intrusion. We retreated back to the porch where I had more questions, but it was time for him to go to work, as he had cast all the pearls of wisdom for the day. Dick started pulling the young Kudzu vines from the dune. I sat down on the porch and began thinking of questions for next week. I was thinking about the purple martins.

PURPLE MARTINS

$\mathcal{D}$ick returned later that week, and together we painted the columns of the porch. It was early May and the purple martins were busy with their nest building in the birdhouse near the ocean. Several had lit on the little railing on top. Earlier in the spring, we had taken the house down to clean and repair the roof. We took a break to watch while some took off for their characteristic flight consisting of short glides then rapid flapping, swooping here and there, diverting to catch unsuspecting insects, which today were dragonflies. On this day a mosquito didn't have a chance as both the dragonflies and purple martins were feeding on them.

I had endeavored to ask Dick a question about birds to which he didn't know the answer. So I asked him where this bird got a male Christian name. I thought he made up the answer, but it sounded good enough to me. He said that this bird was named for a French saint, St. Martin, because it departs from France to go to Africa about the time of the festival of St. Martin, called Martinmas. Later, I went to the public library to check his story and authenticated it.

Dick told me how these purple martins spend most of the year in the Amazon River valley of Brazil, then send scouts up north in mid-March to check on their nesting places of last year. In some unexplained manner, the ones to follow get the message and the remainders arrive a few days later. After they cross the Gulf of Mexico, they rest and feed in southern Florida or the delta of the Mississippi River. Then they fly to various places in the United States to mate, lay eggs, and hatch their young, living in houses like mine. In past centuries, these birds lived in cavities of trees, in cliffs, in caves, and later in gourds put up by Indians. Today they are spoiled and will inhabit a house only if the holes are the correct size and if the house is located at some distance from the ground or the surrounding trees.

I let Dick ramble on as we sat down for a rest. During a pause, he lit and relit his pipe, and I told him about the town of Manaus, a Brazillian city on the banks of the Amazon River. During the months the purple martins are in Brazil, they fly in the early evening to an oil refinery on the outskirts of Manaus, where untold numbers congregate for a few minutes on the rails, pipes, and ladders of this refinery. Here they seem to ignore the unceasing noise of the flames spurting from hot pipes and the blasts of steam. It is in an environment that is radically different from the pristine rain forest from where they had just come. In the darkening sky they swirl and acrobatically dodge each other in a strange invasion. This spectacle lasts for only a few minutes, and then they scatter back to their roosting places along the river. Nobody has a reasonable explanation for this phenomenon. Dick seemed amazed that I knew such facts, but I am sure that he will reconfirm this, as I did his information, then add it to his repertoire of nature tales.

A few days ago I had the opportunity to inspect one of these birds up close. A screen door had been left open and one flew into the dining room. At first I tried to coach it out with a broom, but it repeatedly flew against the window. Half-stunned, it allowed me to pick it up. I observed that it is a much larger bird than I had thought, with a wingspan of some ten inches. Its purple feathers are iridescent, its eyes are blackish brown, and its tail is forked. It lay loose in my hand for a moment, then started to revive. I took it to the porch where it flew off, ready to catch some more dragonflies or mosquitoes.

HARRIS TEETER'S ROOF

The sea oats are abundant this autumn. They appear fragile and limp with their heavy tassels, but they are not. This morning a red winged blackbird landed and perched on a stem, and it hardly swayed.

I observed a common tern darting like a butterfly above the surf in the late afternoon, and it made me wonder why some birds are called "common:"—common egret, common gallinule, common snipe. There's nothing common about these birds. Perhaps Mr. Audubon and his bird watching friends just ran out of names.

Who knows why a bird as ordinary and obnoxious as a common grackle deserves such an imposing name as *Quicasalus quiscula*? Any bird with such manners shouldn't be iridescent either. I'm pleased when one utters some half lyrical sound, but usually their call is an irritating noise or squawk. They reserve their more pleasant sounds for the females in the spring but communicate with their fellow males by stretching their long necks. These sounds are even worse when their cousins visit, the boat-tailed grackles called *Cassidix mexicanis*. These birds line up on the boardwalk's handrail facing the wind and have a neck stretching contest after feeding. They occasionally stop this nonsense and sing, in Spanish I assume, in a low guttural gargle, but only when the females are near.

My English visitors used to say that Litchfield's Harris-Teeter grocery store reminds them of the Food Hall of Harrods in London. But I reminded my guests that we don't have as many gawking tourists as I see at Harrods. But anyhow, I'm more interested in the gravel roof of Harris-Teeter than their produce section. The U.S. Corps of Engineers built a new jetty over on Huntington Beach. This caused such a commotion with the nesting terns last fall that this spring they moved their nesting site onto the gravel of Harris Teeter's roof, where the slope and texture was just right for them to lay their eggs. Their new abode seems successful, as this year's brood has been raised, and no beach walker has stepped on an egg from this flock.

THE STORKS ARE COMING

$\mathcal{T}$he endangered wood stork recently began visiting the mud flats on the marsh at low tide on Pawleys Island. One evening near sunset as I walked to the crabbing dock on the creek, I sat down and watched a pair glide in, approaching like air liners or perhaps like cranes depicted in Japanese woodblock prints. They landed nearby and seemed oblivious to my presence.

These wading birds—the only stork in America—are a relatively new phenomenon here. Previously, the great blue heron was our largest bird, but now it takes second place. For the last several years these storks have been coming farther and farther north. Their traditional breeding grounds in southwestern Florida are being taken over by human sprawl—parking lots, golf courses, shopping malls . . . concrete. This disruption of wetlands and the natural water cycles is not favorable for the wood stork to feed and reproduce, so as a solution to this problem, they have discovered South Carolina!

As I sat on the dock, this pair of storks stalked closer and closer. They were close enough for me to observe their unusual method of fishing. They waded in the shallow marsh water, submerging their bills, which they snapped to catch some unsuspecting fish or crab. To startle their prey, they stirred the water with dainty pink feet attached to long thin black legs. At this short range I didn't need binoculars to see this great white bird—white winged with a black trailing edge and a sleek black tail. Their heads appeared naked, grey, and too small. They fished as if posing for a National Geographic Society photograph. John James Audubon wouldn't have needed a rifle.

But these wood storks are only visitors to Pawleys Island. They have flown the five miles down here from Sandy Island where they have been living for a year or so. Recently, I visited on the western side of Sandy Island, sat quietly, and observed their ritual activity of courting and nest building. This pair, perhaps from a nesting colony on South Island, east of Georgetown, had found seclusion and the habitat of Sandy Island more to their liking.

At first they were perched in a cypress tree near a nest that appeared unfinished. They flew down to the marshy ground and while one watched, the other waved its long neck, then walked in circles. They clapped their bills together, and then one picked up a stick and flew back to the nest. The other followed and sat on a limb nearby, resting its dark grey bill on its neck while a mate crammed the stick into this home in the top of a cypress. It took the stick out and crammed it back into the nest. It was obvious that more work would have to be done before this nest would hold an egg.

On my way home to Pawleys Island, I went by the public library to read more about them. The wood stork has been proven by DNA studies to be related to the black vulture and the turkey vulture. But how unlike they are, except for their soaring abilities and their great wing spans. Another similarity is their capability to smell their prey, a characteristic rare among birds. As Florida evolves into concrete, we welcome the wood stork and have no fears that Sandy and South Island will suffer the same consequence.

BEETLE JUICE IN THE NIGHT SKY

*W*hen the sky is clear and there is a new moon over the island, it's a good time for star gazing— star gazing and wondering. On one such night I went out on the back deck to look at the constellation Orion in the southeastern sky, where each star tried to outshine the other. Astronomers declare that in this constellation there are innumerable star "nurseries," something these scientist call proliferating nebulae, a term too complicated for most Pawleys Islanders.

But I wasn't interested in new stars because they can't be seen through my little telescope. I'm interested in the bright old stars, the stars I've looked at all my life, the ones I can wonder about. With Orion and its three-starred belt buckle as a skymark, I could rather easily identify four of the brightest stars in the heavens. I could wonder about Capella, Sirius, Rigel, and Betelgeuse, or "Beetle Juice," as this monstrous old star is pronounced. This "Beetle Juice" is the Titanic of our night sky. It's hard to even imagine how big it is, as thousands of our little earths might be placed inside its great sphere. Its brightness suggests that it could be relatively near, but it isn't. It is 527 light-years away.

Its distance made me wonder just how long it takes for its light—the light I saw that night—to reach Pawleys Island. I went back into the house to consult my star recipe book and found that a light-year is five trillion miles. To determine when the light I saw left "Beetle Juice," I punched numbers into my little hand computer, and the figure of 550 years popped up. Five hundred fifty years! The light reaching the island that night left "Beetle Juice" before Christopher Columbus sailed from Spain to the "New World."

I went back out to the deck to do some more wondering. I thought that our own planetary system is compact and even "Beetle Juice" seems close when we consider that our neighbor galaxy, Meissier 31, or the Andromeda Galaxy appear only as a small diffuse smudge of light from billions and billions of suns. I can't even see it without good binoculars, and even then sometimes I have to guess. The smudge of light from the

Andromeda Galaxy left there a very long time ago, before Pawleys was an island.

My wondering had taken me so far that I dared for a moment to think what might lie beyond Andromeda. I staggered back into the house and declared to myself that we're all so insignificant that it really doesn't matter who is elected president of the United States; it doesn't matter who wins the South Carolina–Clemson football game or who becomes mayor of Pawleys Island. It doesn't matter.

The only thing that matters right now is that I have the chance to go back out tonight to do some more wondering. Later tonight I may wonder about Sirius. I might wonder about Capella. I may wonder about those three stars in Orion's Belt.

LAST DAYS OF SUMMER

Rough winds do shake the wilting blooms of fall
From thy faded, once white, now peeling fence.
And summer's lease hath all too short a date.
Thy moonlit naked swims er gone.
Then, too hot the eye of heaven may shine,
And often is his gold complexion dimm'd
While sunset martini vanish into
Squirming guts unbound.

And feline meow, meow, meow fades,
But alas too late.
Nor too early ah thy slivering cunning cat.
And every fair from thy fair sometime
Declines thy wish'd hint.
By chance, or nature's changing course
untrimmed, unbent.

Nor dripped St. Michael underwear of John
Cease to hang on thy grey spindly hammock fair.
Lest damp quilt cease its putrid smell
And head's odoriferous pillow stilled unfair.

Feebly flying gnats yet unseen
Do probe foreign skins of their sweet sap.
Fair faded faces they do slap,
Then retreat to thy Pawleys slumber couch.

But thy eternal summer shall not fade,
Nor lose possession of that fair thou ow'st,
Nor shall death drag thou wander'st in his shade
To quietly imprison duck host of the south.

Nor shall eternal vanish thy cake of crab,
Alas thy grits, thy pie of chess.
Promethean tongue doeth lap thy bread of sourest dough
Til sleepest doest not abate.
Jasonic songs of Listz, thy rapture of St. Cecilia
Mass doest not fade
To some unknown abyss acrost mossd and marshy
Creek unbound
Where long neck of waterfoul doeth glide
And sly fish hawk seek its prey.

Nor shall death drag those wander'st
In his shade
When in eternal lines to
Time thou grow'st.

All gone are not the last days of summer
So long as men can breathe, or eyes can see.

So long lives this, and this gives life
To thee.

Inspired by Shakespeare sonnet XVIII

A WINTER MORNING

*I*t was late February, and the beach was quiet and isolated with hardly a person in sight, sometimes for days. I got up early, at daybreak, and let the Dalmatians, Tom Jones and John Brown, have a run. As the dogs raced off, the early sky was full of gray dawn light mixed with winter's blue and orange colors. They were pleased to chase the foam that forms along the edge of the surf when the wind and the temperature are right. They dashed at it, barking and pawing, then they stood back looking confused when nothing was there. As the sun peeped up, Tom Jones chased two willet who have resided between the groins for years. They flew away, perhaps to the next groin, but their voices could still be heard ringing insistently. A few early sanderlings arrived, and I sat on a groin post and watched them scurry and play tag with the surf, catching some unsuspecting little sea creature.

As the morning brightened, the circus continued. A flock of black skimmers flew by with their bills dipping down to catch some morsel before it reached the sanderlings. A line of brown pelicans sailed by with their wings just touching the crest of the waves, and with only a rare flap they seemed energized by some perpetual motion. A lone stray white pelican followed, not really joining the flock—an isolated bird that looked like an albino. A thermos of coffee helped to awaken and keep me warm. I sat and was joined by the gulls who always come to the beach at this morning hour for sun and whatever they can find to eat. They squawked and lingered, then flew inland, perhaps to the McDonald's parking lot.

After the gulls left, the northern gannets arrived, and soon there were hundreds of them showing off their aerobatics and spectacular high dives out in the ocean. With a wing span of two yards, white pointed tails and black wing tips, there's nothing around here like them. They seem timid and from a distance look like terns or gulls. The bird book says that they never touch land except to nest, and that's up in Nova Scotia or around the Arctic Circle.

Other than the shorebirds, it was just me and the dogs alone with the elusive and ever-changing sea edge. Like me, the dogs don't seem to have an interest in the shells. As puppies they used to pick up the shells, but now they don't bother. By the groin, an American bittersweet shell had washed up, I picked it up and examined it, trying to comprehend the life of the creature who once inhabited this empty domain. How did it find food? Who were its enemies? How did it protect itself and reproduce? But for me, simply to take it home to the shelf is an exercise in futility. The fulfilling moment is knowing the lifecycle of the creature who lived inside this vacated home. But I must be careful when thinking such thoughts, as I have many friends who are "shellers;" and annually go to Captiva Island in Florida to collect these lifeless domains.

We walked slowly down to the next groin southward. Tom and John rested at my feet. These dogs don't wonder about the comings and goings of our coastline like I do. I think that at some point in history, in geological time, the ocean waters will gradually creep westward and cover Pawleys Island. Then I remind myself that these comings and goings have gone on since the days when great reptiles roamed the lands and large sharks swam up and down the deep channel that is now the Waccamaw River. In the past the ocean crept to the mountains westward, paused, and slowly receded again.

Newton's Law, the basic law of the universe, will prevail: For every action there is an equal and opposite reaction. The outline of the shore today is but a moment in the history of the earth. Eventually, these comings and goings will slowly happen again. The coastline will creep eastward, and creatures like us will roam up and down this beach with their dogs. Maybe they'll resemble Tom Jones and John Brown. Maybe they'll run faster—fast enough to catch the willets. Maybe their dogs won't have spots.

THE MAGNETISM OF THE NECK

$\mathcal{T}$he Waccamaw Neck holds a certain magnetism that few areas can claim. When men first walked on this continent twelve thousand years ago, the ancestors of Indian tribes came here—the Winyah, the Sewee, the Cusabo, and the Yamasee. Then more recently in the 1700s the Chicora-Waccamaw and Pee Dee became permanent residents on the Waccamaw Neck.

Just across the creek from Pawleys Island in a new subdivision, amateur archaeologists are unearthing an endless pit of pottery shards along a stream that empties into the marsh. Recently they allowed me to visit, and I saw tables of pottery in a backyard.

Recorded history tells a bit more about the Spanish, who were drawn to this area in the early 1500s. It is not certain, but there is a likelihood that Hobcaw Barony land bordering on Winyah Bay was the site of Francisco Gorodilo's landing point as he arrived from the Dominican Republic. In 1526, he was followed by Spanish and Africans under the leadership of Lucas Vasques de Ayllon in their ill-fated attempt to settle San Miguel de Gualdope—the Spanish called the Waccamaw River "Gualdope."

It was here that the first slaves were brought to America and here the first slave rebellions took place. Had disease and conflict not ended their venture and had these settlements been permanent, the course of American history would have been different.

OLD BEACH GLASS

$\mathcal{O}$ne night a storm washed up bits of old beach glass between here and the groin in front of the Kelly's cottage to the north. As I combed the beach for some of these ignored gems, Ellie Whitworth approached me. I vaguely recognized her as an elderly neighbor I had met at the chapel service in the spring. As she got closer, I looked up and greeted her, then continued with my beach glass business.

"Heavens, just what are you doing? I don't see any shells," she said.

"Just looking for old beach glass," I answered, never looking up. She sounded amazed, "Well, never in my life have I heard of such a thing. Old beach glass! I collect shells."

She came closer, and I handed her a piece of glass. I explained that these old worn pieces might easily be confused with jade, especially the fragments of moss green colored beer bottle pieces that have been smoothed over the years by the sand. To astound her even more I added, "When my ownings are settled, I have deemed that my collection of beach glass be thrown back into this ocean off Pawleys, so somebody else will have the pleasure of finding it."

She held up the fragment I had given her allowing the morning sunlight to shine through. "Old beach glass, I declare." Ellie rubbed the glass in her palm, looked at it again, and said, "I must go straight home and tell my sister about this. Mary Sue will want some to go with our collection of razor clam shells. We also have a collection of prickly cockles and keyhole limpets that this glass'll look good with."

"Well, I don't know about such things as limpets and keyholes, but I do know glass when I see it," I said. Then I showed her a dark blue piece from a Milk of Magnesia bottle. She stroked it, handed it back to me, then wheeled around and faced my house.

"Mary Sue and I are curious as to why you fly that English flag there on your porch. It's even above ours," she pointed. I explained that I spent more than half my time living in London. Almost before I could say London, she responded in a loud shrill voice, "Oh my! I was in London last year with my niece, and I just loved every minute of it. Where do you live in that gorgeous city? Anywhere near our hotel across from the park?" She stopped, and then said, "You know, on down from Harrods and near Lady Di's palace there in the gardens."

I replied that I lived near Victoria Station on Buckingham Palace

Road and added, "That's about two miles from Harrods and Lady Di's. Sometimes I take the tube and go down there to Harrod's Food Hall. But it's terribly expensive, so I don't buy much. Just look mostly."

Ellie quickly asked, "Well living there, have you ever really seen the Queen?" She stopped, thought for a moment, then questioned, "Did you say Buckingham Palace?"

I answered, "Yes, in fact, I did meet Her Majesty once at a neighborhood Christmas party in a mews near Buckingham Palace. I met her, Ellie."

"Well, I don't know why on earth she'd be at a mews. Isn't that a horse stable?" She paused, then said, "She's so precious. How was she dressed? In one of those pretty blue crepe outfits she wears, I'll betcha."

I replied casually, "Not really. She wore an old head scarf, a long green overcoat, and wellies. I hardly recognized her, but I have a photograph taken by me to prove it. Yeah, I talked to her at that party. More or less like I'm talking to you right now."

Ellie placed her hands on her hips, assumed a wide-legged stance, then brushed at her hair, and said disappointedly, "Why heavens be! A scarf, an overcoat and . . .wellies. Wellies!"

No doubt this conversation would still be going on except for the welcome distraction of the neighbor's Labrador retriever who bounded down from the inn. I put the beach glass in a pocket and looked for something for the dog to chase.

Ellie started walking on down the beach toward her home. She stopped, turned, and yelled, "What did you say she was wearing? What kind of shoes did she have on?" She hesitated, then yelled, "What are wellies?"

SAND

*T*houghts of the goings and comings of our coastline on Pawleys

Island are esoteric and sometimes confound one's imagination. But questions about the saltiness of the ocean, about the tides, and, in particular, about the make-up of the beach sand are queries I ask visiting children as we play in the ocean or romp on the beach. I've learned not to discuss such topics with the adults who visit because they don't reply with as clever answers as the children do. They just look at me and then stare into space thinking, "What a silly question."

Children like to hear about grains of sand, and this is why I have an old Bausch and Lomb microscope in the house—the same scope I used in medical school to look at acid-fast bacteria. On a rainy day I'm apt to clean the dust off this instrument and use it. Children gather around and squeeze in to be next to look.

Sometimes I ask the children where these grains of sand came from or what they're made of. Young children may say that these grains came from God, or the rain, or that their mother brought them in a sand pail. Older children may say that this sand came from the river, or that the sand is ground up sea shells. The older ones are closer to the point.

I gather the children in a circle on the floor and place sand in their palms. As they take two little fingers and feel the sand, we talk about where it really came from. They seem interested to know that only a very small percentage of Pawleys Island sand is derived from ground up sea shells—calcareous material. I explain that the beaches of North Carolina, a hundred miles north, contain twice as much calcium material because there are more shells there.

Then I give them the surprise: the great majority of our sand on Pawleys Island is from elsewhere. It comes from west of here, the Piedmont Mountains and points in between. I tell the children that the Waccamaw, the Pee Dee, and the Sampit Rivers, the wind, and the rains bring decaying rock material to our ocean, and that they are seeing tiny bits of quartz derived from granite and such stones. I explain that under the microscope we are seeing this geologic antiquity as a sand flea might. Some grains display sharp and jagged edges, others rounded and smooth edges in colors of black and grey or transparent—all in little worlds of their own.

Children get restless, and before I lose their attention I explain another phenomenon that I can't show them under the microscope. Each grain of wet sand is surrounded by a film of water cushioning it from the next grain. The surrounding water usually contains single cell plants and animals swimming about, and that in these little worlds, the beings are breathing, fighting to survive and reproducing.

Children seem interested to know that there are billions of little worlds surrounding them and that each grain of sand may be the epicenter of these minute universes. These grains were a part of Pawleys Island beaches long before the children loaded into their parents' SUVs to come on vacation. I tell them that their grandchildren and great-grandchildren may play on this same sand someday.

If it rains, we go inside, and the children may ask me about why the ocean is salty. I shall have difficulty showing this under the microscope. Maybe we'll mix some table salt and sand and have a look. Maybe we'll play hide-and-seek under the house, or maybe we'll just sleep.

JELLYFISH

*T*he *Stomolophus meleagris* have arrived on Pawleys Island! The uninitiated and sometimes the knowledgeable may ask, "What's that?" The latter know this creature as the cannonball jellyfish. The former have no idea. Some simply call these "jellyball" or "cabbagehead" jellyfish. To those who live here on the island, they announce that springtime has arrived, as they lie in abundance on the beach in late March and April. It may seem more romantic to announce spring with the arrival of purple martins from the Amazon in Brazil—they're alive and catching our mosquitoes. But some years the purple martins are late in getting here.

These cannonball jellyfish also tell us that the loggerhead sea turtle is out there waiting to come ashore and lay its eggs. Some of these jellyfish have died because of bites from the turtle. To the loggerhead, these jellyfish are like caviar and sour cream, although they're made up of over

90 percent water. (The Chinese eat this jellyfish as a snack—raw or fried.)

A relative to the cannonball arrives earlier on the Pawleys beaches. This creature, actually an animal, is called the mushroom jellyfish and can attain a diameter of a foot, somewhat larger than the cannonball, but less abundant.

Children visiting Pawleys beaches have been taught to avoid all jellyfish because of their sting. Actually these early visitors are innocuous and have no significant sting. Later in the year, the rarer sea wasp, sea nettle, and moon jelly show up on the beaches of Pawleys Island. A dab of meat tenderizer will eradicate their sting. Even more rare is the Portuguese man-of-war, but generally they stay out near the Gulf Stream.

THE HIGH TIDE DINER

$\mathcal{I}$ drove over to Sherald's Store to get groceries and crab bait. Mobie stood behind the meat counter, as usual, wearing a white, bloodstained apron and a blue cotton shirt. In his pocket, as always, were seven colorful ball point pens and two marking pencils. I gathered up some things and then asked him for fish heads and chicken necks for crab bait. He mumbled, "How you doin'?" Around here sometimes this is a question and at other times it is a statement. While I was deciding how to answer, Mobie asked two more questions. Questions about what I do with my time in London and about the resignation of England's woman prime minister. I made a stab at answering while he was busy wrapping my things in white waxed paper and tying the bundles with twine cut from the roll above his head.

Mobie brought my packages to the front of the store, put them into a sack and did the tally. He wet the pencil tip with his tongue, grinned apologetically and said, "Well, I'll swan! That's in the neighborhood of seven dollars. Been that if you'd got another Goo-Goo." I shuffled through some ones and paid my bill. Frank walked me to the car carrying my brown sack, which he carefully placed on the front seat. He told me to call again.

After the amount of time spent at Sherald's Store, I realized that it was too late, and too hot in the kitchen, to prepare a noon meal, so I decided to drive up the highway to the High Tide Diner where the truckers eat. Between the post office and Buddy Vereen's place, my little Ford was nearly sucked into the exhaust of a eighteen-wheeler, then I had to dodge a pick-up that pulled into my path from Waccamaw Road. I adjusted my baseball cap, held tightly to the steering wheel, and pulled into the left turning lane. At Rutledge's vegetable stand, I wheeled across traffic into High Tide's parking lot and came thankfully to a halt.

I got out into the noon heat, looked at myself in the car window and prepared myself for entry into the diner. I undid two more shirt buttons, smoothed my hair and retilted my cap. Walking in, it felt like a plunge into the old Blue Hole. The window air conditioners whined along with the Nashville music playing on the Nickelodeon. They whined through a throng of whiskered truckers and construction workers, through a sea of baseball caps bearing slogans related to large machinery and football teams, and through a mass of sweaty T-shirts bearing remarks about mothers-in-law and the Darlington 500. I found an inconspicuous corner table and sat down, fumbling with my plain red baseball cap, trying not to feel self-conscious about its lack of a slogan. I tried to be nonchalant, but these truckers knew I was not one of them.

The plump waitress, known to the truckers as Pearl, brought me a tall plastic glass of already-sweetened iced tea and slid a menu across the yellow Formica table top. She knew that I didn't need a menu, but this was part of her routine.

"Honey, I haven't seen you since we run out of boiled okra last week. As I remember, we were out of mashed potatoes, too. Where you been? It's mad dog days and I was beginnin' to think you was mad like my neighbor's dog. Mad over the boiled okra and mashed potatoes. I even thought that maybe you'd stripped your gears." She laughed. "You know, like the stripped gears of my love life."

"Naw, Pearl," I answered. "My gears are not stripped too much, but

I have blown a gasket or two since I was here, but not over boiled okra. And I'm not too mad to come back." I pretended to look at the menu.

Pearl gazed across the highway. The traffic caused her green eyes to make little jerks, as if she were watching the Ferris wheel at the county fair or a passing train. She kept gazing out there expectantly. She swiped at her red hair with the hand which held the ball point pen, then she finally refocused her attention on me and my order.

"Honey, you've come late again and the truckers have already eaten all the mashed potatoes and the Kentucky Wonder green beans, and worst of all, there's nothing much left of the pork ribs. Just some ends." She stopped, then added, "But you're in luck. Lurleen's little Billy Boy brought in three pecks of greens, turnip greens I think." She looked back at the kitchen and said, "They've been cookin' in salt pork and they're about ready." Before I could respond, she said, "I'll just bring you a plate lunch with some of Billy Boy's greens, some of that mashed baked squash and whatever meat Lurleen can find in the oven pan." I nodded.

Pearl picked up the menu and slowly walked towards the kitchen, molded into her white-trimmed, orange polyester pant suit. At the kitchen window, she stopped and pulled at the synthetic material cling-ing too tightly to her hips. She yelled in my order so that it could be heard over the noise of the kitchen's exhaust fan. Then she borrowed a quarter from a trucker and inserted the coin into the Nickelodeon. It lit up, and Dolly Parton sang "Nine to Five."

Pearl returned with my plate lunch and slid it along the table, leav-ing a trail of gravy in a neat thin line. As I started eating, she mopped the gravy with her index finger and wiped it on a paper napkin. She stood by my table, gazing across Route 17. "Damn, Hon, it looks hot out there." She continued to stand there jingling through the coin tips in her pocket.

The truckers were thinning out and I was one of the few people left in the diner. Pearl jingled her tips again, took out two quarters and placed one on top of the other on the Formica. She looked at me and winked both eyes like a pleased lady moose. She picked up the coins and said, "Honey, be sure to put plenty of that hot pepper sauce on Billy Boy's greens." I stirred the iced tea and shook some pepper sauce on the greens.

Pearl smiled and stood taller. "Honey, when I get off, Lonnie's comin' by on his big Harley-Davidson, and we're goin' to Myrtle. Just us. Lon's promised to ride us around. Says he'll blow my hair back. Blow it back several times tonight." She hesitated, then added, "But hell, tomorrow I'll be back here servin' plate lunches to the truckers, lookin' out at this highway and, I guess, thinkin' about Lonnie and that big black Harley-Davidson." She turned and walked toward the Nickelodeon.

I finished eating my plate lunch, went to the cash register and paid Wanda the $3.72. I dialed a tooth pick and stood for a moment watching Pearl at the Nickelodeon.

I drove back down Route 17 in the heat. I drove past Buddy Vereen's place, past Buzz's Roost Hardware, and turned left at Sherald's Store, heading for the island. I thought of stripped gears, of blown gaskets, of boiled okra. I thought of red hair, and I thought of Pearl. I rolled down the windows, but my hair wouldn't blow back. My old Ford wasn't a Harley-Davidson, nor was it a pick-up. And I didn't have a Pearl. Only Lonnie had all that.

RUBY'S BEAUTY PARLOR

*R*uby is as bossy as a late summer hen with a string of baby chickens. But I go to Ruby's for haircuts because she's fast, and she's good. Ruby grew up in a family of about ten down around Moncks Corner where, as a girl, she spent a lot of time making spit curls on her younger sisters. She got interested in the beauty business and opened a shop there. But after attending a beauty convention in Myrtle Beach, she decided that Moncks had seen enough of her. She moved up to the mainland of Pawleys Island, to where there was more beauty action.

I had seen Ruby that morning at the post office, standing in a long line to buy stamps. Ruby, with her hair frazzled, looked as if she could use a beautician of her own. She told me that I needed a haircut and that she'd call me as soon as she got back to the shop and looked at her schedule. She bought stamps, cussed the postmaster, got into her VW, and drove off.

When I got home, the telephone was ringing. It was Ruby. "It's a good time right now to work you in for a trim. Let's see, I'm just putting Jeannine under the dryer, doin' some mousse on a curly perm customer, then I can do you a job."

I went across the creek to Ruby's as quick as a dog fight. I stopped momentarily on the front steps to observe a ruby-throated hummingbird at the red plastic feeder in a nearby holly bush and then entered the cold shop. Concentrating on her customer, Ruby greeted me with a mumble through a mouthful of bobby pins.

"You jest have a seat right here by Jeannine, and I'll be with you as soon as I've finished this comb-out." She took the bobby pins from her mouth and introduced me to Jeannine, who was seated under a dryer.

"That's Dr. Minton, who's here to get trimmed from London. He's from England." Ruby put the bobby pins back between her lips and mumbled, "Doctor, that's Jeannine Brown."

"Good morning, ma'am," I said to this fellow customer. I picked up an old issue of *Ladies' Home Journal* and sat down next to her. I held up the magazine to shield myself from the hot air blasting out of the dryer.

"Look's like Ruby's laying one right on you," I said.

"Uh-huh. A tight set to give me a real curly look. It's a Friday, so me and Ruby plan for it to hold at least through the weekend," she said with determination. "Would you get me a mentholated out of my handbag there on the floor?" With a stocking foot, she pushed the green canvas bag towards me, while keeping her head straight and staring ahead. She was evidently afraid to move a muscle in case a pin or a curler fell out and got her in trouble with Ruby.

I placed the bulging handbag in my lap and started opening its roped string. Jeannine suggested, "Just fumble there and get my methane, and you kin just light a cigarette and hand it over to me." I sorted through some battered Baby Ruth bars, some ball point pens, and a wad of lipstick-smeared Kleenex before locating the lighter.

"So, you're a real doctor and not from here on the Neck?" she inquired. Before I could answer, she added, "Hope you-all don't get that awful stomach virus that's goin' around here." She took the cigarette I handed her and kept talking. "One of the kids, me, and Buster been twisted double for two weeks, off and on." Without moving her head, she pointed a long index fingernail to her lower abdomen, "Right here, it'll get you."

Ruby gave her a sharp look. Jeannine took a deep draw from her comforting cigarette, inhaled, and then blew the smoke out through her nose in a long diagonal jet-stream. Through the smoke, I could see her taking a long deliberate blink with both eyes. Ruby squirted Nexus mousse on the curly perm customer and gave Jeannine a piercing but approving look. I sat with the handbag in my lap, occasionally patting it like a puppy, as I waited my turn.

"Whose wedding did you say you're going to, Jeannine? That girl I saw you with at the Piggly Wiggly last week?" Ruby asked.

"Uh-huh. She's my new friend, Ellen Aimsworth, that was livin' next door in the silver Air Stream, until that big wind last Tuesday nearly blew it away. It was a close shave, so Ellen up and moved to Socastee with her mother-in-law to be." Jeannine carefully deposited ashes into her cupped hand.

"Will the wedding be at the Baptist in Socastee?"

"Nope, Ruby. It's an outside wedding in Garden City." Jeannine took another draw from her cigarette. "It's on the concrete basketball court at Irby's Mobile Home Park. Ellen's marryin' a big tall guy, who was a basketball player at Myrtle High." The air conditioner coughed. Ruby walked over and pounded it with her fist while Jeannine talked on.

"Well, the guy wasn't much to look at when I saw him at the Air Stream, but Ellen says he's got a good job at the Kwik Kall in Surfside. Iffen it looks like rain, they'll do the wedding at the Gethsemane Free Will in Myrtle. I hope it's at Gethsemane 'cos I'm sure to look wind-blown at Irby's." Jeannine paused, stretched one leg, then the other, took another drag on the cigarette, and went on, "Have you heard of the Reverend Willard Wooten of the First Baptist Church in Myrtle? Well, Ellen tells me he is presiding if he kin get back from Aiken where he's doin' a revival."

"Buster going up for the wedding?"

"He said he was, and I ironed him a fresh shirt—even spray starched it. And I asked Loretta to stay with Randy and Sue Marie. But now I think he's backin' out so he kin watch Big Bo Peep wrestle that trio of fat women on Channel 70. You know, we've got a dish now, and Saturdays Buster aims to watch any channel that has wrestling on. Saturday nights I have to work my way to the bedroom through the empty beer cans. As far as the kids are concerned, they'll be all right. I'll get Randy some boxes of Cracker Jacks to open, and Sue Marie can tussle with her new kitty cat. It'll be a big day out for me, Buster or no Buster."

Ruby had finished with the curly perm customer and made change from a Dutch Master cigar box. She placed her hands on her hips and looked at me. My time had finally come. I walked to her chair cradling Jeannine's handbag. She impatiently took it from me, replaced it at Jeannine's feet, and draped me in a pink cape. I sat dead still. Ruby turned the radio up to listen to Georgetown's Swap and Shop program. The window air conditioner grumbled and the dryer hummed.

Ruby's next customer—her eleven-forty-five—arrived and sat down next to Jeannine. Through the mirror in front of me I saw a stocking foot push the handbag towards the newcomer. Ruby turned, glared at Jeannine and told her to keep her head straight.

In no time, Ruby finished my hair cut, undraped me, and I put my $4.50 in the cigar box. I thanked her and nodded to Jeannine. As I walked out, Ruby came to the window and stood with her scissors dangling from an index finger. She was watching the hummingbird at the plastic feeder.

Two weeks later, I went back to Ruby's. I was her only customer and had arrived considerably before her twelve o'clock. As usual the radio was on and the air conditioner was grumbling. Ruby started on my hair. After a moment I asked her, "Ruby, have you seen that customer you were doing up to go to a wedding last time I was here?"

"Oh, you mean Jeannine Brown. Yeah, I heard through Mabel Tucker, and then, Tuesday, Jeannine was in here." She stopped, and in a different and lower voice said, "Take your glasses off. Hold your head straight and still, if you can." Then she continued in her beauty parlor social voice, "Oh, I've got to tell you, that no-count Buster husband of hers let Jeannine drive his Ford Maverick up to the wedding. It rained something terrible, so they had it at the Gethsemane. After it was all over with, and Ellen and her man had gone, Jeannine couldn't get the Maverick started. She looked in the trunk and there was only one jumper cable. Then she remembered that she had seen Sue Marie lead-ing the neighbor's German shepherd with the other one." Ruby pushed my head to one side, told me again to hold still. She continued, "Now according to Mabel Tucker, the Reverend Wooten volunteered to drive Jeannine back down to get the other cable. She said Jeannine ran into the trailer all excited, while Buster was high and full of Old Milwaukee. Mabel said that Jeannine announced to him something like, 'I got car trouble. Need the other cable. Reverend Wooten's givin' me a jump.' Buster proceeded to hit Jeannine in the head with a can of corn, then he went out and roughed up the Reverend."

By now there was only an occasional clip of the scissors, as I sat dead still. "Jeannine snatched up Randy and Sue Marie and took them to the neighbors. She called the law in Georgetown, and Sammy Holkum and a new deputy Sheriff come up and arrested Buster for disturbing the peace. Finally, she and the Reverend went back to the Gethsemane and started the Maverick."

Ruby circled the chair, looking at my hair from various angles, but she was clearly more absorbed in Jeannine's story.

"Well, that Reverend Willard Wooten is a tall, good-looking preacher, but Jeannine didn't have any mind to him, at least I don't think so and neither does Mabel. But that Buster was full of beer and the meanness, like a snake just come out of him." Ruby paused again and looked at me through the mirror. "Jeannine come in here Tuesday for a comb-out and said she'd moved her things and the kids' over to her uncle's place in Hagley. She'd won some money in the WGMB bingo. She said she'd won a Bingo Ringo, whatever that means, and was buying Randy, Sue Marie, and herself some decent clothes." Little ticks could be heard from the air conditioner, which stopped when Ruby whammed it with her fist. "Jeannine was all grins when she came in. Said Reverend Wooten had worked her out a paying job on the River Queen, the sightseeing boat that goes up and down the Waccamaw. I fluffed her hair and she looked right good. She had on a nice red dress, and she didn't smoke a lick. And you know how she was smoking. 'Goin' to wean myself. It's not scriptural,' she told me."

With the comb in one hand and the scissors dangling from the other, Ruby commanded, "Tilt your head up. No, no, that's too much. Now don't you move a muscle until I get around your ears. Don't squirm." She went back to her clipping. "Jeannine's always had it bad, grew up hard, come from a half-way respectable family down around Bonetown, near Moncks Corner where I come from. She up and married that Buster guy who wouldn't work a lick. And they say that he beat Jeannine now and then as they moved from here to there, from Deep Creek to Sampit Run, with her trying to raise those kids."

The air conditioner was acting up again. Ruby pressed the button to turn it off, and when this didn't work, she jerked the cord loose from the outlet. She continued, "I was talking to Horace and Mabel Tucker. They're right close with Reverend Wooten and are guest members of his church in Myrtle. They live right over yonder." She pointed across the road. "Horace is the one who bought the River Queen up at the dock on the Wachesaw Plantation and he's giving Jeannine a job as ticket taker and refreshment salesgirl, sort of a river hostess I guess you might say. Horace told me that he's providing her with a place to live, too. She and the kids are going to live in Horace's lighthouse over on North Inlet, the one that the government has turned over to him to keep lit."

All was quiet for a moment. I glanced in the mirror, and Ruby was looking out the window. I turned just long enough to see a hummingbird fly from the feeder.

"Mabel tells me that Reverend Wooten lost his wife two years ago in August while she was having a C-section up in Myrtle, when their baby came. Since then he's been helping Horace with the lighthouse some, that is when he's not looking after that baby or doing revivals. Mabel and me suspect that he feels more like a shepherd or something, just keeping that lighthouse lit. And just think, Jeannine will be helping them see to that light."

Ruby finished my haircut, sprinkled lilac talc powder on a soft shaving brush, blustered it about the back of my neck, resprinkled the brush and whisked it about my temples. I tried not to choke. Through the cloud of lilac-perfumed powder I could see Ruby's twelve o'clock customer coming through the door.

"How you doin'?" Ruby asked.

"How's it going with you?" the customer replied.

"Great, just great," Ruby answered.

She removed the pink cape and popped it like a whip. As the hair fell and the lilac powder drifted, she pitched the cape across her shoulder and reconnected the air conditioner. She took my five dollar bill, made change, and heaved a sigh. "Honey, I guess Jeannine's Jesus just sent her to Ellen's wedding at the Gethsemane."

I walked out into the noon-day heat with all this on my mind. I paused on the steps to watch that hummingbird again. It swung like a pendulum in a wide arc, back and forth, back and forth, by the feeder in the holly bush. Then it flew sideways to a white hibiscus bloom and seemed to stop in mid-air. It hummed and quickly pierced the yellow stipes with its long bill. I looked up, and Ruby was watching too.

PLUTARCH'S LIVES

A northeaster wind bore down on the island that late January morning. A misty rain didn't fall as much as it was blown sideways. It was steely cold. Few shorebirds ventured out.

I swathed myself in a quilt and got on the hammock, wrapped up like a mummy. I lay there and watched a lone cormorant flying northward against the wind, flapping and determined, but alone. The words of William Cullen Bryant's poem, "To a Waterfowl," raced through my mind. I could remember distinctly its last stanza:

He, who, from zone to zone,
Guides through the boundless sky thy certain flight,
In the long way that I must tread alone,
Will lead my steps aright.

As I pondered these words, the rain blew in more fiercely, like wet saplings whipping me. My cocoon was getting soaked, and I retreated inside. I thought this might be an appropriate time to read something uplifting, something noble. I stood on my toes and reached to the highest shelf, a place dusty and rarely disturbed. I found Plutarch's Lives and decided that this was a deserving book to be read on such a day.

Was it silliness that came over me when I started wondering what was Plutarch's other name—his first or given name? Could it have been Bernard Plutarch? Sam Plutarch? Leroy Plutarch? J. D. Plutarch? Or was it Plutarch Goldstein? But then it dawned on me that a Greek as virtuous as Plutarch didn't need two names. One was enough. After all, Pericles was Pericles, nothing else.

Retreating to the nearest chair, I sat and read what Plutarch said about Pericles. Back then, around Athens, poets were more important and respected than they are now. Learned people studied poetry and paid attention to it. Plutarch says that the poets of Athens called Pericles "Schinocephalos," a seemingly respectable name until it is deciphered. This amusing word means "squill head" or "onion head." Plutarch knew all about Pericles from his beginnings. He says that Pericles' mother, being near term, fancied in a dream that she was brought to the bed of a lion, and just a few days later, she was delivered of Pericles. He was a cute little baby and perfectly formed, except that his head was longish and greatly out of proportion.

Pericles grew up doing good things for the Greeks. He went out and saved Athens from the Persians and eventually built the Parthenon. His Athenian buddies would gather there on its steps, look up, swish their togas and say, "Old Onion Head did it!"

But as the late afternoon wore on I did try to read more from Plutarch's *Lives*, delving into Themistocles, Alcibiades, and Philopomen, but it just didn't work. Maybe there was something about the island air. More likely, it was just me.

The January rain slackened, and I went back to my damp cocoon in the hammock, hoping to see another lone cormorant—some shorebird, so I might have another chance to wonder about boundless skies and about treading alone.

I lay there, but my mind wouldn't leave Plutarch, and it wouldn't leave Pericles. I was stuck with old Onion Head.

AM I SHEPHERD OR A POET?

That particular day moved as lazily as a blue moon, but the breeze was good enough to fly a new dragon kite that a visitor had presented as a house present. I finally got it up in the air and was happily flying it when two pretty little girls stopped their beach play to follow along and giggle. The late May wind settled, and I wound in the kite and sat down on the groin to watch a diving fish hawk pluck a fish from the ocean and fly toward the creek. All was quiet for a moment. Then the nearest little girl looked up at me and, after whispering something to her friend, said, "I'm Sally and this is Susie." She looked down and wiggled her toes in the sand. She seemed to be searching for a comment to entice me to talk. Finally she said, "Daddy keeps people's books or something. Besides flying kites, what do you do?"

When I am asked this question, I usually answer that I am a shepherd. But I guessed that Sally and Susie had probably been in a Christmas play at church and knew precisely what a shepherd was—that man in the long night gown who carried the crooked walking stick. Then they would probe and ask unanswerable questions about the wise men, swaddling clothes, mangers, and Bethlehem. So I thought for a moment and then said, "I am a poet." Without a word, the little girls ran off towards the surf. I retreated to the Duck's Nest with my dragon kite.

A few minutes later there was a gentle tap and then a louder knock on the screen door. I greeted two giggling little girls. Sally, standing in front, placed her hand over her mouth, looked down at her sandy feet, and said between giggles, "Mister, will you write us a-a," she giggled again, "a poem?"

I pleaded, "But little girls, I am on vacation. I don't work on vacations. I fly kites. Things like that."

Susie, stretching from behind her friend, tried to peer into my living room. She looked up at me and said, "We only want a little one. Maybe only one or two verses. A real little one for me and Sally."

I hadn't written a poem since the fifth grade, but now I was caught. Caught like a crab in a net, so I said, "Well, you come back after a while, and I'll try to have a verse or two for you."

They ran like elks back to the beach, and I sat down to call up all my creative powers. Struggling with words, I wrote:

Oh distant wave once chilling,
You seem now to possess us.
Oh soft sand, once dry, once hot
Now cool, now soaked, now dark
For Sally and Susan's bathing.

I wrote about sea birds, about soaring kites, about the ocean wind. I wrote about anything I could think of. Just before dark, I heard a tap on the door. I picked up the labored verses and went to open it. Sally took her hand away from her giggling mouth just long enough to snatch the piece of paper from me. Not a word was said. They vanished towards the rented house next door.

During the remainder of the week, daily love letters appeared under my screen door, notes—descriptions of Archibald, Sally's cat, and their exploits of the previous day as well as the dates of their ninth birthdays— printed neatly on lined paper. Now, no doubt, I had life-long friends, the kind made only on an early summer beach on Pawleys Island.

They visited me again before leaving for home. Sally asked for my London address. In mid-December a Christmas card, hand made, arrived in my London mail in an envelope postmarked Aiken, South Carolina. Inside the little Christmas card, on a piece of lined notebook paper, Sally had written:

"Dear Dr. Minton,
How are you fine I hope. Archibald and Susie say Hi. Can you come to my school's Christmas play? Susie is a girl shepherd or something. But I am Mary.
Love, Sally

DINING ALONE

*I*t is not unusual that I prepare Fagioli ed Orzo or Petites Tourtes de Fruits de Mer Ostendaises for myself, but sometimes I have had enough of my own cooking. One Monday night, when I was pretty sure things were fresh, I ventured over to Frank's Restaurant on Route 17, as I quite often do. It's the same old building I used to go to when Frank Marlow presided over his butcher's shop and wrapped the meat in white waxed paper and tied it with string. I sat at the bar waiting my turn for a table. Sitting there alone was a guarantee to draw attention and comments from the two twenty-something blondes along the bar. They whispered to each other, cast me a fleeting glance, and then went back to their lipstick-smeared fuzzy navel straws. They knew and I knew that a lone male drinker should be sitting over in front of the Texaco stop, sipping a Bud. But not being a beer drinker, I just sat there drinking a house Merlot instead. It was I who would be in bed by 10:30. It was the blondes who would be hung over the next day.

Upon entering Frank's, I had requested from Irene, "A table for one, please." I could read her mind: "He'll have a table for two, but since there's just one of him, I'll only get 50 percent of the potential revenue. As for tips, well, he's eating on his own, so he's likely to be generous." Being interpreted, this means that if I get a table at all, it will be right in the back, behind the Ficus benjaminum.

As I sipped the Merlot and awaited my seat behind the dusty ficus, I had plenty of time to think about my position in this South Carolina society—the society between Debordieu Colony and North Litchfield, between Georgetown and Wachesaw Plantation. The only way I would really fit in would be to take Holy Orders, like Father Pat over at the Catholic Church. Since I'm not the preacher type, I'll make do with my life on the island. Living alone suits me like the black spots suit Tom Jones and John Brown, my Dalmatians. I can drop everything at a moment's notice and go to the Inlet Square cinema or up to the Cracker Barrel for a bowl of white bean soup. I can decide exactly how many inches of dust shall be allowed to accumulate before cranking up the vacuum. At dinner I relish being able to enjoy the food rather than having to hold a conversation over it. And I don't mind putting things in the dishwasher as I hum a little something from La Traviata because neither Tom Jones nor John Brown recognize that I'm not in tune.

Well, it was now half an hour and two glasses of Merlot later, so I asked Irene about my chances of a table behind the ficus. When she said it would be thirty more minutes, I stood up, winked at the two blondes, and decided to drive up Route 17 to the Piggy Wiggly.

In some respects, going to the Piggly Wiggly is better than going to Frank's. The Eine Kleine Nachtmusik playing on the PA of the Piggly is much more pleasing than the drone of drinkers and eaters at Frank's. There I can listen to myself shopping for food and at Frank's I can't hear myself eat. I can't hear myself think. I can't hear Irene when she comes around and asks how I'm doing.

Even at the Piggly Wiggly, a single man shopping may create some curiosity. I ask myself, "Why, when most chefs are men, does this come as a surprise to people, to the grocery clerks, to my occasional guest? Do they expect me to live on microwaved beans on toast?" I can hear my guest saying, "You mean, you did all this yourself?" as if my arms were broken. "Of course I did, it's only souffle de pommes de terre. It's only cacciucco con battuto alla livornese. I got up a 4:30 this morning to start it. I have nothing else to do. I am single."

Anyhow, as I listened to Mozart, the grocery cart started filling. Reluctantly, I asked the clerk stocking the shelves for passilla chillies and Szechuan peppercorns. She searched the shelves and found only the peppercorns, but from her expression you would have thought I had asked for a bra. I pushed the cart to the poultry counter and selected two rock Cornish hens, those very small fowl which are little more than ambitious eggs. I put the little hens in my cart thinking that, even dead, they look cute. Just about this time a young woman walked by and had a look into my cart. She said quietly to the lady with her, "Poor little things." I could hear the older lady, "He's a callous brute. Anybody who would cook those poor little things . . ."

By the time I had pushed the cart over to the wine department, I was thinking gloomily, "Maybe I look like a callous brute, maybe I look shifty." I am, of course, acutely aware that serial killers and mad bombers tend to have domestic arrangements similar to mine. Whenever I read a psychological profile of a suspect on the post office bulletin board, it is apt to read: "The authorities are looking for a single man in his late forties, who lives alone, is not gregarious, and almost certainly eats Cornish hens, grilled, not roasted." They lump us all together in the same boat.

I selected two bottles of 1992 Sangiovese and a small bottle of White Xynisteri Cyprus brandy. I checked the grocery cart. There were the chillies, celery, red onions, lemons, rosemary Grissini bread, two fennel bulbs, some cherries for clafouti aux cerises, and the "poor little things," the rock Cornish hens. Then I went back and circled again, while the music changed to Vivaldi's Le Quattro Stagione. I picked up some sandwich bread and a package of bacon, and over at the vegetable section I found a nice head of lettuce and a large tomato.

It was late when I approached Lorrita at the check-out.

"How you doin'?" she said. Then she looked into my shopping cart. "I bet I know what you're having for supper."

I said, "Yeah, Lorrita. I'm having bacon, lettuce, and tomato. I'm having a B.L.T."

LETTERS TO THE SOUTH PACIFIC

A late winter storm, a northeaster, had raged over the island for the past two days. With nothing much else to do, I ventured to the attic to organize and clean it. I was greeted with cobwebs, dust, and piles of faded cardboard boxes filled with an accumulation of worthless correspondence, canceled checks, and bank statements. I crawled across to a green military trunk in which I have stored significant letters over the years. When I opened it, some letters bulged forward and on top was a manila envelope marked "Letters to the South Pacific." Then I remembered that these were most of the letters I had written to my older brother when I was fourteen years old, when he was a seaman on a destroyer, the USS *Farragut*, in the Pacific during 1944. To my surprise he had kept these letters and a few years ago had presented them to me in a neat bundle in this same manila envelope. At the time I hardly looked at these epistles, feeling somewhat embarrassed at what I might have written to my big brother so long ago. The letters were stowed away in the trunk, and I thought they might stay there forever. However, on this day, I decided to take them downstairs and read them.

March 10, 1944

Dear Ralph: I will write another letter as I have just received the biggest letter I bet you have ever wrote. Four pages. I didn't think you could ever write that much. Are you seeing the world? I wish I could. How many Japs have you seen? Mama says you can't kill any from your ship. In today's paper there was a real good write up and picture of all the boys that put the flag up on Iwo Jima. I will try and send it to you.

Out of the six that put the flag up I think that three are killed by the Japs and one is wounded. That picture really was a dramatic scene."

August 5, 1944

Dear Ralph: I just thought that I would write to you as I have nothing to do, much. How is the navy treating you? We haven't heard from you in over a month. I don't know why. Do you? Can you really tell me if you are in the Third Fleet? We heard a lot about it until our radio broke or the battery went dead. What number is your ship? I'm always seeing pictures of destroyers and they always have numbers. I guess there are hundreds of them. I would like to fly a Hell Cat airplane from a carrier.

I think Millard Sherald has been freed from the Germans and is not dead. His mother told Mama in the post office. He was a real good basketball player. Fowler Stanton is back from Germany or somewhere because I saw him in the Baxter post office on Sunday with his uniform on. He was a gunner on a navy bomber or something. WHUB on the radio said he was shot down once and I guess that's why he's home. He walked away from the post office with your gal Jean Green. But I guess I'm not supposed to tell you that. She didn't know I saw her.

August 15, 1944

Dear Ralph: It's my birthday and I'll write another letter as Mama mailed the other one unfinished. Mama let me get a dog for my birthday. I call it Duckie because I traded a duck and a nu-grape drink to get it from Walter Wheeler, that boy who lives out on the Baxter road by the Sewells. He's the boy whose mother cusses me so much. I bet you remember her, don't you? I also traded for us some ration coupons with Buttermilk and William Maynard.[1] To get them I traded ten of the marble aggit you gave me before you left for the war. But two marbles were chipped real bad. Do you remember those? Lizzie Maynard still washes our clothes in her back yard like she used to when you were home. She still gets the Holy Ghost and shouts in the back yard sometimes. Yesterday we heard her yelling Jesus, Jesus in the backyard. Daddy went out there to see if she was okay, and she was, I guess.

January 28, 1944

Dear Ralph: How are you? Guess you are still seeing the world? Do you sleep in the hammock on your ship? I would really like to know how you like the ocean, and are

---

[1]. Buttermilk Maynard was killed in the Korean War.

you swimming in it? You had a terrible time with that in boot camp, you said. I'm reading a navy book now to report on in Miss Hill's English class. I'm on the main sophomore basketball team now. We beat the freshman 12 to 40. I scored 12 points. But I can't do that every time. I am coming out for the main team next year, but Daddy says I'm too little. I've got a good chance if Bud Keisler joins up with the navy. (Also, he's taller than me.) This six weeks I made an A in algebra, an A in ancient history, an A in Miss Hall's English, and a B in Biology. (Mr. Bertram on the final said my drawing of an amoebae looked like a Paramecium and shouldn't have whiskers.) Miss Hall said to the class that I was first this six weeks and it made Eleanor Scout mad. She's the Jehovah Witness girl from the Low Gap who is usually first. Miss Hall said on the final that she misspelled Zerxes in ancient history, the Persian man. I just told about him and didn't try to spell him. Eleanor won't speak to me now.

May 12, 1944

Dear Ralph: I will write another letter because we got one from you yesterday with a lot cut out of it. I'll bet you saw another suicide Jap plane. It's hot here and we are raising a tobacco patch now that school is out. We are raising it where the peanut crop used to be because tobacco costs more. It is my first and last I hope. It's awful to set out. We have to reset it today. I wet the roots of the awful smelling plants, dropped them and then set them out while Daddy just makes the holes in the right places. He is the slowest man I ever saw. Junior Bice rode by on his bicycle and yelled at me that we would have to catch big green tobacco worms this summer.

March 28, 1944

Dear Ralph: Our radio is fixed and it came over WHUB that Webster Lewis has killed 155 Japs and captured thirty. Do you remember when he went squirrel hunting with Daddy? I don't believe he could kill that many.

October 30, 1944

Dear Ralph: I'm getting ready for the Halloween party in the gym tomorrow night and I'm writing this letter from the study hall. But I'm really afraid Miss Hall will see me writing. I'm supposed to be doing her Bible assignment on the Bee Attitudes. But I'm not. She stands up there behind the desk looking mad and jingling her keys. I think Bud and Harold have slipped out to go to the gym where they crawl through the back window and play basketball. I'd like to slip out but I guess I'd get caught and then she'd make me write sentences. I've learned to hold three pencils in one hand and write 500 sentences in no time. Bud teaches me and I've caught on. The bell is ringing and I can't wait to get to the gym. Bye bye.

November 2, 1944
    Dear Ralph: The Halloween party was fine and Mama said I didn't spend too much money. I am a sophomore now and we've finally had the election and guess what? I'm the class president over Harold Denny and Martha Sue Herrin. (Sam Denny was the president last year, but he fainted and fell over at the second class meeting. Miss Hall helped him up, but he wasn't even nominated this year.) I hope I don't forget when our class has the chapel and I have to say a poem. But I don't think I will. At the party I saw your girls Charlie Mae and Jean. I gave them some chewing gum for you. Well that's about all this time.

December 1, 1944
    Dear Ralph: I'm playing on a team now in basketball. I play with the Future Farmers, although I'm not one. We have FFA in white on our blue uniforms and black leather kneepads. We played the main second team last week. I didn't score, but my man didn't either. Our coach, the fat FFA teacher, said that was alright.

April 7, 1945
    Dear Ralph: Dock Johnson has been killed in Belgium. You know Kenneth McBroom that was in our class, he has his arm off. He is back. A. V. Randolph was on the USS *Maryland*, but he isn't on it now. It blew up.
    I fixed a flat tire on Daddy's car yesterday and have a blister on my hand. I have really been working lately. Daddy let me drive the car with him up to Ward's Mill to get our tractor back from Uncle Wiley. But we got ready to leave with it and when we put the water in it the pipe was broken, so we had to pull it home by hand. After we got home I put the water in it and we could hear it pouring through the motor or something. Daddy took the oil stick out and water poured out of it. So we don't know what's wrong. I bet you would.
    The last letter we got from you two pieces were cut out, about the flag hoist and what forces you are in. I am sending you some pictures of the Iwo battle. I don't know whether you have seen them or not.

March 19, 1945

Dear Ralph: I was sick last week and Mama made me stay in bed and take sulfa drug and castor oil. But I got better. Some boys and girls were starting to walk out here to see me from the seminary while I was sick and Miss Hall caught them and they had to write a few hundred sentences. Like, "I will not skip class. I will not skip class."

June 1, 1945

Dear Ralph: Daddy is always having problems with our radio, but it is fixed now. Lillian and Mable came to visit on Saturday night, and we listened to the Hit Parade and then Evelyn and her magic violin, I guess. They brought cheese and crackers. I also like Kay Kaiser. Do you ever hear him? My favorite program of all is *Dr. IQ*. I send in questions to him sometimes like what does the word Tennessee mean? I will close now as I have to get ready for Sunday School, but I don't like our teacher Mr. Maxwell.

P.S. I am almost as big as you now. I wear your shirts and kakki pants.

September 1, 1945

Dear Ralph: The infantry soldiers from Fort Knock, KY, are camping in the Stewart field where we used to raise corn. About five hundred are on a bibwack there and most are sleeping in little pup tents. I go over every day and sell them Mr. Goodbars and Milky Ways for ten cents, and I buy them for five cents at the Campbell's store. I have made a lot of money. One soldier talks to me every day. He is from Virginia and says he will write to me if he goes overseas. He wrote down my address. I took him and showed him the Ford spring and the blue hole. We went swimming in the blue hole, but it was too cold to take my clothes off.

CASH REGISTER RAGE

"Why can't a woman be like a man?"

—"My Fair Lady"

$\mathcal{I}$ had intended to remain quiet about this, but since I have heard both women and men talk about it I shall feel free to express an opinion. I have experienced this in the United States, England, France, and the Far East. Men rarely do it. This is the phenomenon of some women's delaying and fumbling when it is time to pay at the grocery store.

I was reminded of this recently at the Food Lion grocery store here. I had dashed into the store to pick up a few items at a time when I was late for an appointment. I got into the shortest line I could find (which, for me, proves to always be the slowest) and stood there trying not to be impatient, trying not to appear to be in a hurry. I stood behind a lady who had a cart bulging with groceries, and as Julina Alston tabulated her purchases, she stood and gazed at the shoes of a fellow customer, then fastened her attention across the parking lot. Julina concluded, "That'll be $44.17," as a young high school student finished sacking this lady's groceries.

She said surprisingly, "Oh, my!" and only then decided to pull the bag from her shoulder and search for a checkbook. It was finally located and she started writing the check, then stopped and asked for the total again. With this, she returned the checkbook to her bag and decided to pay with cash, fumbling for the money. She was two dollars short. Julina and I continued to wait as she was deciding which credit card to use.

My impatience finally overcame me, and I suggested that we play, "eny, meny, miny, moe," to select a card. She glared at me and told me that she would be pleased if I got into another line. I retreated as she reached for a grapefruit to throw at me, having learned my lesson.

There was a similar occurrence in Georgetown, D.C. recently. I read in the Washington Post about a prominent U.S. Senator who had gone to the "social Safeway" to do on-the-way-home grocery shopping when a delaying lady blew a gasket and slung her shoulder bag at him. The Senator wasn't as lucky as me. He was taken to the emergency room at Bethesda Naval Hospital for suturing of facial lacerations.

Bill Crowley recently visited from London. He told me of his experience at the food hall of Marks and Spencers on King's Road. Something of a fight ensued when his impatience overtook him—he and the delaying young lady were taken to the police station around the corner.

Everyone who frequents grocery stores, markets, and department stores should be aware. There's a new epidemic, Cash Register Rage, or in England it's more commonly known as Till Rage.

HEALTH FOOD

*L*ately I've been stopping at Pawleys Plaza to pick up the free publication *Over 50*—the magazine depicting people like Martha Stewart and Barbara Bush on the cover. It's not like the magazines at the Piggly Wiggly check-out counter with Leonardo Di Caprio holding court on their pages.

I've finally convinced myself that I should read the articles in *Over 50*. Some of these articles have reminded me that we should watch what we eat, which doesn't mean that we should look at this food as it goes down our goozel. It means that we should analyze, just a bit, what we are eating. Most everything I had picked up at the Piggly Wiggly had listed innumerable additives, such as preservatives, coloring, and bio-things which made me start wondering. Should I try some things from the local health food store, To Your Health, which advertises in the county newspaper?

I drove down Route 17, and when I was sure that nobody was looking, I pulled into the health food store's parking lot. I noted that it shared a duplex with a chiropractor who advertises on a Myrtle Beach television station. Having only a moment to spare, I quickly surveyed the bulging shelves, then purchased a box of Kombucha green tea, thinking that anything named Kombucha would automatically guarantee long life and happiness.

Later, I made my first cup of the tea, and I must say that it was rather pleasing, not as tasty as some of the tea brought by English friends but better than the tired-tasting Lipton—the American standard tea.

Before putting the box on the shelf I read about the kombucha I had been drinking, and the surprise came. Here is a list of the ingredients in this tea: organically grown spearmint leaf, natural passion fruit flavors, natural plum flavors, Kombucha-pure extract which contains Oriental ginseng, licorice root, peony root, ginger root, eucommia bark, cinnamon bark, reishi mushroom, Dong Quai root, rehmannia root, lycii barbarum fruit, and twenty-nine millograms of caffeine per heaping teaspoon.

Standing there, it dawned on me that I had violated my mother's trust. My mother had warned me about mushrooms, she had warned me about ginseng, and she had told me to be careful about roots and barks. She had impressed on me that I should never eat anything with a name like Dong Quai. My mother had told me that I would grow hairs in the palms of my hand if I ever ate passion fruit.

My mother was from southern California, and she was so old that she had been an extra in the film *Birth of a Nation*. My mother never knew about health food stores. If she knew about passion fruit, she should have known about kombucha.

But I'll forgive her, she was too old to have known about *Over 50* magazine.

SANDY ISLAND

I could have gone by myself, but I felt that it would be more appropriate to go to South Carolina's "Garden of Eden" with a black friend. Zachary Allston had relatives—a cousin—living there, and he agreed to go with me, provided that I take him to see his girlfriend in Georgetown afterwards. Zachary was eighty years old!

It was a fine October morning and summer was just beginning to fade, so there was a certain crispness in the air. Indian summer was here, and it was a good day to go to Sandy Island, not only because of my company, but because the cottonmouth snakes were supposed to have returned to their dens. It is well known that Sandy Island is the epicenter for this poisonous snake. Snake fearing people shouldn't go there.

I picked up Zachary from his home on Bess Lane, and we drove northward on the highway for three miles. Just before reaching Brookgreen Gardens, we turned westward onto an asphalt road as straight and level as an old truck bed. Zachary talked constantly, telling me tales of Sandy Island, tales involving his elderly cousin, Moses Murray. As a boy he had spent many summers on the island with Moses.

We drove these three miles through a forest of long leaf pines that thinned out into a marshy swamp leaving sweet gums, cedars, and chinaberry trees draped in a green gauze of kudzu vines, making them appear like large animals—dinosaurs and elephants. Banks of welcoming black-eyed Susans grew along the road. Late summer blue chrysanthemums grew tall and stalky with their withering October leaves, a preamble to Sandy Island.[2]

We parked, got out of the car, and I stood looking back down this road and thought, "If this road could talk, what would it say?" For centuries the blacks, on their way to and from the King's Highway, used these paths, as had the Waccamaw Indians before them. Plantation owners on the island a hundred years ago had parked their buggies and carriages along the eastern banks of the Waccamaw—the Allstons, the Petigrus, and the Heriots.

Before we could straighten ourselves out, old Moses Murray greeted us. He and Zachary began jabbering in their brand of English, with Moses speaking in a Sandy Island dialect different from the mainland lingo. These cousins hadn't seen each other in a year, and there was much to talk about. We got into the small fishing boat he had brought over, and like most of the other families who live on the island his boat was powered by a no-nonsense outboard motor. It whined low as we crossed the Waccamaw, low enough so that he and Zachary could talk.

Moses turned to me, cut the whine of the motor lower, and asked me where I lived. When I told him that my home was on Pawleys Island, he said proudly, "Sandy be over ten times bigger dan Pawleys. We have

2. The original trail and road was a mile north of here, near Brookgreen Plantation.

thirteen thousand acres here," and with this he sped up, finishing the quarter of a mile across the river to the island. Moses cut the engine and we floated in to a primitive dock and tied up with several other similar boats.

I continued to sit in the bow of the boat and surveyed the island I had only read and heard tales about. The land was flat, dark, and unbroken, sweeping away in both directions—a great pine forest interrupted by only one house that I could see. A lonesome dirt road curved gently around up toward a knoll and out of sight from a parking area, which was occupied by three dilapidated pick-up trucks.

As Moses secured the boat, he told me that the school boat crossed the river to and from the island twice each day, and after that the islanders were on their own. "When I grows up we don't have such a school boat. Go to school on de island in that two-room school house dats gone now." I asked Moses about crossing the Pee Dee River westward from the island, and he told me that in no time one could be over to Plantersville. Then quickly added, "Nobody want to go to Plantersville. Nothin' der."

We got out of the boat, and Moses insisted that he would give us a tour. He walked in front, up a narrow sandy road that curved gently to the left, then past a small bright blue house with a rusty tin roof. Its front yard was enclosed with a white faded picket fence and two white-washed truck tires serving as flowerbeds for dusty chrysanthemums. An old woman came onto the porch, surprised by visitors. Zachary and Moses talked to her in a dialect I didn't understand. Moses introduced me and she said, "Won' you come en?" But he answered that we didn't have time to linger.

We walked on as the lane meandered through a cedar thicket. We went up a slightly elevated knoll with a clearing, and suddenly there was a stuccoed brick building with two towers: Bethel Baptist Church, the highest point in the county. Moses, being a deacon in the church had a key. He opened the door and then explained why it was such an imposing church for the few families who inhabited the island. He said that it would be filled on anniversary Sundays and at homecomings. He added, "Dat's when we have singin's and dinner on de ground, and it last all day and everbody whos ever lived here come back. We keep dat ferry boat busy all day with de comin's and goin's. Even past sundown."

I stopped to get a sniff of the country church aroma—a characteristic smell of cleanliness, of lilac powder, of sweat, of freshly-washed Sunday clothes. It was a smell that I recalled from when I went to some country church as a little boy, clinging to the secure hand of my mother. I stood there remembering as Moses and Zachary awaited me at the doorway. I finally turned and left the church, with this nostalgic aroma still lingering lightly.

We walked the few steps down a pathway toward the cemetery, where late summer gold and yellow chrysanthemums were struggling to bloom. A light wind caused a weary sound to come from the pines above. Moses took us to the grave of "Aunt Lula Belle," as Zachary called her. She was his aunt and the mother of Moses. Wasps clung to the rim of an overturned flower vase as Moses carefully righted it and rearranged the faded plastic red roses, trying not to disturb the wasps. The simple white marble tomb-stone was inscribed: "Lula Belle Murray, the devoted wife of Ebinezer Murray, 1875–August 12, 1960," and below this: "Gone but not forgotten." Neither of the old patriarchs said anything as we walked on through the graveyard.

We walked back down to where the sandy lane forked and took the right turn leading westward across the island, passing two more houses brightly painted in shades of blue. Each house had a fence with a frantically barking dog who clamored at the fence to get at us, snarling and half climbing the wire mesh. The lane wound its way through a sweet gum thicket mingled with scrubby cedars. Moses and Zachary walked in front a few steps, both talking and paying no attention to their surroundings. Then I saw something that appeared to be a tree limb in the middle of the sandy lane. As I came closer, it became obvious that this obstruction was a large snake. I yelled just before Moses stepped on it. They stopped and backed off as it coiled and opened its wide white mouth before crawling down the lane and into the weeds—a remaining cottonmouth with insomnia.

Moses proposed that we should go no further, so we retraced our steps. He stopped and pointed in the direction of the snake and said, "Dat be a bad warnin'. In October see a snake, dat means a den here. More snakes, more snakes." Then he came closer and said, "I don't want to mess wid anybody's cottonmouth. A big un strike at me this spring while I cuttin' de graveyard. Too big for me to kill wid anything I could get my hands on and he crawled back in de weeds and I left dat grave-yard to him."

Our guide decided to take us in another direction to get over to Indian Lake, a northward route through a more swampy terrain laden with live oaks draped with Spanish moss. We stopped to watch a gliding wood stork. We walked on, finally reaching the lake at the end of the lane that looked even more snake infested. We sat and rested on the trunk of an uprooted live oak on the edge of this lagoon.

Moses was in a talkative mood, telling us about his maternal great-grandfather, Phillip Washington, who after the War Between the States was able to buy Mount Arena Plantation for a few dollars. He said that other ex-slave families—Pyatts, Collins, and Nelsons—joined his great-grandfather along with other freed slaves from Brookgreen and Spring-field Plantations. Washington, an industrious man, sold small parcels of land he had purchased to these former slaves. They fished, hunted, and farmed in a primitive existence, threatened mainly by the swamp fever—malaria.

I asked Moses about the islander's relationship with the mainland, and he said that they traded with the Eason family, who owned a country store up near Murrells Inlet. This involved a trip to the mainland across the river and then a buggy ride northward, a trip which might take most of a day. Their children were schooled at home until, eventually, a two-room school house was erected.

Three turtles sunned on the bare trunk of a tree that had fallen into the lake. Intermittently, frogs croaked in the marsh nearby as a flock of red winged blackbirds sang a chorus from a tamarisk thicket. Zachary reminded me that I had promised to take him to Georgetown to see Sadie Johnson. As we walked back, Moses led us by an old rice field now slumbering in weeds and occasional cypress trees that stood like awkward sentinels guarding a forgotten nothingness.

With Sandy Island hospitality, Moses invited us to come by his home before leaving, and I agreed to do this when he said, "We eat somethin' from my truck patch. I git you a piece of late watermelon that I raised." I told Zachary not to worry. I would get him to Georgetown in plenty of time to go courting, so we walked on toward Moses' home, which was in a part of the island called Ruinsville. We walked by swampland and a clearing where great poplar and hickory trees played host to twisting grapevines winding their way upward into tangled masses. Moses' truck patch was manicured, tidy and raked, with piles of cut weeds here and there.

Zachary and I stood on the sandy road while Moses went into his patch and thumped watermelons. He picked one and carried it to his house. It was a simple home painted bright green with a tin roof, a roof one might imagine sounding rhythmic and reassuring in the rain. Moses cut the melon, and it made a crackling sound. "It'll be a good un," he said. He brought Zachary and me each a quarter of the melon and encouraged us to spit the seeds over the edge of the porch to three Rhode Island reds, chickens who stood there waiting expectantly.

Moses wasn't ready to quit talking. All he needed was the encouragement of a question. I asked about Mount Arena Plantation. With this cue he pointed in the direction of the landing dock and said, "Where I puts de boat be de place where Mount Rena was. I remember Mamma Lula Belle tell about her great uncle who be Gabe Lance, de old slave driver at Mount Rena. Dat plantation be owned by Mister Here It [Edward Heriot] before de war." He continued, "Ol Miz Petigru [Mary LaBruce Petigru], she owned bout three plantations here, according to Mamma Lula Belle. She had Groze [Grove Hill Plantation] and she own Hazel Hill [Hasell Hill Plantation] and she own anoder up by de church and dey call it Pipe Dream, I think. But she sold it to old Gobenor All-ston [Gov. Robert F. W. Allston] when she git old. Old Doc Flagg, he and his boys owned a place here, too, and it be called Oak Lon [Oak Lawn Plantation] and it be where Brickwell be now." He spit a mouthful of seeds toward the chickens and continued, "Now de slave driver for Miz Petigru at Pipe Dream be another cousin, Phillip Washington, and he a smart man 'cause after dat war he buy up plantations for little of notin' and sell 'em to other freed folks and let em pay as they could. I guess he sit back den and raise watermelons." Moses paused then said, "Now Mamma Lula Belle tell me all dis cause her daddy, Prince, be one of de freed slaves."

The Rhode Island reds were now sated with watermelon seeds, and Zachary was anxious to go. Moses walked us back toward the dock, stopping to point toward the old school house that had a hand written sign, "Welcome to Sandy Island Community Center." Moses ferried us back across the Waccamaw River and walked us to the car. I shook his hand and thanked him for his hospitality. He stood watching us as we drove toward the highway.

In Georgetown, I delivered Zachary to Sadie Johnson's home. I went shopping down the road at Wal-Mart.

LITTLE BLACK GIRLS

Over to the St. John's A.M.E. Church
I went
For a blessing this morning.

I sat on an ennobled pew
A pew encrusted with
Little black pearls.

I sat by a row of little black girls,

Who wiggled and smiled
In the bliss of youth.

Little black girls in full panoply
On this shining morning.
Light streaming through stained glass,
Prismatic rays beaming onto the skin of
Little chocolate girls
Sweet and shining,
The color of wet indigo ink.

Black little girls,
In ribboned pigtails,
Proudly polished little girls,
Befrilled in starch dresses,
As white as a boll in September.

THE LOST AFRICAN-AMERICAN REPUBLIC OF McKENZIE

Since Dick Crayton is now in his mid-eighties, he is no longer everybody's handyman. He's spending more time making joggling boards. For the past three years Frank Sherald had worked for me. He can do most anything from donning a black tie and serving drinks, to carpentry and housework, but sometimes I have a problem finding jobs to keep him busy. Frank is a handsome African-American who stands six feet four inches tall and has lived around Pawleys Island for most of his eighty-three years, except for a tour of duty in the U.S. Army when he was stationed in Europe during World War II. He is so respected in this community that he is the head elder in his church. As with Dick, we do a lot of talking, with Frank telling me how it "used to be" around here. Frank Sherald has become my best friend.

Last week we worked together gathering straw from the pine thicket in front of my house at Litchfield Plantation to take to the flower garden at the Duck's Nest on Pawleys. We raked the straw and placed it in plastic bags that were in trash cans. We were nearly through when Frank yelled, "Ad damn!" He threw the rake in one direction and almost knocked me down as he ran from the pine thicket, exclaiming "It's a big copperhead!" I don't particularly care for such snakes but felt compelled to investigate. There it was, lying coiled and ready to strike. A yard worker heard the commotion and came to take a look. He pinned the snake down with a forked limb and placed it into a sack. He took it to his truck, saying that he would add it to his collection of such snakes at his home in Garden City.

Frank had adjourned to the house and wouldn't even watch. Realizing that he was still dazed by the event and that I wouldn't get much more work out of him on this day, I suggested that we drive up Route 17 to a place I had just read about in *Low Country Companion* called McKenzie Beach. I recalled that Frank had told me that he worked there in the 1930s.

We drove northward two miles across the road near Miss Ruby's School, then turned right onto an overgrown lane and drove a few feet toward the marsh. Before getting out of the car, Frank explained that there had been two McKenzie Beaches and here we were at the first, dated from 1936. We walked toward a clearing at the edge of the marsh and could look across to the spit of land now called South Litchfield. It was lined with a row of million dollar houses facing the ocean to the east and the wide marshy creek to the west. He said that this area had been called Magnolia Beach until it was wiped out by the hurricane of 1893.

It was here that Frank commenced his narrative of the lost "African-American Republic of McKenzie." He was quick to say that what little had been written about this place was virtually true, but that much had been left out. Through the clearing at the creek's edge he showed me an overgrown broad walkway that had led across the marsh and creek toward South Litchfield. He knew it was there because as a late teenager in 1936 he had helped excavate the mire from the marsh to construct this walkway. While this primitive road was being built, Frank McKenzie had another crew constructing a building on this spit of land that would become known as McKenzie Pavilion. It was a two-story building housing the pavilion and restaurant on the first floor and the "hotel" on the second floor.

There was one catch to all this. Frank McKenzie did *not* own the land. He, more or less, borrowed it from relatives, including a distant cousin, Lillian Pyatt. Back in 1936, just north of this property, were six or seven rather substantial summer houses owned by African-American physicians from the west part of the state. One of the physicians was Dr. Bernie, so it became known as Bernie's Beach. They had their own walkway, but it was private.

We went back to the car and before driving to the second McKenzie compound, he told me a few facts about this Frank McKenzie. It seems that McKenzie, a mulatto, was the son of a prominent white man in Georgetown from the Foxwood family, a fact that was common knowledge. He had not inherited any of the Foxwood money, but had gained some of their entrepreneurial genes. At an early age he went up north and got a job during the day with the New York Central Railroad, and at night, he played the saxophone in nightclubs in Harlem. In New York he spent some time with a distant cousin and fellow South Carolinian, Lillian Pyatt. Lillian was a savvy businesswoman who had dreams of a beach for the African-American community of Pawleys Island. A plot of land became available with beach access and she snapped it up. She returned to South Carolina with Frank, who by then had a little bit of money. They were set on establishing their "republic."

Soon Frank McKenzie married one of the Morris Sumpter daughters, Lizzie, who was as industrious as he was a smooth talker. The Sumpters owned forty acres of land, so when McKenzie married Lizzie, he was able to "buy" a narrow strip of ocean front property reaching westward from the ocean to Parkersville Road. This would eventually become the second "republic."

We drove southward and turned left, across from James Wallace's

"Christmas Palace," onto an overgrown jungle-like lane. Just visible on the right was a dilapidated pink stucco building covered with ivy, Virginia creeper, and kudzu. Frank explained that this was the old Brookgreen Motel constructed by McKenzie after Hurricane Hazel. We drove on and suddenly there was a clearing that revealed a road leading across the marsh with the tip of South Litchfield Beach in full view. When the road became impassable, we parked and walked on a concrete structure where we sat down. We were seated on the water cistern, which had been constructed in 1945 when McKenzie started his second project. As we sat there looking northward toward McKenzie's first domain, Frank said that McKenzie had given him his first jobs. As an eighteen year old, he had been placed in charge of collecting the 10¢ admission for visitors to cross the twenty-foot boardwalk at the end of the road. And as a whopping six-foot-four young man not many failed to hand him a dime.

At times, McKenzie utilized Frank as a "jammer." He went into the creek with other boys and "jammed" for flounder by using a two-pronged fork. At night, Frank came inside the pavilion to become the "ketchup boy," going from table to table to place ketchup on guests' plates—a bottle of ketchup cost 25¢, therefore no bottle was ever left on any table. Lizzie, the cook, charged not more than 10¢ for anything—a flounder sandwich, a plate of shrimp, pigs' feet, each was 10¢. Upstairs McKenzie leased rooms for 75¢ an evening. Indeed, business at the first McKenzie Beach thrived, and Lillian Pyatt kept her eye on things, getting a small percentage of the earnings. After ten years this all changed as McKenzie's relatives, including Lillian Pyatt, demanded rent for the land. McKenzie decided it was time to move a half-mile south to the property he had "purchased" from his in-laws. He realized that the war was over, and the servicemen, who had a bit of departing pay in their pockets, would be returning soon. He also realized that there would be more African-Americans traveling, and with segregation still in full force, they would need lodging.

At his new "republic" he constructed a one-story pavilion and separate cottages on the beach for overnight guests. By 1945, the complex was completed with a water supply from the cistern, which received its water from a well near the highway. The pavilion rocked seven nights a week, and it was said that his establishment made the pavilion at Pawleys Island sound like a monastery.

When McKenzie didn't have a live band, the "Picollo," a jukebox, provided music. He usually filled in as a saxophonist for the live bands. McKenzie Pavilion and McKenzie Beach were the places for an African-American to see and be seen. Frank and Lizzie made a little money and provided their community with a sense of pride. For twenty years there had been a diversion from Mt. Zion Baptist Church and St. John's A.M.E. Church, and many were able to partake of both. The churchgoers could sit on their side of the pavilion and enjoy a flounder sandwich and let the 10¢ beer drinkers sit on the other. They could all walk or lounge on the beach.

The "republic" was nearing its end when Hurricane Hazel approached the South Carolina coast in October 1954. As the skies darkened and the winds howled, Frank and Lizzie fled inland. Two days later they returned to find virtually nothing left of the pavilion or cottages. Everything had been leveled. The "African-American Republic of McKenzie" had vanished.

But Frank McKenzie made one last effort, trying to re-establish nearer to Route 17. He constructed the Brookgreen Motel, a tavern, and restaurant. But a few years later he was forced to sell because of mounting debt. The new owners were Walter Manigault, Sr. of Georgetown and Modjeska Simpkins of Columbia. The property remains in the ownership of many members of these families now. On any day they can come up Route 17 and turn into that little road, and with some difficulty they might see the skeleton remains of that pink stucco building. The Brookgreen Motel has been taken over by a jungle of vines.

It is somewhat easier to get to the site of McKenzie Pavilion. Frank Sherald says that he has been there. He was checked at the gate of the community by a uniformed security guard. He was in his black tie going to the home of Sophie McKissick. He was serving at her grand party. Entry into "million dollar row" didn't cost Frank a dime.

MIZ ANGEL'S BUSINESS

$\mathcal{M}$iz Angel was the color of dark chestnuts. She had come over to the island to do some housekeeping and cooking, but she told me she had grown up in Charleston near the Piggly Wiggly grocery store on North Meeting Street. She was proud of her Charleston blood. Ageless and small, with pipe-stem arms and legs, Miz Angel carried on in a high, squeaky chatter —squeaky like some old, rust-bitten door hinge that had endlessly swayed in the wind. This chatter came from a head wrapped in a neat bandanna of assorted bits of fabric with colors mixed like early summer asters. And from under these bandannas her hair corkscrewed out like twisted icicles of jet.

Miz Angel lived over on Shell Road, where she supervised a grey asbestos-shingled house—a house with a manicured and swept dirt yard where there were beds of pink amaryllis. Two whitewashed truck tires served as flower beds for blue and white petunias in the spring and for yellow chrysanthemums in September and October. These islands of color seemed too close to the front door, obstructing the entrance to Angel's front porch, which was full of a variety of potted plants. Miz Angel grew Jerusalem cherries, mother-in-law's tongues, and ferns as ageless as herself. An old, moss-green rocking chair was crowded in, empty like an unused throne, dusty and only for looks.

The front door was for night spirits and dream visitors maybe, for Miz Angel greeted callers at the door of the back porch, which served as the main entrance to her domain. In this domain there was, at least sometimes, the solemn and robust Big Richard, the brick-laying husband who had brought her to the Neck from Charleston. Big Richard was like an apparition, for he was rarely seen by anyone except Miz Angel and then only at late hours and for his five o'clock breakfast, which she had grown tired of cooking: two fried eggs, two patties of sausage, gravy and grits, plus several biscuits.

Then there was Little Richard, their son, who had returned to Shell Road from a stay in the U.S. Army. He sat endlessly spit-polishing his black military boots, working away until he could see his reflection in the shine. Little Richard had no other job.

The rest of the household consisted of two daughters and a variable number of their children, depending on the day of the week. The daughters, Virginia and Carabelle, both worked as waitresses at Oliver's Back Porch Restaurant in Murrell's Inlet. Their working hours were convenient for Miz Angel to raise a growing number of their children. Carabelle had three little girls: fat Little Maybelline and her sisters, Scarlet and Teensie Spice.

I frequently visited this domain on Shell Road, sometimes to pass the day, stopping by after mulberry picking or turnip green collecting over on the Waverley Plantation. Sometimes it was after a trip to the post office, when I needed some of Miz Angel's philosophical thoughts. Then there were times when I just needed reassurance, when I just needed to be hugged tight.

My crab delivery visits were the practical, business-like encounters when I presented catches of crabs for Miz Angel's approval. On one such occasion I sat, as usual, at my assigned place at the end of the oil-cloth-covered kitchen table, drinking iced tea from a tall, frosted, plastic cup. Solemn Little Maybelline stood close by, quietly gazing at me until Miz Angel told her to stop staring and go outside and play with Teensie Spice. Spice had a June bug that flew around with a long string attached by its leg. With the child gone, I could give my full attention to Miz Angel, who was standing over a wash pan inspecting my crabs. There she stood like old stiff molasses inspecting, smelling, squeezing, frowning, resqueezing, rejecting and accepting but never smiling for this was serious business. This was Miz Angel's business. Finally I was told she had made her selection and that I should come back next day, but not before she had watched her *General Hospital* on the television. Those crabs would be stuffed with young scallions, green pepper, and her own bread crumbs. They would be heavily dusted with paprika, for Miz Angel liked to match the carnelian color of the cooked shells.

After my visits, she always accompanied me out the back door and to my car, stopping briefly to chide one child or another. Fat Little May-belline would stand, with her arms behind her back, staring. Miz Angel always hugged me and then waved as I drove off towards the island.

On the day after I had returned from my annual winter migration, Big Richard knocked on the door. I greeted him and fat Little May-belline and asked them to come in. We stood on the porch in the early April wind looking towards the dune, discussing the damage done by the March northeaster and high tide. I pointed toward a flock of pine sisken, which had just landed on a telephone wire by Sea View Inn next door. Big Richard stood as quiet and as still as a standing stone while I poured sunflower seeds onto the bird feeder. Little Maybelline leaned against a column with her hands behind her back while braided strands of hair with white plastic bows swayed in the wind. She was expression-less, staring intently as I went about my morning bird-feeding ritual. I said, "Honey, I like your pretty striped dress and your belt to match." She peered down at her belt and felt the hem of her dress and then stared back at me. Big Richard had moved closer.

"Richard, thanks for the brick wall you've built for the new flower bed. Miz Angel sent me a card that she'd planted some seeds, verbena I think, and they're coming up. Rich, speaking of Miz Angel, I'm about unpacked and would be much obliged if, after a while, you'd drop her off to help get the house straightened up."

He did not answer.

"How's Miz Angel? And how's Spicy and how's Scarlet? I'll bet the grandchildren have grown and grown, gained some pounds like Little Maybelline."

I looked at Big Richard. His face had withdrawn into rigidity. He stood somber and silent for a long moment.

"Doc, she's passed."

"What do you mean, 'she's passed?' Passed what? Passed!" I didn't understand.

"Why Angel up and died. Died, dead, and buried. If Angel had lived til Tuesday she'd be dead three weeks tomorrow. Angel just gave out."

I fumbled for words, then collecting myself I murmured, "God rest Miz Angel's dear soul. I can't believe it."

Richard said nothing and Little Maybelline stared.

"Richard, was she sick long? Did she suffer? What was she sick with?"

"Naw, Angel wasn't sick to me. Just up and died. She died. Doc, 'bout the time of the cold spell in March, Angel started tellin' me her dreams. She kept tellin' about a big black bus that was arrivin' in her dreams, like a dreamt vision would be, and each mornin' while she'd be cookin' breakfast, she'd say, 'Big Rich, it was here again, outside on the road' 'What's here again, Angel?' I'd ask. 'Dat big black bus be here. Why, it just drives up in front of the house and lingers and lingers. Nobody gets on and precious nobody ever gets off. Then after a while it drives away, sometimes backin' up and sometimes goin' on forward. And I never sees a driver.'"

Big Richard shuffled about, looked out towards the creek, then back at Little Maybelline.

"Next mornin' she'd tell me all this again. 'Drempt dat big black bus here again, and I got up, went to the window, and I yelled at it, Who bees you black bus? But nobody say any answer.' She say to me, 'I'm dead to know what all this means, Rich.' Then a Friday, two weeks ago, first thing in the mornin' while she's making my breakfast she say, 'Finally somebody get off dat big black bus, and you know who it was? Rich, it was Little Maybelline. And she carried a big bouquet of them white oleander. She carried them across my front porch and clean into the house. Carried them to me. Come to my bed wearin' a white dress she doesn't have like that. Maybelline gave me the flowers, then I felt good. And I woked.'"

I glanced at Little Maybelline. She gave an angular, confirming nod.

Richard went on, "Well, Auntie Juliet had been right sick and on her death bed. She up and died a Friday. So me and Angel took Little Maybelline, Teensie Spice, and Scarlet to the wake in Awandaw. On the way down there, while everythin' was quiet, Angel say, 'Rich, you may have to make your own supper tomorrow night, and some for the girls.' I didn't understand. I just looked at her, and we drove on."

At the crabbing dock with the creek and mainland in the background

Above: The Duck's
Nest on Pawleys Island

Right: Miz Angel

Above: The dining room at The Duck's Nest

Left: Yum Yum Young, the Bar-B-Q man, was for many years houseboy for George Vanderbilt

John Brown, Pericles, and Tom Jones at The
Duck's Nest II

Above: Dick Crayton, Homelite, and Titus
at The Duck's Nest

Below: The Vicountess Hampden inspecting Dickie's
pipe at The Duck's Nest

Above: The lawn of The Duck's Nest the spring after Hurricane Hugo

Top left: Remains of The Duck's Nest after Hurricane Hugo, 1989

Bottom left: Reforming the dune on Pawleys Island after Hurricane Hugo

Top right: Three of the twelve Maxwell family children after Hurricane Hugo, McClellanville

Bottom right: With Tom Sutton and Mary Linen, McClellanville, six months after Hurricane Hugo

Below: A home on Sandy Island

Dame Eva Turner at The Crown Equerry House

Above: The Queen and Sir John Miller at a Christmas party, The Royal Mews

Below: My garden on Eaton Square, London, just before a July 4th party

At the Crown Equerry House with the door keeper,
Chelsea Pensioner, Edward Wood, and Dr. Fred Akel

Going to the Garter Service at St.
George's Church, Windsor Castle

With actress
Sophie Sigall
at my home
in London

Rosita Conway at a picnic at Royal Ascot

Above: Hiding behind a lion, Shotover House, Oxfordshire

Below: A picnic with friends at Royal Ascot

With Sir John Miller at Shotover Estate, Oxfordshire

"And that was Saturday?"

He nodded. "And on Sunday at the Jericho Graveyard, at the buryin,' Angel asked to stand behind me while Auntie Juliet was bein' lowered, while Reverend Nelson was sayin' the last words, while Cousin Nathaniel was doin' the shovelin', while things was quiet. Then I heard somethin' and Brother Frazier put his hand on my shoulder, sayin', 'Richard, Angel's down.' So I turned quick an' picked her up. Her arms was hangin' like wet wash rags and all limped. But while I was standin' holdin' her, she roused, tightened up, and I think she say, 'Rich, dat black bus. Who bees dat black bus?' She limped again and that was all."

He sighed and said, "Angel passed right there."

For a moment all was quiet except for the rustling of the myrtle thicket and the monotonous surf below us. Little Maybelline moved towards the steps, and Big Richard followed. I walked down behind them, past the new flower bed of verbena seedlings and the white oleander bush with its early flowers.

"Richard, what do I owe you for the brick laying you've done?"

He answered quietly, "'Bout twenty dollars, I guess. You can pay me sometime."

They got into the old, rusty green pick-up. The girl faced backwards in the seat, on her knees, never taking her eyes off me. They moved out of the driveway and drove northward. A few yards down the road, Little Maybelline stuck her head out and waved. Along near the church she waved again.

ABLE CALHOUN

*O*ne Easter Sunday I went to the services at St. John's A.M.E. Church with Page Oberlin, the innkeeper next door. It was a wonderful and warm sunshiny morning. The sanctuary was filled, but the usher made room for us near the front. Light filtered through the simple stained glass windows, casting a certain mellowness on the white dresses of three little girls seated beside us. As the service proceeded, they were fidgety, examining each other's white purses and their contents. They occasionally looked up at us but were quick to get back to their business.

After the message, at a time when we had no doubts that He had risen, offering time had come. This part of the service was presided over in a kingly manner by a handsome elderly layman, who was big in stature and appropriately dressed in a navy blue jacket, a crispy starched white shirt, and trousers as white as an albino polar bear. This layman wasn't dark black, nor indigo; he had the color of a mulatto. There was most certainly some Caucasian blood in his veins, and one imagined that every drop of it was aristocratic. Standing there with a silver offering plate, he gave an oration. He admitted to Jehovah and explained to us Philistines that money was the root of all evil. He talked about talents, about prodigal sons returning home, and he reminded us that it was better to give than receive.

I just had to whisper to Page, "The presiding layman looks and talks like he could be chairman of the board."

She whispered back, "That's Able Calhoun, our garbage collector. He can be difficult, even impossible if there's an extra lettuce leaf in the garbage can."

Finally the service ended, and we made our way toward the door. Being relatively new to the community I did not recognize anyone in the congregation, but Page seemed at home and received greetings and warm hugs from several of the sisters. We returned to Sea View Inn for Easter lunch.

Later that week I was attending to the future of the dandelion crop in the front yard as a big green garbage truck drove up. I recognized Able Calhoun as he stopped the truck, and we had a chat, small talk at first about the late spring, the pitiful strawberry season, and then about President Reagan's prostate operation. I looked down, chopped at a dandelion, paused and said, "By the way, I was at your church on Sunday. You looked mighty good, and you presided like you had a place in glory awaiting you." I wiggled the conversation from strawberries and prostate operations to his ancestors. "Able, you carry the good South Carolina name of Calhoun. It's always been a family to be admired in this state. Do you know much about your forebears?" I asked.

"Well, I don't know much, but some say we are of a plantation down on the South Santee River. Uncle Jib says we sprung from old Sabe Calhoun, the black slave driver at the plantation they called The Ark, up the Neck from here. Mammy declared that I take after her family, the Allstons. You know, the people up at Brookgreen. Doc, I don't know, and there's no telling on God's earth who all my ancestors was. Maybe somebody knows and maybe they don't." He looked down at the overflowing garbage cans then back at me. "Guess now it don't make no difference. I'm free and happy and the Lord will provide. Got myself a good garbage route."

He slowly placed the contents of the cans on his truck and said, "I've talked too long and it's time to go." He walked around, and before climbing in he said, "I'm pleased to talk to you. Hope you'll come back to the A.M.E. next Sunday. The Miracles will sing, a visiting preacher from Mingo Creek will give the message, and I'll supervise the offering." He drove off toward his next stop up the island.

I continued to lean on my hoe then chopped more dandelions and thought about Able. He may be difficult about what we put into the garbage, and sometimes he leaves the garbage can lids off allowing the possums to have their supper from leftovers. He may be black or he may be white or he might be in-between and not know exactly who he is. But I'll bet my life that Able Calhoun is a good man. I'll go to his church any Sunday.

I went back into the house and reread *Black Majority*, a book I had checked out from the Georgetown Public Library. According to this book, in 1800 there were 18,000 blacks and only 2,000 whites in the county. There were few white female settlers, and in general, white women had been discouraged from settling because of reports of the deaths of several white women soon after arrival.

This book reprinted a 1736 advertisement from a Georgetown bulletin—an advertisement aimed at the county's white bachelors:

> . . .that if they are in a Strait for women, to wait for
> the next shipment from the Coast of Guinny [sic]. Those
> ladies are of a strong robust constitution; not easily
> jaded out, able to serve them by Night as well as Day.
> When they are sick, they are not costly, when dead their
> funeral charges are but an old Matt, one bottle of Rum
> and a pound of sugar.

So goes some of the hidden and shady history of Georgetown
County!

MOTHER'S DAY AT THE A.M.E.

$\mathcal{I}$didn't spring out of bed this morning. I simply got up. On this
May morning it didn't seem like Mother's Day for it was raining and
windy. I felt all at sea. I felt droopy and sad. I tried to arrange myself and
get a better attitude. And then I remembered that Octavia Ivory, the
African-American lady who attends to Rutledge's vegetable stand over
on the highway, had invited me several times to attend her church, St.
Ephesus A.M.E. Thinking that it might be a good day to do this, I put
on my navy blue suit. I reminded myself that two years before I had
attended an Easter service and an anniversary service at St. Ephesus, and
they had made me feel welcome. I didn't feel afterwards as if I had been
to some country club for socializing.

I drove in the late spring rain, through fog, up the highway, and
then left at the faded sign pointing the way to the church two miles
toward the Waccamaw River. As I approached the white clapboard
church, I was greeted by a wet hen followed by a string of bedraggled
baby chicks running in front of the car.

I parked as near to the door as possible, stepped over and around
puddles of water, and entered the church. Octavia was the official white-
gloved greeter. She welcomed me and showed me to a seat near the
back. The gospel choir hummed "We Shall Gather at the River" while

we awaited the start of the service. They sat under a white cross embellished with light bulbs, matching the white dresses the mostly female choir members were wearing. Some of the ladies wore a red rose, others a white rose. The only man in the choir wore a dark suit and a red rose.

I suppose that on any other Sunday, St. Ephesus is the domain of the pastor, Reverend Elijah Brown, but it soon became apparent that on this Sunday a man wouldn't get in a whimper. For this was Mother's Day, and St. Ephesus was transposed into a matriarchal kingdom of colorfully dressed women, some of them canopied in hats with such wide brims that they had to tilt their heads back to see the altar.

I read the program Octavia had handed me until the adult choir marched in like a troop of lively angels singing "Hush, Hush, Somebody's Calling My Name." They seated themselves opposite the Gospel Choir. Sister Leota Williams presided and said the opening prayer. She introduced Sister Wandalena, who would say the main prayer. Seated on the aisle of the second row of the gospel choir, Sister Wandalena gave herself three of four brisk waves with her McKnight Funeral Home fan, stood slowly, and then walked with dignity to the rostrum. I was told later that she had never done this before, but in her watermelon-pink dress she uttered the long prayer with aplomb, fanned herself, and ended, "Let the Lord touch the vocal cords of the speaker. Amen."

With Sister Leota back at the rostrum, there were welcomes and announcements and two offerings, one for missionaries and the other for the weekly budget. They were taken up in sweetgrass baskets by sisters dressed and gloved in white, each carefully keeping one hand behind her back. As the money was counted, we sang, "There is a Balm in Gilead." After announcing the amount of the collections, Sister Leota introduced Sister Marlena Washington of Little River, who would give the message.

Sister Marlena was a lady of generous and majestic proportions clothed in a long white crepe dress. This sister did not simply give the message, she preached! She preached about each letter of the word "mother." Sister Marlena preached about the virtues of mothers and in particular she preached about her own mother. Her own mother, "Over there across the River Jordan. Across the River Jordan where my mother sits with other black angels on snow white marble pews so wide that she can rest comfortably in her golden slippers." The message ended with a chorus of "Yeses" and "Amens." The adult choir stood and sang, "We're Marching to Zion." These sisters did not just sing, they marched. Back and forth they went, looking up at that white cross with their arms raised. "We're marchin' to where we got freedom and a restin' place," they sang.

After the congregation sang another hymn, Sister Leota presided over the memorial service honoring the mothers who had "passed" since the previous year: Sister Elizabeth Allston, Sister Mary "Queenie" Alston, Sister Angel Brown, and Sister Althea Brown. Sister Leota insisted that they were all across the Jordan and happily at rest. The service was interrupted by a woman in the second row who sprang up and started shouting. Two sisters fanned her and hugged her until she calmed down.

The service was nearing an end and the Reverend Brown had his opportunity to say a few words. He said he realized that this day at St. Ephesus belonged to the women, so his remarks would be brief. He lamented in the words of the hymn, "On Jordan's stormy banks I stand and cast a wishful eye." "Yes, yes!" shouted Sister Leota.

To the tune of "Blessed Assurance," the gospel choir marched out singing, "O dearest mother, you are my star. I shall strive daily to be like you are. Your wholesome teachings, your words of praise will keep me careful all of my days."

I turned slowly to leave with all these glorious images in my head. As I stepped into the aisle, a smiling black face greeted me. A black angel dressed in white. This sister hugged me tightly and then hugged me again. I left the church and was walking toward the car when Octavia called out, "Be sure to come by the vegetable stand tomorrow. Fresh strawberries from Orangeburg are coming in. I'll hold you some."

I drove back to the island feeling much better.

UNCLE ZACHARY

$\mathscr{I}$ had known Uncle Zachary Allston for only three or four years but it seemed like ages, as I had visited him so often.

We first met one Sunday morning after the service in the churchyard of St. John's A.M.E. We had a pleasant chat. Uncle Zachary, nearly ninety years old then, pointed across to his home on Bess Lane and insisted that I should come visit him. A few days later I was passing by in mid morning and saw him sitting on the front porch. Realizing that the mail was not yet sorted at the post office, I decided to stop by. I parked my car in front of the rickety garage, which had a faded sign above its door—"Jesus Saves." Uncle Zachary didn't get out of his glider rocker but motioned that I come on to the porch. As I got nearer he said, "De ole artut ritis bees got at me." I sat in a worn-out over-stuffed chair facing him. This beady-eyed little man looked at me piercingly, speaking rapidly in a Gullah-ish style of English. Sometimes I could hardly understand him. He told me about his grandfather, who had been a slave on the Springfield Plantation. His grandfather had difficulty in coping with freedom, so he went back to the William Allston family.

These visits became ritualistic, joining neighbors on the porch to hear Uncle Zachary tell tales of ghosts and haunts and, worst of all, his stories of plat-eyes. Eventually I took a video camera and recorded him telling about Caesar Hog, his great uncle, who had shot and killed a cousin. Uncle Zachary would squint his eyes and tell about this mean uncle who eventually "got his own throat slitted out on de road til he's dead hisself," he would say. Then pointing out toward Bess Lane, "Uncle Caesar Hog bees a frog gigger and after he's killed he still be roamin' up an down de road at de nite wid out his head." He would stop talking and after the silence had sunk in, he would add, "But he only bees out der a walkin if in spring and de bull frogs bees singing and croaking."

Uncle Zachary gradually became more feeble, and finally his doctor placed him on digitalis. Weeks later his daughter Julia called me saying, "Daddy's not stirring around, and he's acting sleepy. Won't talk. Can you come to see him?" I drove over and was careful to park under the "Jesus Saves" sign. I went in and found Uncle Zachary in bed, barely able to be roused. Julia stood over us as I checked his pulse. It was thirty-eight, half the normal rate. I asked to see his medication bottles and found that he had been taking double the amount of digitalis that his doctor had prescribed. I suggested that she stop the digitalis for a few days. Two days later I called on him and found him on the front porch in his glider. From that time on he declared that I "had snatched him from de jaw of death." The following Sunday I went back to the A.M.E. After church, as we were leaving the building, I checked his pulse, and it was seventy-four. Finally I asked why he had doubled his dose of digitalis, and he answered, "It bees such a wee tablet, it can't do no good."

Several months later Julia called to tell me that her father was in the Georgetown Memorial Hospital, and that he wanted me to come and treat him. I knew and Julia knew that I couldn't do this, but I agreed to go see him socially. My trip to Georgetown was delayed until the following day. I found his room and gave a slight knock as I stood holding a little bouquet of wild petunias I had gathered before leaving the island. There was no answer, so I peeped inside and saw an African-American woman slowly mopping the floor. The bed had been made up, but Uncle Zachary was nowhere to be seen. She didn't look up as I inquired about his whereabouts. She said, "Uncle Zachary have gone home to his precious Jesus." She continued to mop and added, "He passed about thirty minutes ago." As I turned to leave she said, "Guess his body's at the McKnight now. Uncle Zachary have passed."

With my bouquet of half-wilted petunias, I walked back toward the parking lot, realizing that I had waited too long to go to see my friend. I drove back northward toward Pawleys Island, crossing the lazy Waccamaw and Pee Dee Rivers. These rivers reminded me of his tales about catching sturgeon weighing four and five hundred pounds, and how he had refined lard cans of roe into caviar. I thought of the times I had brought him down this road to go courting his eighty-four-year-old girl-friend, Louisa Mae Robinson. I thought of the times I had left them alone at her home for an hour or so as I shopped at Wal-Mart. I thought of how pleased he looked after these visits, and Louisa Mae, too.

I drove back to the island, went to the north end where the wild petunias grow, and gathered a fresh bouquet. I drove over to Uncle Zachary's home and gave them to his daughter. By then the neighbors were gathering, but there was no sadness. As I left, Julia said, as if to comfort me, "Daddy's gone home to his precious Jesus. Daddy's gone home." She shed a tear and seemed to cry, then straightened up and greeted more neighbors. I drove back to the island.

Four days later, in the afternoon, I went to St. John's A.M.E. Church for the funeral service. Hazel Smalls, dressed in a white uniform and white gloves, greeted me at the door and presented a two-page program entitled, "Home Going Service for Mr. Zachary Allston." The obituary read:

"Zachary Allston, son of the late Abraham and Mary Jane Allston, was born on March 1, 1902, at Pawleys Island, South Carolina. He departed this life on April 8, 1992 at 1:30 p.m. at Georgetown Memorial Hospital.

He was joined in holy wedlock in 1919 to the late Daisy Johnson. They were blessed with six children, three of whom preceded him to the grave. He confessed his faith in Christ and joined the A.M.E. Church where he served as Class Leader No. 14, president of the No. 1 Usher Board for many years, and the Willing Work Club, to which he gave his dedication and untiring service even when his health was failing. His love and concern for his church's welfare was ever strong. He was well loved and known to all. He had a beautiful personality and never met a stranger. Most of all, he liked to fish and tell old fish stories.

He leaves two daughters, Julia of the home, and Eliza of Hope, NJ, one son Nathaniel, twelve grandchildren and eight great-grand children, and a host of other sorryful relatives and friends."

On the cover of the program was a photograph of Uncle Zachary smartly dressed in a navy blue suit. On its lapel was pinned a long color-ful badge imprinted, "Usher President." He stood looking like Moses holding the Book, but his book had the title, "Roll Book Sunday School Class No. 14." I remembered his proud pose because I took this photograph after church service last September.

I was seated near the back of the vestibule, one of the few white faces present. The gospel choir sang, "Roll Out the Chariot," as the handsomely dressed family filled in to occupy one side of the nave. There were prayers and a chorus of "Amens" echoing from all parts of the sanctuary. Remarks were made by Jake Young of Usher Board No. 1 and by Norman Reid of Class 14. Sister Betty Nash, his niece, sang "Deep River," then each of us marched to the front after being invited to "view the remains." The Gospel Choir hummed "Swing Low Sweet Chariot;" I went forward and looked at Uncle Zachary, turned, and nodded toward Julia and Eliza before going back to my seat.

I slowly walked out of the church, made my way over to the little graveyard nearby, and stood by the open grave that awaited Uncle Zachary. Pink and white dogwood bloomed all around and a pine warbler sang from the limb of a live oak. Uncle Zachary had indeed gone home to his precious Jesus. And I had lost a friend.

HURRICANES

*E*nglish guests are sometimes a problem when they arrive during the hurricane season because our storms are covered in detail by the British press. Some of my British friends arrived recently: Patricia Ellison and her friend Tom Windsor, Veronica Hurst, and Cynthia Colburn–Martin. They arrived in mid afternoon from New York where they had spent the evening. None had visited South Carolina before, and they didn't know what to expect, except possibly a hurricane.

Before unpacking, they came out on the cypress boardwalk to view the dune and ocean and then, as I was helping Lizzie in the kitchen, I could see them pointing westward toward a brewing storm. Tom, who Patricia told me had been a decorated navigator on a Lancaster bomber during World War II, seemed to be leading some discussion. He was adept at this since he was a retired meteorologist for BBC Radio, Southeast. Although it was September, the height of hurricane season, Tom knew there were no hurricanes churning in the Atlantic. He was obviously having some problem convincing the other guests.

I finished the kitchen tasks and decided that it was time to join the discussion. Returning to the porch, I suggested that they unpack, and come back to the porch to discuss hurricanes and storms over tea. The word "tea" seemed magical, and in a few minutes they were back on the porch; Patricia brought a notebook and pencil.

Hurricane of 1822

I was most truthful with them as I sat with the *Hurricane Album* in my lap. I held it up and told them that this was a book I had prepared over the years that explained our history of hurricanes going back to 1822. I told them that English guests do seem to accompany these storms, for during my last six fleeings from hurricanes, I have had English guests on five occasions. I also noted that although these guests were apprehensive, they seemed to have derived some pleasure and excitement from riding out these storms over at Waverly Place three miles inland.

With the *Hurricane Album* opened, I showed them articles printed in the Georgetown newspapers since the early eighteen hundreds. Then I circulated the book. I explained that the South Carolina coast has been hit by five great hurricanes since records were kept during the last two hundred years, and that all of these except one occurred between mid September and mid October. I preceded to tell them about our close calls with Connie and Diane in 1955, Helene in 1958, Donna in 1960, David in 1979, and Floyd in 1999.

By now Patricia seemed calmer, and Tom, seated beside her, was glued to the album. Veronica and Cynthia gazed toward the ocean in a jet-lagged trance. Tom, never looking up from the album, asked me a question about the 1822 hurricane that swallowed the whole town of

North Island, just southeast of Pawleys Island. I told him that the three hundred people who disappeared with that town had probably heard stories of previous hurricanes that had devastated this area of the coast in 1752 and 1804. I mentioned the tragedy of the Withers family who lived on North Island. They didn't have the benefit of The Weather Channel. When the wind and water swept in that late September evening in 1822, they and visiting twenty people had no place to flee. They would have been glad to have been in the 1999 snarled traffic west of Charleston on Route 26, fleeing Hurricane Floyd in an air-conditioned SUV, sipping an iced Pepsi from the cooler. Instead, the Withers family, who were celebrating their new home on North Island, were among the fourteen drowned out of the group of twenty that evening. They were the last residents from a town that has never been rebuilt since.

I pointed out a copy of a narrative in the album where a Mrs. Johnstone foretold of this hurricane, and its consequences, years beforehand:

Georgetonian Recalls Story
Handed Down In Her Family

WHERE NOW BREAKS THE SURF ONCE STOOD A FLOURISHING
VILLAGE OF NORTH INLET.
Foretold Coming Of The Hurricane

A weird tale of how a woman foretold the storm years before it happened, and how her daughter and grandchildren were lost when the hurricane washed their house from its moorings is recalled by a member of the Johnstone family, a grand niece of one of the storm's victims, now living in Georgetown. This story has been handed down in the Johnstone family for several generations.

It seems that seven years or so before the disaster Mrs. Andrew Johnstone, who was then living with her son-in-law, Robert Francis Withers, and his wife, formerly Miss Esther Johnstone, drempt [sic] one night that a terrible storm had visited North Inlet, and that her daughter and grandchildren perished in the waves. Mrs. Johnstone said that the dream had made a great impression on her for she

saw Mrs. Withers and the children struggling in the tur-
bulent water for several minutes before being carried
under by a foaming wave that blotted everything from
sight. She implored her son-in-law to sell the property
on the island and move far inland, and after much persua-
sion, Mr. Withers followed her advice. He purchased a
home in Statesburg, and there he lived with his family for
several years, far from the sound of the surf that was to
bring tragedy to his life.

In 1817, Mrs. Johnstone died, and the family decided
there was no use to continue their residence in the
upcountry for they were all longing for a sight of the
sea, and the place where they had spent so many happy
years.

Mr. Withers purchased an attractive lot near the water's
edge and immediately employed a carpenter to build a comfortable and commodious summer cottage. At last the house
was completed, and the owner planned to hold a house warm-
ing. Everybody was in high spirits. Dainties had been purchased from Georgetown. "Creek boys" had been engaged to
secure fish and shrimp, and the women of the family had
been busily sewing for several weeks on brilliant evening
gowns and gay little dresses for the young ladies of the
family. On the night of September 25, 1822, many a guest
had assembled in the new abode, and the merriment begun.
Myriad candles were lit and soon was heard the sound of
the violin and drum, summoning the young people to the
dance. No one heeded the howling of the wind and the dash
of rain on the windows, for they thought it was just
another summer squall. But the clouds gathered thick and
fast, and the rain came in torrents, and the tide rose to
an alarming height. Preparations were then made to abandon
the house, but while some of the occupants were making
ready, the crash came. With a thud the structure rested on
the ground, but the swirling waters had no mercy. Slowly
the building drifted to sea, with all of the lights burning in the inky darkness—a funeral pyre, it seemed to the
more fortunate ones on the island who had made good their

escape to the sand hills. Mrs. Withers and her children
found a watery grave as did many of the island's pop-
ulation, and Mrs. Johnstone's vision was fulfilled even to
the smallest detail.

Then I mentioned the slave rebellion of 1822, two months before this hurricane. On July 2, 1822 Denmark Vesey, a Sunday school teacher, and thirty-four other Negroes, as they were called then, were hung in Charleston on charges that they instigated a slave rebellion. Negroes claimed that this storm was "God's getting even with the whites."

I showed them a two-page article from Georgetown's *Winyah Intelligencer*, which was written during the first week of October 1822, telling in some detail of the death and destruction on North Island.

September 30, October 3, 1822

AN ACCOUNT OF THE 1822 HURRICANE AT NORTH INLET

The weather had been for a week or ten days very unpleasant, the wind blowing occasionally fresh from the E. and
S.E., but as there appeared none of those indications
which usually precede a Hurricane, and as the mercury in
the thermometer continued low, very little apprehension
was entertained — even at sunset on Friday evening the
27th although the weather was bad yet still there
appeared no cause to apprehend a gale; at the close of the
day there was a heavy shower from the S.E. accompanied by
some wind, after which the weather appeared better,
between ten and eleven o'clock. However, we had a squall
from the N.E. from which quarter the wind continued to
blow high till about twelve, when we experienced another,
more violent squall from about E.; the mercury about this
hour had risen to 79 and continued to rise for sometime
after. From twelve, the wind continued gradually to
change to the S.E. and S., increasing in violence as it
shifted. From S.E., it blew with frightful and unprece-
dented violence; most of the injury caused by the wind
must have occurred about two o'clock in the morning and
while it blew from this quarter. As the time of high water
had been about seven o'clock in the evening, the inhabi-

tants apprehended no danger from the view as from the violence of the gale; it was presumed that it could not continue. However, it pleased the Almighty to disappoint them and by the awful result to prove how fallacious are all human calculations.

The tide could have ebbed very little, if at all, when the waters returned with irresistible violence between three and four o'clock in the morning and reached a height far exceeding that in the great gale of 1804 and we believe of any other tide within the memory of the oldest inhabitants; a very small portion indeed of the uninhabited part of the Island remained above the ocean. The gale began to subside we believe about half after three, the wind blowing then from S.W. It was oppressively warm during the gale and many of those luminous bodies, or meteors unusual in our fall gales, passed near the surface of the earth. The gale was of shorter duration and accompanied by less rain than usual.

The dwelling House, a very large new building and [unintelligible] lot; vestige remaining. Here again, it is our melancholy duty to state the loss of many valuable lives. There were in this house eighteen persons, of whom four have been most miraculously saved. Those are Mr. R.F. Withers and three Negroes.

Those lost, we lament to say are Mrs. Withers; her four amiable daughters; her son; Mr. Shackelford, nephew of Mr. Withers; Mr. Wish, and five Negroes. Mr. Withers, about daylight, was heard calling for help in Dubourdieu [sic] Creek near the ocean, a little above the settlement on that island, and was rescued we understand by Lieut. Levy of the U.S. Navy. It appears that he had clung to a piece of timber. Mr. Withers, who had been long in a very bad state of health, finding himself chilled and exhausted, called to one of his Negro men, who was endeavoring to gain some time but whom he did not know to secure himself on it.

As he was about to relinquish it through inability to contend any longer, he heard the voice of his affectionate little girl of twelve or thirteen years of age, of whose presence he was before ignorant, cheering him and entreating him to persevere in his exertions and assuring her father that she believed he would be able to retain his grasp of the timber till it should please God to cast them on shore — this instantly restored to the father animation and strength. But, in a few minutes after, an overwhelming surge separated them forever in this world. The Negro was afterwards taken up alive in the marsh opposite to that island; a Negro boy of Mr. Withers was driven across to Dubourdieu's Island on a pair of steps, landed and took refuge in a house, which was shortly after blown down. He survives uninjured. Another Negro man whose arm was broken in the fall of the house has also been taken up alive.

Hurricane of 1893

During tea time I talked about the Flagg Storm, the Great Storm of 1893 that occurred on Friday the 13th of October. I told them that this storm, possibly the worst hurricane to impact our coast, had been written about in several books, but each story seemed to be embellished somewhat with subtle differences. I suggested that it is like the game "Pass the Word" where the initial phrase becomes so misconstrued as it is passed along that finally we do not know fact from fiction. I suggested that there are two sources of fairly accurate information—the tombstones at All Saints Waccamaw Episcopal Church Cemetery and three articles published in *Georgetown Times* immediately after the storm. Then I read from the album inscriptions from All Saints cemetery tombstones:

Sacred to the memory of Joseph G. Taylor who departed life on 13 October 1893, Age 15, 6 months and 3 days.
In loving memory of Arthur B. Flagg, his wife Martha and Albert, Ward, Alice, Ebin and Mattie who were lost in the storm on Magnolia Beach 13 October 1893.

In Memorium to Arthur Belin Flagg and Georginia

Ward Flagg, my father and mother who were swept
away by the Tidal Wave on Magnolia Beach 13
October 1893.

I pointed northward and explained that Magnolia Beach is just
north of Pawleys Island and is now called Litchfield Beach. On Magnolia, about thirty people lost their lives in that 1893 storm. So many of
the Flagg family were drowned that the storm was sometimes referred to
as the Flagg Storm. This prominent family mourned the deaths of Dr.
and Mrs. Arthur Flagg and their five children; Trial Judge Flagg and all
of his family, including visiting young cousins who had come to romp on
the beach—Alice LaBruce, Bet LaBruce, Bessie Weston, and three servants, Adele, Vitrim and Sallie. I explained that all homes on Magnolia
Beach were washed away and floated off except for one, the Hasel home
which had just been completed, then referred them to the article printed
in Georgetown's newspaper the next day:

GEORGETOWN, S. C., OCTOBER 14, 1893.

E X T R A

MAGNOLIA SWEPT AWAY!

15 Lives Lost

DURING FRIDAY'S STORM

LIVES AND PROPERTY SWEPT AWAY
LIKE CHAFF BEFORE THE WIND

PAWLEYS ISLAND

THE END OF THE ISLAND COMPLETELY SWEPT AWAY
Georgetown awake [sic] this Saturday morning to a full
realization of the damage by the late storm.

The streets were full of all kinds of rumors — that one
half of Pawley's Island was washed away; that Magnolia
Beach was gone, with all of its inhabitants, and that desolation and death were hand in hand. For on this morning,
Capt. A. A. Springs arrived at the wharf with the distressing news of one of the greatest disasters that has
ever overtaken our sorely distressed community.

As severe as the storm was in our city, we were merci-
fully saved any loss of life, the damage being strictly
confined to property.

On Pawleys Island it was different, however. The upper end
of the island received the worst part of the blow. There
people had to go to the upper story of their houses for
safety; in others, the houses were blown down and swept
away, causing considerable loss in articles of furniture.

The news from Magnolia Beach struck terror to every
heart. Then it was asserted that the whole of Dr. Flagg's
folks were washed away and drowned; that John Dozier's
family were also lost, as well as others; that nothing had
been heard of Robert J. Donaldson and family, on Goat
Island; that Wm White and Josh Ward had been drowned while
attempting to rescue people at Magnolia Beach; and numerous other rumors of a more or less distressing character.

At midday a colored man arrived at the post office
directly from Magnolia Beach and gave us the following
particulars of the loss of life at that place:

Old Dr. A. B. Flagg and his wife are drowned.

Trial Justice Flagg and his wife and children are
drowned.

Miss Alice LaBruce

Miss Bet LaBruce

Miss Bessie Weston

A little girl, name unknown.

Three servants: Adele, Vitrim and Sallie.

Our informant stated that Mr. Wm White and Josh Ward were
safe.

All the houses on Magnolia were washed away, with the
exception of the Hasel house.

Dr. Ward Flagg was only saved by holding on to a bush,
but he managed to save one of the children also.

There were questions from Tom about what happened to Pawelys
Island since it is so near Magnolia Beach. I explained that on the north
end of Pawleys there were five houses in 1893, three of these belonged
to the Tucker, Freeman, and Fraser families, and that they all lost their
homes.

Storm of 1916

This captive audience wanted more, so I gathered my thoughts of the Hurricane of 1916. I mentioned that my stories had their source in newspaper articles and hearsay, but that finally I could tell them about a hurricane where I had actually talked to someone who was in it.

Very few people are living who remember the 1916 storm, but eighty-five-year-old Dick Crayton and his twin brother, Sammy, were one-year-old boys living on Pawleys Island that mid July evening. Dick remembers his mother, Pearl, telling the story of that evening. A few hours before the storm a telegram arrived in Georgetown warning of an impending storm. Edward Kaminski hurriedly made his way up to the island, crossing the Waccamaw River on his tugboat, *Palmetto*, then walked to the island to warn the residents. He arrived after most everybody had gone to bed, and had to awaken families at each house.

Pearl Crayton was at home with the twin boys, her five-year-old daughter Alice, and Justina, a teenage servant. Mr. Crayton was away for the day and evening. Mrs. Crayton and Justina threw some clothes on the twins then hitched the horse and buggy and they were off northward on the dark island road.

From Mrs. Crayton's description, the scene must have appeared much like the episode from the film *Gone With the Wind*, when Scarlet and her servant, Prissy, flee in the rainstorm from Union troops, but this was no movie. Pearl Crayton was fleeing in the horse and buggy through the beginning of a hurricane as Justina gripped the children.

They headed northward on the island road. The frightened horse reared up as they turned westward on the north causeway, and the buggy nearly overturned. Angry winds, now coming from the northeast, virtually blew them across the creek, which was a raging river by now. Pearl, with her family and Justina, arrived at the refuge place of Mr. R. C. Allen's home, situated just north of the causeway. They joined about twenty other islanders who had congregated there while Allen struggled to get the horses into the barn. Like a flock of wet chickens, the Craytons were welcomed. They joined the other neighbors on the second floor to bed down on pallets for the night. Pearl said that nobody slept much that evening as the Allen house shook and swayed. She commented on how stoic the teenage Justina was, and how she attended to the children as if this storm was a routine affair.

The following morning the sun was shining, and Pearl's buggy was all hitched and ready. She drove her cargo through debris on the island road back to their island home, which was still standing. They were all alive, and Dick lived to tell the story eighty-five years later. The *Georgetown Times* told the story a day later on July 26, 1916:

Severe Hurricane

SUMMER COLONY ON Pawleys ISLAND
LEAVE THE BEACH IN STORM

Pawleys Island and the immediate vicinity got a full share of the hurricane Thursday night and Friday. This storm will go down in history as second only to the storm of '93, when so many memorable tragedies took place.

The northeast wind set in before midnight Wednesday. Before morning it had become a stiff gale, and the weatherwise and the timorous began to seriously question the final outcome. Usually these northeast storms are supposed to last for 36 hours. But the fishermen, as well as the lifelong dwellers in the neighborhood, gave their opinion on that dark Thursday, about which time the tide would be running out, would see the finish of the "blow." However, instead of subsiding, the wind continued to increase in violence, and the tide, drawn by the full moon, rose alarmingly fast. Before dark, the causeway connecting island and mainland was submerged. The water reaching almost to the boards on the bridge, dashing in waves waist high over the lower parts of the roadway. Business men coming in cars and buggies from Waverly found it impractical to cross to the island until lower tide. But the islanders still felt themselves safe, and with the gale rising to a hurricane, most of them went to bed, secure in the protection of their fortification of sandhills.

By midnight a message—brought over on Mr. Kaminski's launch, the *Palmetto* — reached the pavilion from Georgetown, saying that the government warned all inhabitants of the island to flee to the mainland to escape a hurricane that was on the way and would reach its maximum about three o'clock. Then began the exodus of dwellers in homes and boarding houses along the beach — men in bathing suits, women attired likewise with caps pulled tightly down over their heads, carrying suit cases and valuable — fathers and mothers carrying babies wrapped in blankets, and wee children walking as best they could. Also, old inhabitants began to remark that the tide was behaving as it did in '93, which hastened the movement to the mainland.

The wind blew a hurricane for hours and tides as high as the storm of 1893 were swept into the inlet behind the island. There were about four hundred people on the island and all of them left and spent the night and the following day on the mainland in vacant houses and the homes of those summering at Ocean View. The islanders left the island at midnight without excitement or great inconvenience.

No warning was received of the hurricane's approach until 11 o'clock at night. Mr. E. W. Kaminski was the bearer of the news. He braved the fearful wind and waves in the bay and walked across from the river, three miles, in a blinding rain and went from house to house warning the people. It was the work of a real hero, and the islanders will never forget Mr. Kaminski. The *Palmetto*, under great difficulty, returned to the city only to go down a few hours later.

Following the *Palmetto*, the ocean tug *Williams*, Capt. Porter, fought her way across the bay and up the river to give assistance to the island. Capt. Porter says he never encountered such seas in all his long career. It required the best of seamanship to handle the big tug even up the river.

Exodus From Island

The cottages and visitors received the news of the storm calmly, and in fifteen minutes the exodus began. Some walked, some used carriages and machines. Special mention should be made of splendid work of several auto drivers, who took great risks in seeing that all were off the island: Messrs Herman Carraway, Belton Brockinton, and Master Ben Munnerlyn. Perhaps a hundred people spent the night in what is locally called the "House of Refuge" at Ocean View. Others went to the homes of cottages, who opened their doors and warmly received them.

Hurricane Hazel—1954

Toward the end of my narrative about the 1916 hurricane, Hattie Carrington walked up the boardwalk. Hattie could sense that I had English guests and had brought a bag of chocolate chip cookies.

I asked her to have a seat and told her that we were discussing hurricanes. "Oh Lordy, Horace and I were staying right down there in the third house," she pointed southward, "that Friday in October '54. They called that one 'Hazel,' the name of my sister." My English guests seemed captivated by Hattie's South Carolina accent. "It was a close shave for us. When Horace and I realized that it was a big storm, we snatched up our things and went over to our son's place in Manning where it was rough enough. We drove back over the next day, and the house we had stayed in was clear across the creek." She hesitated, looked at Patricia and said, "In 1952 we had vacationed in the house which stood right here," pointing to the floor of my house. "The only thing left of this Tinklescale House was some two by fours. I also remember seeing a sink and a commode on the beach. Everything was clear gone."

Hattie finally handed me the cookies, which I passed around. As she changed the subject to her London visit, I pointed out the October 21, 1954, article from the *Georgetown Times*:

Hurricane Wrecks Island, Small Damage In City

Hurricane "Hazel" left a debris of destruction on Georgetown's nearest ocean front resort, Pawleys Island, after her visit last Friday. Summer homes irrespective of style from the modern, gaily painted pinks and green houses, some of concrete blocks to the quaint wide siding rambling summer homes of fifty years ago were shattered. Some were carried into the marsh, some dumped into the ocean, some so completely destroyed that how and where they went may always remain a mystery.

A new development at the south end of the island where approximately twenty houses had been built, or were in the process of building, were wiped out, excepting two houses on stilts: one, known as the "roost" and one belonging to Mr. and Mrs. John C. Heinemann. These remain but are completely separated from the other part of the island by a new inlet cut through the sand dunes by the ocean.

Houses that stood behind sand dunes thirty to forty feet are now in full view of the ocean, in fact within a few feet of the water's edge at high tide.

In other places the sand was washed and deposited in such a way that the houses seem half way buried in the sand. One large home on the north end was placed in the middle of the island's only road.

It is believed that every house on the island was affected in some way of the approximate 600 . . . and a great number were completely destroyed. It is estimated that two thirds of the property was badly damaged and one third completely destroyed. Five homes on the island were destroyed by fire on Friday.

Hurricane Hugo—1989

I had intended to say nothing more about storms or hurricanes but two days later Patricia, at tea time, brought up the subject again. She said, "I remember when you returned to London in the fall of 1989, I think it was. You looked a bit shattered and said you had been through a storm here. I remember the pictures you brought back. Pictures of this house you had made for the insurance company. It looked like London after the Blitz."

I told Patricia how I'd watched reports on the weather station for five days before that storm. I told her that this hurricane had aimed at us from the beginning—a bee line straight at us, while everybody, including John Hope, the hurricane expert, kept saying that it would go this way or that way. But Hurricane Hugo had its mind made up, and it didn't veer. Early that September morning I drove over to Shell Road and enticed two African-American men to come over to the island where I had a supply of plywood waiting. While the wind was blowing the ladders around, I was loading the car with things I wanted to see again after the storm. At noon Deputy Sheriff Claude Roundtree drove by and announced, "You have thirty minutes to leave this island." I fled to Charles and Squeaky Swenson's home off King's River Road where I had arranged to stay. I discovered that I left my reading glasses on the island and returned to find Deputy Roundtree blocking the north causeway. After some persuasive pleading he allowed me to return to my home. I had a video camera conveniently hidden in the car and was able to photograph the incoming storm. By the time I left the island, troops from the National Guard manned the causeway. I returned to the Swenson cocoon where the electricity soon failed as pine trees flew here and there. With the winds howling and trees falling, it was a restless night.

The following morning I worked my way down various unblocked roads and back ways to the north causeway where U.S. Marines had replaced the National Guard. A sergeant laughed at me when I said I wanted to go back to my home. About noon, after showing proper identification, I was allowed to return home, or to what was left. The island was devastated. The roof of my home was in the driveway and the ceiling on the top floor was caved in. But worse, there was no dune or vegetation left on the island. Sand from the dune had been deposited between my house and the road. I next drove toward the south end of the island to find two Pawleys Islands, as a breach had severed the island in two. I felt better about my house when I looked westward and could see about a dozen houses that had been blown across the creek. The Bird's Nest section of the island was unrecognizable, all stirred around like scrambled eggs.

I drove to the north end of the island where the Swado home had been blown and washed toward the creek and tipped over. I told them about walking up the beach to the Tip Top Inn, which had also toppled, but in the opposite direction, toward the ocean.

Patricia asked, "Oh my, where did you live with all this going on, without a roof over your head?" I explained to her that I lived in a house at Litchfield whose occupants had fled the hurricane. I mentioned McClellanville, a town thirty miles south of here, where the African-American section of the town had been devastated. Sixty or seventy families were made homeless. I told Patricia that I went to this town three days after the storm intending to adopt one family. A week later I had adopted seventy families. But I was not in the mood to continue to talk about McClellanville and tried to drop the subject, referring them to a thick album I had prepared on the McClellanville experience.

The guests sipped their Jasmine tea and all was quiet for a moment, then Patricia said, almost with finality, "Well I'm just glad you don't have earthquakes here."

I thought for a moment and replied, "Earthquakes, earthquakes. No, no we don't have earthquakes," knowing that I was telling an untruth, knowing that I wanted to go in the ocean, and knowing that these guests would never return again had they known about the evening the earth convulsed on Pawleys Island. Had I been completely truthful I could have said that many of us who live on Pawleys Island have noticed that our homes shake. But we pay little attention because we have become accustomed to it. When a visitor notices this shaking I tell them not to be concerned. When a picture falls off the wall, I just put it back and change the subject to the Gray Man or perhaps to Alice Flagg.

I know something about the earthquake which shook the island on August 31, 1886, but I never mention this to my guests. I don't tell them that we're located on a fault line that has devastated Charleston and the surrounding area several times. I never tell my guests that we might be safer in San Francisco or the Napa Valley. When my house shakes I never suggest that we might be safer in Bangladesh or eastern Turkey.

But if a clever history-minded guest should mention 1886, I might comment on the admirable conduct of the women that night, or I might repeat bits of the article about the 1886 earthquake that appeared in the *Georgetown Times* two days later. I could tell about the chickens falling out of trees where they roosted, but I would try to change the subject. If I am pressed, or if more pictures fall from the wall, I might go and get the following article and read it to them:

The Earth Convulsed!

September 8, 1886

THE SHOCK AT Pawleys ISLAND

Signs of the Impending Quake — The Island Badly Shaken Up — Men and Women Terribly Alarmed — Admirable Conduct of the Women

We are indebted to Mr. W. St. J. Mazyck for the following graphic and comprehensive account of the earthquake shock and its effect on Pawleys Island, as observed by him. August 31 will always be remembered by the inhabitants of Pawleys Island. The early morning was bright and clear. By 10 o'clock the heavens were overcast with long dark ridgy clouds. By 12 noon it was clear again; but it clouded up and rained from three to four in the afternoon. The heaviest clouds seemed to pass down the river and go to sea over the Winyah Bay. During the early part of the day, there were frequent gusts of wind, which seemed to portent an autumnal gale. The afternoon and evening were intensely close, the thermometer recording eighty-four degrees at 7 p.m. There was nothing, however, to create uneasiness, and little did we expect to get such a shaking up as occurred from the earthquake—an experience entirely novel, and most assuredly not agreeable. Nobody hankers for more. As some persons had already gone to bed and others were just going, attention had been called to the clocks. Ten minutes of 10 p.m. were pretty well to be agreed upon, though my observation made it seven minutes, when the first ominous noise began. This noise resembled the approach of a heavy train of cars or a high wind and was observed some

seconds, perhaps ten, before the actual shock. I remember
distinctly asking twice, "What is that noise?" and the
answer, "It must be an earthquake." I replied, "Well, let
us notice the effect," before the house (a neighbor's) in
which I was began to heave and rock.

The motion was up and down and from side to side, so that
every portion of the house was under a violent strain. It
seemed to me and others that it must fall and nothing
could save it. The duration, from the first evidence to
the termination of the shock, is variously estimated from
one and a half to three minutes. I am inclined to think
the latter is nearest the fact: but it was not a time for
nice calculation. This shock, which was by far the sever-
est, was followed by two pretty sharp ones within twenty
minutes. Several others were distinctly felt. I think
eight in all, ending about ten minutes of 11 o'clock. Some
think there were two others. I was inclined to believe it
was thunder, as there was some lightning up north. I am
quite satisfied that during that hour there was a constant
trembling, with occasional heavings of the earth's surface. Unfortunately, I failed to observe the thermometer.
High tide in the creek back of the island occurred very
soon after the first three shocks. It was a full tide, but
not excessive. It was soon falling and went out rapidly.

I visited several houses. There was, of course, considerable apprehension but nothing like a panic. The compar-
ative calmness of the women was admirable, and they
deserve credit for it was a novel and trying experience.
My sympathy was particularly aroused for the little children who had been taken hurriedly from their beds to the
yards. The poor little fellows could not comprehend the
situation, but they behaved well.

About midnight it seemed to be considered that all danger was over, and most persons retired, hoping to spend
the rest of the night in quietude. Alas, they were sadly
disappointed! At three minutes 'til one, there was a rum-
bling and sharp shock for six to eight seconds.

That was too much. Sleep was gone; everybody was on the

alert, with rather widespread demoralization. People freely indulged in grave apprehensions and serious specu- lations as to more violent disturbances. The tension was too great, and some of my fair friends gave way.

All went reasonably well the rest of the night until twenty minutes to five, Wednesday morning, September 1. There was another shock and another at twenty minutes after eight. There was another shock at 12:30 and another at 5:15 P.M. and still another at midnight. Several minor shocks closely followed, which seemed to me to be rather a continuation of the greater shocks. In twenty-six hours, we had one nearly every hour, and it seemed that during that time there were constant, or very frequent, tremors with slight undulations particularly noticeable on the rice field banks. The Negroes were constantly remarking upon the different directions of the passages of the undu- lations. The worst shock came a few moments after the dis- turbances in the water. One young lady was positive she saw the fowls falling from the trees in which they had roosted.

The uncertainty and violence of the shocks was the painful part—that terrible feeling of uncertainty entirely different from anything I ever felt. One young friend remarked that the lengthened intervals was a great relief, and he hoped the next interval would be a hundred years away. So, with all of our troubles, there were a few bits of fun here and there. Man is an elastic creature. Under the most trying circumstances he will often do or say something to divert and amuse his fellow man. What a won- derfully good Providence it was to make him so.

Patricia, Tom, Veronica, and Cynthia became absorbed in the ocean, beach boules, bird watching, and the usual nothings we do here. Tom painted the old columns which hold up the porches. Veronica and Cyn- thia became adept at crabbing; Patricia avoided it because she was afraid of their pinching claws. When finished with the columns, Tom flew a kite when the wind was right.

With this activity they forgot about hurricanes and earthquakes and never mentioned weather again, except on the way to the airport Patricia said rather surprisingly, "Well, we didn't have a hurricane, but I almost wish we had."

THE MUCH TRAVELED HOUSE

Sumwalt and Eileen lived in a 1930s faded, white-shingled house which usually was located toward the north end of the island across from the Greene's place on Atlantic Boulevard, a street undeserving of its name. Boulevard doesn't apply to anything up there, except maybe the Greene's house. A few years ago it got a new foundation and a coat of paint, plus some green decorative aluminum shutters. It was reasonably deserving of a boulevard address.

Back then all the island homes had to have a name so the mail carrier would know where to deliver letters and boxes. Sumwalt's house was called "The Creek Bed" because it was near the creek to the west. This two-and-a-half-bedroom, one-story house had rested, but not too sturdily, on greyish-black concrete blocks anywhere from two to three feet off the ground, just enough room for some of the island's varmints, such as raccoons, opossums and maybe cats who nobody claimed. Sumwalt referred to them as "fertile cats."

This elevation also allowed for water to flow under the house in case of storms or the high tides of a northeaster. Upstairs— five steps—there were the bedrooms, a living room, and a large kitchen and a screened porch both facing the creek. All in all, "The Creek Bed" was called a comfortable home, where Sumwalt and Eileen raised two daughters, Sweets and Sophie.

The Swados, who worked hard in their filling station over on route 17 at the crossroads, also owned pets: Chyna Dynette, a Siamese cat and Leonardo, their toy schnauzer. Sumwalt did not like the pets but put up with them because the girls liked to tussle with them, and he also felt that in spite of his small size, Leonardo made a fairly good watchdog due to his ability to bark loudly.

On the morning of October 15, 1954, just after daybreak, Eileen got up to make breakfast, and before going into the bedroom to awaken Sweets and Sophie, she turned on the radio. WGSM Georgetown was announcing that Hurricane Hazel had, surprisingly, turned westward and no longer was "out yonder." The storm was headed straight for the South Carolina coast.

Eileen rushed into the bedrooms and shook Sumwalt, who still lay curled up like a ground worm. She went to the other bedroom and woke the girls. When she told Swado what was going on, he rushed out, took a look at the greying sky to the south, then snatched up the whole family never bothering to take his pajamas off. They all jumped into the '52 Plymouth and fled westward across the causeway.

They were on their way to Moncks Corner to stay with Inez, Eileen's sister who was a prominent beautician there. Passing through Georgetown, Sweets, who was just now getting her eyes open, tapped Sumwalt on the shoulder and asked about Chyna Dynette and Leonardo. Sumwalt didn't answer. Eileen cupped a hand over her mouth and said "Mercy."

An hour later when they arrived in Moncks Corner, Inez had already heard about the hurricane. As the Swados pulled into the driveway, Inez stood at the back window looking eastward and listening to a Charleston radio station. She hugged Sweets and Sophie, then found a pair of her husband's overalls for Sumwalt.

That day Inez stayed away from her beauty parlor. She, Eileen, Sweets, and Sophie played Monopoly. Fred, Eileen's husband, came home from work early. He and Sumwalt listened to the radio. That night the house shook, but not too badly. They all listened to the radio.

The next morning, without electricity, they ate cold cereal, and Sumwalt loaded the family into the Plymouth. At the last minute, Inez decided not to open the shop. Instead, she drove with the Swados back to Pawleys Island to help clean up the mess. Sweets and Sophie rode with Inez. They followed Sumwalt and Eileen on Route 701, turned through Francis Marion National Forest and through Shulerville, where they had to detour toward McClellanville because of downed telephone poles and lines. They came through Honey Hill and finally reached Route 17 south of the Santee Rivers. They got to Pawleys Island three hours later.

There was a convoy at the north causeway with heads sticking out of all the car windows, looking toward the island, surveying houses on the west side of the creek—houses which belonged on the east side of the creek. Then Sumwalt held out his arm and motioned for Inez to stop. He announced to Eileen, "I see it." He pointed northeastward, "I see it, but it's half in the creek." He yelled to Inez and the children, "There it is!" They all craned to look. He had spotted "The Creek Bed," tilted over into the creek. The rest of the island was a jumbled mess—houses scattered like children's building blocks. They crossed the causeway and turned left, driving around the Foster house, which was perched in the middle of the road. Eileen said, "Mercy!"

They arrived at the site where "The Creek Bed" had previously stood. They pulled into the driveway where several greyish-black concrete blocks stood, looking like tombstones. "The Creek Bed" was on the other side of the road. Sweets ran toward the sound of a barking dog. Sophie followed closely behind and then the rest of the Swados.

Sumwalt stood in a daze, while Eileen and Inez stacked two concrete blocks up by the door. It was jammed tight and Leonardo barked louder. Swado went back to the car to get a crow bar. He stood there while Inez pried the door open. Leonardo leaped out, but Chyna Dynette lay quietly on the tilted sofa. She had six kittens during the storm.

Eileen and Inez spent the afternoon straightening things out, sweeping up mud and dead fish, and drying out the quilts. Sumwalt went to the filling station, but there was no electricity so he came back home with a Coleman stove that he propped up level in the kitchen. They tugged at the beds and aimed the feet toward the downward slope. Sweets and Sophie ran up and down the road as if it were some holiday. Leonardo barked and followed them.

Late in the afternoon, an exhausted Sumwalt was sitting in an old damp recliner in the yard beside "The Creek Bed," when Dick Crayton drove up in his pick-up. He told Sumwalt that "The Creek Bed" had been seen just after daybreak floating around on the creek, and one of the Lachicotte boys had seen it float back here to where it had started. Too exhausted to be surprised, Sumwalt just said, "Well, I'll be durned."

Dick and Sumwalt made plans to move the house back across the road when things dried out. They made plans to jack it up two feet higher and place it on new concrete blocks.

All went well as they got accustomed to walking around in a tilted house and using the Coleman stove. The next day Sumwalt opened the filling station, and two days later Inez returned to her beauty parlor in Moncks Corner. Lilo Crayton visited and brought a little ceramic plaque for the kitchen—HOME SWEET HOME. It was placed over the sink. A week later Dick and Sumwalt, with some help from the neighbors, moved the house back to its original spot, and the Swados were level again.

The Swados lived an uneventful and happy life on the island for the next twenty-five years. Soon after moving their house back to its previous site, Dick suggested that they change the name of their house to "The Ark," and Eileen agreed. Sweets and Sophie grew up, finished high school, and both graduated from Horry-Georgetown Tech. Sweets moved to Conway, and Sophie went to Little River, both working as medical technicians. They married and soon grandchildren were visiting "The Ark."

Chyna Dynette raised several more litters of kittens but finally met her doom under the wheels of Zenith Allston's garbage truck. Leonardo probably died a natural death as an old dog, but Sumwalt declared that a neighbor had poisoned him because of his barking. They kept talking about getting another cat or dog but never did.

Business at the filling station thrived. Sumwalt delved into the caviar business on the side, but nobody ever knew much about this, not even Eileen. He looked more prosperous, became bald and gained weight. Eileen took on pounds too, and had several new dresses made by her sister in Moncks Corner. Things were going along smoothly.

Then, early on the morning of September 19, 1989, once again they had to evacuate to Moncks Corner as Hurricane Hugo swept up the coast. This time Sumwalt had enough time to get into his camouflage coveralls before jumping into their new Dodge.

Three days later the post office had reopened, and I stood talking to Mae Ellerby when Dick Crayton drove up. He got out of his pick-up, came and patted me on the shoulder, and expressed his regrets that my house had had its roof and porches blown away. Then he asked me if I had seen the Swados and "The Ark." He suggested that I drive up the island to visit them.

Later that day I drove up there and long before reaching the Swados' place, I could see "The Ark" back where it had rested twenty-five years before—tipped over into the creek. Sumwalt had found a chair and sat rocking, looking toward his house, still dressed in his camouflage outfit. The old recliner was draped in a mildewed quilt. As I drove up he yelled that he was sorry that I had lost my porches and told me that he had seen my columns and spindles scattered down around the chapel. I got out of my car and trying to be sympathetic, told him that my house didn't look half as bad as his.

I looked toward the concrete blocks on which his house had stood three days before. I looked at the tilted and warped house. I asked if he and Eileen would move to the mainland.

Swado gazed up at me as though I had asked a ridiculous question. He pointed at "The Ark" and said, "That's the most traveled house on this island. They tell me that it was again seen circling around in the creek, and it had floated right back here, near where it came from." He paused to lick his lips and said, "Dick and I plan to move her right back across the road. We'll jack her up and build another foundation and stick her on it." He hesitated, then added, "Eileen and me will live in her another twenty-five years. We may get some more cats and dogs. We'll start over." Swado pretended to look down and spit, put the cigar back in his mouth and mumbled, "The mainland! Shoot."

About that time Eileen worked her way out of "The Ark" carrying something. I asked what she had found. She held up a ceramic plaque inscribed, "HOME SWEET HOME."

THE McCLELLANVILLE EXPERIMENT

I have not told this story before because it awakens in me depressing thoughts about the fury of nature and its consequences. During the third week of September 1989, Hurricane Hugo slammed into the coast of South Carolina. The eye of this storm was centered over Sullivan's Island a few miles north of Charleston. Its devastating winds reached a hundred miles north. Pawleys Island was on the northern limits of these winds. Thankfully, I was in residence at my island home during this period and was able to prepare. At noon, on the day of the storm I fled the island and went inland a few miles to stay with friends in a safer place.

After the storm, Pawleys Island was uninhabitable. It was without water and electricity, and telephone and electric wires were down on the island road. My house had lost its roof and porches. I could only visit and was not allowed to stay.

Three days later the *Sun News* of Myrtle Beach published a front-page story and photograph about the town of McClellanville, nestled between Charleston and Pawleys Island. The article featured resident Mary Linen who had survived the storm. The night of the storm, she and her children, Lisa and Robbie, had left her mobile home to go next door and stay with her elderly mother-in-law. As water rushed through the house, Mary tied her children to the column of the back porch using an electric cord. It was a miracle that they survived.

The article explained that the residents of McClellanville, a predominantly black community lying thirty miles north of the storm's eye, had been told to come to Lincoln High School as an evacuation place. Five hundred of them gathered there that evening. Officials did not know that this school building was in the flood plane. The 140-mile-an-hour winds brought the ocean to the school. By midnight the evacuees had fled their pallets on the cafeteria floor and had gone onto the stage of the auditorium. Five hundred people were crammed into an area that could confortably accommodate less than a hundred. In the darkness the wind had brought the ocean water to the stage where they stood on tables and chairs. As the water rose and covered them up to their waists, fathers held children on their shoulders. The wind howled outside, children screamed, and mothers cried. Everybody prayed. Gradually, the water reached their shoulders. Suddenly, the wind subsided and the water stopped rising. By daybreak, they were able to go back to the village to find their devastated homes scattered and washed off their foundations. Hardly anybody had insurance.

I reread the article and knew that I had to do something to help this community. Later that day, I drove the thirty miles to McClellanville, but guards from the U.S. Marines would not allow me in the town. I had a restless night, and the next morning I decided to try to find this Mary Linen I had read about. I would "adopt" Mary and her family if I could. I returned to McClellanville, and with a specific person and purpose, I was allowed into the village.

After much searching and being sent here and there, I was directed to a small house on Dupre Road. Wet homemade quilts hung across a rusty fence in front. I knocked on the door and a bedraggled and sad-eyed Mary Linen greeted me. She carried a broom and continued to half-heartedly sweep. I introduced myself and asked if she was Mary Linen. She answered, "Yes, is I in trouble?" Mary seemed surprised that I was a doctor, telling me that she worked as a housekeeper in a Charleston hospital, and that I was the first doctor who had ever spoken to her. She told me that her husband, who was a truck driver, had returned from the Midwest yesterday. They slept in the bed of his truck last night. She had sent the children and her mother-in-law to stay with relatives in Charleston. She took me outside, laid down her broom, and pointing toward an overturned mobile home in the field, she said, "That's our home."

We went into the house, and she showed me the watermarks on the wall, the soaked bedrooms, the overturned furniture, the kitchen appliances that had been washed to the back porch, and then she pointed to the electric cable that had held her children during the storm. The house reeked of mildew. Still, Mary did not know why I had appeared on the scene.

Trying to become better acquainted with her, I asked why she and her family had not gone to the Lincoln High School the night of the storm. She answered, "God had told us not to," and we dropped this subject. We went outside and sat on the edge of the porch. While Mary rested, we talked, and I tried to decipher this despondent black woman. I finally said, "Mary, I want to help you and your family. I'll return tomorrow to meet your husband." She asked me to come back in the house where she reached the highest shelf and took from it a dry handmade quilt. She gave me the quilt. Shaken, I drove back toward Pawleys Island determined to help Mary Linen and her family.

I spent that evening on the telephone, calling friends whom I knew would help in this emergency. The first objective was to find a dry home for the Linen family. I called a friend in Spartanburg who said he would send a mobile home there the following day. Late the next morning, I was back in McClellanville to meet the truck pulling this home. I directed it to the Linen yard where I met her husband Robert. Mary stood in the yard, wearing a camouflage outfit. Tears streamed down her face when I told her that this was her new home. Robert stood with his hands on his hips, speechless. Neighbors left their damp homes and gathered in the yard as the mobile home was pulled into place. I was introduced to several of the Linen cousins—everybody on Dupre Road was related. I was pulled here and there by these cousins, each telling me to come and see what was left of their homes. My adoptions soon extended to six families.

Overwhelmed, I fled back to where I was now staying in Litchfield. It was Saturday night, and I was back on the telephone. I called a physician friend in Atlanta who agreed to donate another mobile home and pull it to McClellanville. He arrived two days later. I made another important call to my brother-in-law, asking him to have a special contribution at his church the following day. He agreed.

The following morning, Sunday, I decided to attend an African Methodist Episcopal Church on Pawleys mainland. I arrived early and sat near the front, alone for a few minutes, trying to collect my thoughts. What do I do next? On the previous day, I had driven through the African-American section of the McClellanville community and had seen its devastation. I had seen these black people standing helpless in front of wrecked homes, I had seen them wondering aimlessly along the roads, and I had heard them telling me of their uncertain future. I had seen the chaos on Dupre Road.

Toward the end of the service it dawned on me. I would form D.A.R.E., Dupre Area Recovery Enterprise. It would be under the auspices of the already organized Minton Foundation, using their 501-C3 charitable donation number. When I returned back to my residence the telephone was ringing. It was my brother-in-law. He informed me that the collected funds from his church and all other churches of Christ funds were going to a central church in Greenville, South Carolina. Immediately I called this church and talked to Tom Sutton, who happened to answer the telephone. I explained the situation in McClellanville. He said that funds were already arriving at his church from Churches of Christ all over the country. He asked me if he could bring the elders over in two days. I gave directions to find me in McClellanville.

Things were falling in place! On Sunday afternoon I returned to McClellanville with my camera and photographed some twenty families standing in front of their devastated homes. On Monday, the film was developed, and that night an album was prepared with a page devoted to each family.

By noon on Tuesday, I had Mary Linen installed in her new mobile home. Her aunt, Minnie Adams, who had floated around McClellanville on a sofa the night of the storm, came to meet the visiting elders from

Greenville. We served them Kentucky Fried Chicken, which I had
brought from Georgetown. Afterwards we drove about the neighborhood before returning to Mary's mobile home. The elders were in tears.
Before leaving, they had a private conference and returned to tell me
that they would pledge a quarter of a million dollars in financial support
and, within a week, would have a party of five volunteers from their
church in place at McClellanville to continue the recovery process. I
returned to Pawleys Island and went directly to the island sign company
and had a large sign printed "D.A.R.E.—Dupre Area Recovery Enterprise—Help Us Help Ourselves."

Things moved fast. I borrowed a mobile office from a friend at Pawleys, and Robert Linen pulled it to a vacant lot in the corner of McClellanville. The telephone didn't stop ringing. On Thursday, Oprah Winfrey
called to ask me to bring Mary to Charleston to be on her television
program. I declined when she said that we couldn't make a direct pitch
to ask for money for D.A.R.E. She seemed astounded and said nobody
had ever refused an offer to appear on her program. I replied that we
were too busy with the job before us. The following day I flew to
Nashville on a fund-raising mission, returning in time to meet the volunteers from Greenville. Their mobile office awaited them.

I greeted the affable and efficient Tom Sutton who had taken a six-
month leave of absence from his well-drilling company to oversee the
McClellanville recovery operation. This church had named their efforts
"Hugo Project Relief," and this organization would join D.A.R.E. in a
combined operation. That afternoon, Tom and I drove throughout the
community, surveying and setting the boundaries for the recovery project. It included seventy homes and families in four square miles—the
entire African-American community. To our surprise, we discovered that
this community was outside the boundary lines of the city limits of
McClellanville. There would be no allotment for this community when
federal funds came to McClellanville.

We called for a town meeting for the following Saturday, then left
notices at each house and at the National Guard Armory in George-

town, where many townspeople were staying. We could sense concern among these people about who we were. They had never heard of the Churches of Christ. They had not experienced white people trying to help African-Americans. "What were we up to?" some questioned.

On Saturday morning we stopped the buzzing of chain saws and the pounding of hammers. The sound of sweeping fell silent as two hundred fifty townspeople gathered in the vacant lot in front of the mobile office. They sat in folding chairs and on the ground, curious to hear what we had to say.

I was first on the agenda. Speaking from the bed of a pick-up, I welcomed them and handed back a large stack of clean, dry quilts that I had gathered earlier in the week, soaking wet, from their fences. This gesture seemed to have set a good tone for the meeting. Tom Sutton spoke next, giving them reassurance that we had no ulterior motive other than to help. He introduced representatives from the Red Cross, Federal Emergency Management Authority, insurance companies, and legal assistants. Each made a short presentation. By the end of the meeting, there seemed to be few who doubted our intentions. That morning we registered sixty families.

D.A.R.E and Hugo Project Relief proceeded. I had obtained post office box 400 in the village, and each day more and more checks arrived. Tom and I had closely observed Mary and Robert Linen and decided to place them on a payroll, giving Mary executive responsibility to represent the community and paying Robert for his eighteen-hour days of hauling refuse to the dump.

Truckloads of supplies were flowing in so fast that Tom had to obtain the trades building of Lincoln High School, converting it into a commissary. Each member of the seventy families was given an identification card that authorized food and provisions.

The community now hummed with activity. Mary learned to use a computer and manned the office telephone. Volunteer workers represented twelve states, along with student groups from Vanderbilt University, South Carolina State University, and the University of South

Carolina. They were housed wherever we could find a dry spot. In the evenings, or after work (whichever came first), Tom—"St. Thomas"—held court by a fire built on a vacant lot on Dupre Road. Townspeople came by to talk. A basketball court was set up and sometimes there were late games that were lit up by car lights. By now, Tom and his group from the Churches of Christ had gained the confidence of the community.

My visits became more sporadic as the time was approaching for me to return to England. One afternoon I went down to welcome the arrival of six large modular homes donated by a builder in Sumpter. I avoided the issue of which family was to receive these homes. Tom, in his tactful manner, solved this problem but not without some controversy within the community. We learned that everybody could not be pleased.

One morning in late October, after I had finally been able to return to my Pawleys Island home, I received a call telling me that I was needed in McClellanville that afternoon. I agreed to come down and went there expecting some emergency. Someone at the office directed me to the trades building commissary. There, in the late afternoon, I found most of the community gathered. As I walked in they sang "Battle Hymn of the Republic." They placed Tom Sutton and me in the center of a great circle. Minnie Adams, Mary's aunt, presided. She read from Corinthians about love. There were prayers, speeches, and singing. Tom and I felt embarrassed as we were presented with quilts which had been made by Minnie. I was asked to respond. I fumbled for words and said that I had done no more than my father would have expected of me. Then I added that I was simply trying to take my mind away from the destruction of my own home. The townspeople joined hands, and we all sang "God be with You 'til We Meet Again." I left the farewell party feeling very humble.

The next day I flew off to London and left McClellanville with Tom and his staff, many volunteers, and my brother-in-law, Henry Schmid, who had come from Atlanta to join our efforts.

I returned in April to find the black section of McClellanville look-ing like a new town. Mary and Robert Linen and their children occupied a new home, which had been constructed on the site of their mobile home. An old grocery store had been converted to a community center where there was a buzz of activity. The children gathered there for supervised activities in the afternoons. In the mornings, the senior citi-zens met there. I recruited a coach and organized both a boys' and a girls' soccer team. Mary and I drove to Charleston and enticed Boy Scout officials to come up, and soon a McClellanville troop was organ-ized with the state's first lady scoutmaster, Elizabeth Young. The com-munity center housed a children's library that was donated by friends. I pretended not to notice the sign painted on the front of the building—Minton Community Center. In May, I hosted a barbecue by Yum Yum Young at Lincoln High School for the community. We ate in that same cafeteria where six months earlier many of these people had crowded onto this stage and barely escaped drowning.

Before leaving for London in the fall, I was invited back for the anniversary of Hurricane Hugo. I arrived at the community center at sunset as townspeople were gathering, each bringing a covered dish of food. We were given a white candle and formed four abreast along the road in front. Daisy Washington, a local singer, led the group toward Lincoln High School. Strings of small white lights glowed along the roadway. We marched and sang. Sometimes the chant would erupt into some spiritual, then return to a chant. In front of Lincoln High School we formed a circle where three local ministers, a Methodist, a Baptist, and a Pentecostal, each said prayers thanking the Almighty that no life was lost during that terrible night, and for the recovery of the black community of McClellanville.

Daisy sang as we marched back to the community center where we stayed until midnight eating, talking, and reliving this experience of Hurricane Hugo.

THE BURIAL OF A PHARAOH

*T*his morning, with nothing much else to do, I read entries in the Eckerd Pen Pal notebook, which serves as a guest book at the Duck's Nest. A week ago, Olga Hirshhorn wrote, "I treasure your friendship and the hours spent talking about our lives."

This entry brought back memories of an early morning conversation—between short periods of watching the ocean—with Olga, as we rocked on the porch while having coffee. Invariably our talk reverted to Joe Hirshhorn, her late husband, the noted art collector and patron who gave the museum in Washington, named in his honor. Joe died a few months earlier and Olga discussed his burial.

"I had decided to bury Joe in his tux, as he always appeared so dapper when dressed formally. He was only five feet tall, as you remember." Olga paused, took a sip of coffee, then said, "I mentioned this to callers the morning after he had suddenly died. Everybody said 'No, you shouldn't do this. It isn't proper.' Then I consulted a more trusted friend, and he said, 'Olga, you dress Joe exactly as you like.' With this encouragement I changed my mind and decided to bury him in his favorite plaid suit, a bow tie, and a red vest. So I sent these things to the funeral home."

Olga stood, retied the belt of her robe, and looked down at the old windmill that flopped hesitantly in the wind. She said in a more serious, but still joking tone, "Joe always said that he wanted to be buried with three things—a *Wall Street Journal*, a telephone, and his first significant art purchase, which were two Durer etchings.

"I went over to the museum, got the etchings out of storage, and took them to the funeral home where I placed them, the newspaper, and the telephone in the casket beside Joe." She brushed her hair back, then said, "But I became concerned on the way to the funeral home about the Durer etchings. So I called our curator and asked his advice. He insisted, 'No, you should not do this. You will be destroying art, and besides, someone might rob the grave.' I thought about it, and decided that in place of the etchings I would put Joe's favorite candy—three Hershey bars—in the casket." Olga went on, "Then Andy, our Chinese house boy, came by with a colorful Chinese doll. So I placed that in the casket too."

Olga smiled, looked out toward the dune and continued. "I must admit that it was a little bit like the Tomb of Ramses II. There was Joe dressed in his favorite plaid suit, a blue bow tie, and a red vest, with his *Wall Street Journal*, a telephone, and three Hershey bars. I stood there looking at him and held the Durer etchings under my arm."

I encouraged her with another cup of coffee. "So Mr. Goldsmith of the funeral home closed the casket for the final time, and Joe was taken to the Temple, where I met his sister, Rozalita, who had just arrived from Newark. Tearfully, she asked to see her brother. I agreed but was terribly concerned about her reaction to this spectacle. She's so Orthodox. You know how they want such sober finalities, and everybody buried in black? Well, we opened the casket again, and with all her weeping and carrying on she never even noticed how Joe was dressed. She didn't notice the *Wall Street Journal*, nor the telephone, nor the chocolate bars. Rozalita didn't notice Andy's Chinese doll. We closed Joe up again, and I breathed a sigh of relief."

Olga stood there, then looked down and patted the neighbor's dog who had joined us. She walked toward the door, stopped, and said happily, "I know Joe would have been pleased, buried like a pharaoh." She went inside to the bedroom to pack for her trip to Washington.

I sat looking at the Eckerd Pen Pal guest book, motionless and thinking. Then I recalled the first time I met Joe Hirshhorn. The memory returned quickly. We were on a safari in the deepest of Africa, out in some jungle. This bright-eyed little man and a smiling Olga joined me at breakfast. As if I should have known, he asked me if I might tell him how the New York Stock Exchange had fared the last three days. Before I could think of an answer he smiled at Olga, patted her on the hand, and said, "Darling, I don't want to see the giraffes until I call my broker in Toronto." Then he repeated his favorite three words, "God Bless

America." I remembered that even in an African jungle he was dapper, dressed in a plaid suit and blue bow tie. I suppose it was too hot for his red vest.

I squeezed fresh orange juice; we ate breakfast and were off to Myrtle Beach for her flight to Washington. Olga checked in at the US Air counter while I stood holding her heavy carry-on bag—a Salvation Army bag from her home in Naples, Florida. At the security check point, the pistol carrying young woman insisted that she open the bag, as it had turned on a red security light. Olga unwrapped the *Naples Times* from eleven small pieces of sculpture she was taking to Washington. She took from the bag three Picassos, two animal figures by Alexander Calder, two reclining figures by Henry Moore and others by Niki de St. Phalle, Kadishman, Alaman, and a highly polished silver erect phallus attached to two perfectly sculpted spheres by Man Ray. Olga rewrapped the sculptures as the young security guard stood, unmoved and without expression. At the gate, Olga stopped and gave me a hug and a kiss, then walked to the plane. She waved and yelled, "I'll be back for some more rocking and crabbing in October."

I waved goodbye and shouted, "God Bless America!"

WOUND-UP TOYS ON THE BEACH

This morning I noticed the year's first sanderlings on the beach. Out near the groin a small flock of these tiny shorebirds ran nimbly just in front of the incoming surf, then rushed back toward the ocean to snatch some little waif of sea life or an unlucky sand flea. They never seem to stop their game of tag with the incoming waves.

This ubiquitous bird can be found chasing these sand fleas and plankton almost anywhere on the coasts of the earth—from the North Sea to the coasts of New Zealand and Australia to Peru and Argentina.

The most amazing fact about this bird is its unbelievable migration distances. It is only a visitor to Pawleys Island, stopping over for feeding on its migratory journey from South American beaches to breeding grounds above the Arctic Circle, sometimes to within five hundred miles of the North Pole. At the Arctic site it mates and lays eggs on the barren tundra. The young chicks start flying in two weeks, and after a month they start their migration southward. On their way they again visit the beach at Pawleys Island, feeding and resting.

I've ceased to think of these peripatetic little shorebirds as just another sandpiper, for they deserve a gaze and a wonder. How many creatures, great or small, travel 15,000 miles for a summer vacation, then tow back several new family members, who must be taught to play tag with the Atlantic surf from the Arctic Circle to Argentina? And who, by the way, entertain people like me along the way.

A JOURNEY TO CHARLESTON

*T*hat morning the alarm clock cruelly sounded. It rang and interrupted some blurred dream of going to Charleston. Once awake, I savored the anticipated joy of driving a borrowed pick-up truck to fetch old columns and spindles from the Charleston Demolition Company out on North Market Street. I promised Peter Porcher that I would have them ready to nail on to my house by tomorrow.

I felt unusually confident about the trip. The old truck had recently been serviced. It had new recaps, and I had filled it up with premium Texaco gasoline. The weather was good, even hot. Most importantly, I was being accompanied by an English friend, Nigel Seymour-Egerton, a jolly and engaging retired schoolmaster from Islington.

We rested and rocked on the porch after breakfast, discussing our trip as the piercing, late May sun caused my guest to shield his eyes with his hand as we talked. He was smartly dressed in a fresh blue shirt with a white collar and pin striped trousers. It was easy to see that he was not a Pawleys Islander, with his light grey sweater, a Jersey, neatly tied around his shoulders. He had borrowed my old Stetson hat which was embellished with a narrow blue and red bandanna. The retired headmaster was ready to go!

I handed him the Amoco road map of South Carolina, then pointed to Route 17 and all the rivers we would cross going to Charleston—the Waccamaw, Pee Dee, and Black Rivers before Georgetown, the Sampit and Santee Rivers to the south, and the Ashley and Cooper Rivers nearer to Charleston. I pointed out McClellanville and Awendaw and told him that these were the only towns between Georgetown and the suburbs of Charleston. Then I told him to keep a lookout for state highway patrolmen, particularly near Georgetown because speeding tickets are expensive. He looked at me quizzingly, then nodded.

Nigel looked more closely at the road map, took off his wire rim bifocals, and held the map even closer. With an index finger he slowly retraced the straight route southward, then back again northward, as if we might be going through some jungle. He asked, "What's this threatening looking green section below this Awendow village—right there?"

I answered, "Oh, that's the Francis Marion Forest. Marion was the Swamp Fox who fought the British around here during the revolution." I continued, "There's only thirty-eight miles across these woods, and there's a filing station right here."

He asked, "Is this red dot right here a menace, this red dot here just beyond the green section?"

"Oh no, no, that's only the warning about the bridge across that part of the swamp around Bull's Island. Our pick-up isn't heavy enough to be of any concern. No problem, we can handle that Nigel," I said with assurance.

He retraced the route again, and finally, without looking up, he stated, "I'm ready." He got up, retied the arms of his sweater, turned to go, and then asked if he would need a car coat.

We walked down the back steps to the pick-up. I circled it, kicking each tire. Nigel followed with his arms behind his back. He made an abortive attempt to get in the truck on the left side, then smiled apologetically and got in on the right.

As we crossed the south causeway, he rolled the window down, and someone catching minnows waved at us. Nigel held his arm out and pretended to catch wind with his cupped hand. He looked straight ahead and readjusted my Stetson hat, its bandanna fluttering in the passing wind. South Carolina belonged to Nigel.

Below Hobcaw Barony, before reaching Georgetown and the Waccamaw River, a siren whined. It sounded again. I looked in the rear view mirror, then at Nigel, who continued to gaze straight ahead, his mind oblivious to any distraction. I pulled over and said, "Nigel, we're caught. You know, caught for speeding. You were supposed to be looking out for this."

He looked at me, then turned and looked out the back window and with mild concern said, "Gracious, how thoughtless."

We got out of the truck, and I recognized the patrolman, J. T. Mooney, the black man who used to run the Red and White grocery store up on the highway. "Howdy. How's it goin'? It's goin' to be a hot day, isn't it?" I said with some familiarity to J. T., as Nigel and I stood side by side in front of the patrol car that had its blue light still blinking. I searched for my driver's license as Nigel stood at attention. I said, "Sorry, I must have been going over 55. Trying to get to Charleston before it gets too hot. By-the-way, meet Nigel Seymour-Egerton who's visiting me up on the island." J. T. never looked up, said nothing, and continued to write. I wiggled about and said, "Prices are a lot higher at the Red and White now, but their Icees are still good. Aren't they J. T.?"

Nigel bent over and slapped at his ankles, I looked down, and then he slapped with both hands and quickly resumed his attention stance. J. T.'s big, black hand continued to write, the blue lights flashed, and the patrol car's radio jabbered with static. I had left the truck's radio on, and I could hear Kate Smith singing "Beautiful Dreamer" over the roar of the passing traffic. Again, Nigel raised one foot, then the other and slapped at his ankles. J. T. finished writing the ticket, finally looked up, then down at Nigel's feet. He handed me the ticket and matter-of-factly stated, "Mr. Seymour, you're standing in a hill of South American fire ants. You-all have a good day." While getting back in the patrol car, he added, "Now, I'm going up the road for an Icee." He waved as he drove off.

Nigel took three steps backwards, looked down, and slapped at his ankles again, then we got back in the truck. As we pulled back on the highway, Nigel was fidgety. He took off my hat and untied the arms of the sweater draped around his shoulders. He slapped at his ankles and legs again. Then he unbuckled his belt, wiggled out of his trousers, and as we crossed the Waccamaw River, he waved his blue pin stripes in the wind. He sat in his jockey shorts as we drove through Georgetown and on southward.

Down where the road goes over to Belle Isle, the radio played loudly and Kate Smith sang "America the Beautiful." The record stuck on "across the fruited plains." Then I saw another blue flashing light behind us. I heard the wailing of a siren. We stopped, got out and stood at attention once again between the pick-up truck and the patrol car. The patrolman finally handed Nigel the ticket. He had been cited for "Indecent Exposure."

Just as we were returning defeatedly to the pick-up, J. T. Mooney's car pulled in behind. We turned, and J. T. got out of his patrol car, grinning and licking an Icee.

AN OCTOBER AFTERNOON
IN A GRAVEYARD

*Y*esterday afternoon was one of those October times when there's a threatening feeling in the air—an uncertain time when one wishes the day would hurry and leave.

After lunch I rocked on the porch with Pierre Monteau, a visiting friend from Quebec. We discussed my shaking house and hurricanes as he addressed Christmas cards, something he always did in October. I realized that there's not much to do around here, but it was certainly too early for me to be addressing cards. With that threatening feeling hanging over the island, I wasn't going to just sit here. I said, "Pierre, lets hop in the car. we'll go to the post office, and then I'll take you to the graveyard at All Saints Church over on King's River Road." I added, "I feel like going to a graveyard this afternoon."

Pierre seemed unusually pleased that I suggested this. He jumped up, put the envelopes into a paper sack, stuffed them under the cushion of the wicker chair and said, "Let's go. I feel like graveyards too."

At the post office, Julia Smalls, the African-American clerk, looked in the general delivery box and said that I had nothing, then handed me a circular about the revival at the A.M.E., which would start next Sunday. She looked out at my car toward Pierre and said, "Oh, I see that you have more company. Bring him to church on Sunday. We'd like to have you-all." I thanked her for the invitation and said we'd think about it. We drove down the highway and turned right onto Shell Road, went on the mile or so to All Saints Episcopal Church, and parked by the rarely-used Greek Revival Church that sits in the corner of the cemetery. We proceeded through the squeaking gates as a stiff October breeze rhythmically swayed the Spanish moss hanging from the live oaks and pines. The sun hid behind a cloud and cast a Victorian gloom over the grey tombstones and little iron fences that separated some of the plots like the Wards and the Belins and the Lachicottes. We walked slowly through the graveyard, and I pointed out the graves of Percival and Paul Pawleys which dated from the early 1800s but had tombstones that appeared to be of a much later date, with Victorian embellishments. I showed Pierre the large flat tombstone that had only one inscription, "Alice," and as usual someone had thrown some red and white plastic roses on it, now faded and mixed with a cheap beaded necklace, several pennies, and two nickels.

Pierre paused at the small headstone of someone called Joseph G. Taylor, a boy of fifteen who had been drowned in the 1893 hurricane. He stood nearby, looking at the family tombstone of the Flaggs, all "washed away by the Tidal Wave of 1893," from Magnolia Beach—all nine drowned on October 13, 1893.

As yet, Pierre had not spoken a word while in the cemetery, he walked on slowly and stopped to look at the little angel headstone on Mary Elizabeth Collins' grave. I told him that it had been sculpted by Will Edmonds, a primitive black artist living in Nashville in the 1930s. I added that nobody seemed to know how this ended up here in All Saints cemetery.

While I stopped to listen to a flock of red winged blackbirds singing a dissonant chorus from a bare sweet gum tree, Pierre walked on then stopped again at one last tombstone. He whispered through the inscription, then read aloud:

BEHOLD AND SEE, NOW HERE I LIE,
AS YOU ARE NOW, SO ONCE WAS I,
AS I AM NOW, SO MUST YOU BE,
THEREFORE PREPARE TO FOLLOW ME.

The late afternoon wind had freshened, but every minute seemed more threatening—threatening for reasons that could only be felt and not explained. We drove back toward the island. Everything was quiet, but Pierre was fidgety and I could sense some unrest gnawing at my guest. Finally, as we waited at the traffic light on Route 17, I asked what was bothering him. Pierre said calmly, "I just want to get back to the island. I want to finish addressing my Christmas cards and putting on these stamps I've brought." He hesitated, then asked, "After all, do you realize what day this is? It's the 13th. This is Friday the 13th. This is the 13th of October."

After a while the traffic light turned green and we drove on to the island.

GARBAGE CAN TOPS
AND WINDMILLS

*I*t was seething hot and humid on that early June morning. The birds were thirsty. There had been a constant parade of birds going to the feeder and then to the water baths out on the cypress walkway toward the beach—red wing black birds, boat tailed grackles and cardinals. The rufous-sided towhees and the little sand doves didn't seem to drink, but occasionally a brown thrush prodded its bill into this warm water. The grackle's usual routine was to drink out of the first container, then waddle to the second for a bath and a flutter. Had these baths been made out of anything except old tin garbage can tops, I suspected, the birds would not have been nearly as pleased.

Above these waterbaths the windmills struggle with the changeable hot breeze. Both little windmills seem confused as to which way to turn next. The old windmill had been through this for many years and it doesn't have much of a problem, but the younger one, which I found at an old store on a country road in Kentucky, was halting and appeared weary. Its propeller blades fell off. Now they're tied on with strings and duct tape.

I try to find things to keep guests busy, and these windmills help serve this purpose—they're always in need of repair. Nigel was a recent visitor, and he sat on the porch drinking tea and observing these struggling windmills. He was a R.A.F. (Royal Air Force) bomber pilot during World War II and had some knowledge of propellers. He approached the one I had brought down from Kentucky and said, "It's front heavy, and I can set it right." He proceeded to dangle three golf balls, which he rigged and attached to its tail, and to our amazement the windmill perked up and was able to keep up with the older one. Nigel sat back on the porch and looked unusually satisfied. I painted the golf balls bright crimson, and now we call it the tritesticated windmill, the only one of its kind on the island.

TEA AND SYMPATHY

*T*he English seem to have had an affinity for the Low Country and the Waccamaw Neck—ever since old John Allston visited up here after he moved from Brookgreen, England to Charles Town in the 1600s. There are a few others that might be added to that list of English people who came here, some stayed and some visited, like Lord Cornwallis who was an unwelcome visitor to Brookgreen Plantation in the 1700s. These English people do add spice to our scene.

It wasn't always spice, however, as I recovered from an episode of yesterday. A London doctor friend, although he was jet lagged, wanted to go crabbing. I decided that it was a proper introduction to the island. I looked at the creek and the chart and time was right, so we gathered the crab lines. I took the chicken neck bait from the freezer, thawed it, and we went to the crabbing dock.

It was a fine afternoon for crabbing, everything looked perfect and I told him that we'd catch a dish pan full. I taught him how to bait the lines and explained this uncomplicated way of catching crabs. But the crabbing excitement was slow, after a while my guest perched himself on the top rail of the crabbing dock for some afternoon sun and some sleepy cogitation, while I did the crabbing. Ten minutes had elapsed, and I had caught only two crabs, then I heard a resounding splash. I looked and saw my guest emerging from the creek with blood dripping from the side of his head. As my borrowed Stetson hat floated away, the creek looked like one of the plagues of Egypt.

He gripped the floor of the dock, and I helped pull him back up between the broken railings, carefully avoiding the rusty hinge that had caught the side of his forehead as he fell. He took a handkerchief from his pocket and tried to stop the flow of blood from the imposing laceration. He was calm and said, "Just give me a cup of tea and I'll be jolly well again."

I pulled in the crab lines, released the two crabs, and we crossed back to the Duck's Nest. He held rightly to the handkerchief, putting pressure on the side of his head, and sat on the porch as I made tea. With one hand he held the cup of tea, and with the other he attended his wound. I tried to be sympathetic and encouraging, but it soon became evident that Earl Gray and comforting words did not slow the bleeding. He took another handkerchief and pressed tighter.

Soon we were on our way to the emergency room at Georgetown Memorial Hospital—I called from my mobile telephone, hoping to avoid the crowded Sunday afternoon confusion. I said, "This is Doctor Minton of Vanderbilt Medical School, and I am bringing a visiting English doctor who is bleeding—he's bleeding from the head." The emergency room clerk answered, "Well, that's alright," and she hung up.

We walked into the crowded emergency room—it smelled of sick babies and stale unventilated air. It was hot. There were sounds of crying infants and of people coughing. A telephone rang. A young man dressed in a green scrub suit walked through this commotion with a Coke and a casual expression, a stethoscope dangling around his neck. He avoided a black baby crawling on the floor.

The visiting guest filled in forms with one hand and held tightly to the handkerchief with the other. The clerk seemed oblivious to our presence and hardly looked up. The telephone rang again and before answering it she said, "It's a hot afternoon, isn't it. You-all just have a seat out there, and the doctor will be with you when he gets caught up. It'll be a while."

I was shattered—my telephone call was unheeded, the words *Vanderbilt, doctor* and *London* had made no impression. Before we searched for a seat, she handed him several more forms—waivers, agreements, compliances, organ donor forms, and two insurance forms. Then we sat and waited and waited in this smoldering afternoon heat.

Thirty minutes later another handkerchief was soaked with blood, and I approached the clerk. She handed me a wad of gauze and said, "Dr. Abernathy will be with you when he catches up. You-all just be patient, Honey." I looked closely at her name badge and said, "Hazel," trying to get familiar, "I can sew him up if you'll get me a suture tray. As I told you, I'm a doctor." She replied, "Honey, you're not on the Memorial staff, and you can't sew nobody up here. That's the rule. The rule." I took the wad of fresh gauze back to my friend.

Eventually Dr. Abernathy called us back into a small examining room and hastily but efficiently sutured the wound. I walked out of that emergency room with my friend. His head was wrapped in gauze; he looked like an Egyptian mummy.

We drove northward on Route 17. As we crossed the Pee Dee and Waccamaw Rivers there was the pink glow of sunset. The air was cool and fresh—except for the odor of Georgetown's paper mill.

The tea and sympathy, plus the several stitches, must have been effective. The next morning I woke early and went to the upper porch to drink my coffee. I hadn't seen my guest since the night before. I looked out in the ocean, toward the gulf stream, and saw the head of a swimmer. I got my binoculars and returned to the porch, focusing in on the bandaged head of a London doctor.

He had survived the night. I called Hazel in the Georgetown emergency room, and told her that they wouldn't need the form about who to notify in case of death.

THE GEORGETOWN LIGHTHOUSE

If I were around the corner at the southern end of Pawleys Island I might see the illumination from the Georgetown lighthouse. This lighthouse, which has been a beacon for over two hundred years, is only twelve miles from Pawleys Island, about the same distance from Georgetown eastward on North Island. Dick Crayton and I had been out there occasionally to gather driftwood. He had tried to give me a lecture on this structure, but I had paid little attention.

Late last summer, while visiting in Providence, Rhode Island, I met a Professor Horatio Schneider of Brown University, who was writing a scholarly book on lighthouses of the Eastern Coast and was in the process of visiting these beacons. I gave him my card and thought nothing more of this casual meeting.

Some time later, the telephone rang, and it was Professor Schneider saying that he wanted to come here to visit the lighthouse before going on to Cape Romaine. A date was fixed and I went to meet him.

I could hardly remember the professor but recognized him at the air terminal. Professor Schneider, in some manner, looked like a person who might be an authority on lighthouses. He was a tall thin man with bushy white hair and thick glasses.

I had made arrangements for a friend, Dr. George Alston, to take us out in his boat to North Island. We set off from Georgetown on the high tide next morning. The Professor sat near the stern of the boat with Dr. Alston as we made our way out into Winyah Bay. Over the roar of the engine, the retired doctor was acting as a tour guide, pointing out Frazier's Point where Capt. Daggett observed the sinking, by his home-made torpedo, of the Union flagship *Harvest Moon*. Then we went by the rusty stack, still visible after a hundred and twenty-five years. Dr. Alston idled the motor so that we might take a closer look. Professor Schneider, knowing about lighthouses but not much about the War Between the States, looked in amazement. Word of the *Harvest Moon* had apparently never reached Rhode Island, and the professor never heard of this flagship. He had never heard of Capt. Daggett and the boys of Georgetown who fashioned this torpedo.

Dr. Alston revved up the engine, and we made our way eastward toward North Island. Winyah Bay was lovely on this morning. A throng of shorebirds greeted us. Royal terns darted up and down, black skimmers flew near the water's surface, a great blue heron swooped low over the boat.

North Island and the lighthouse became visible in the near distance. Dr. Alston eased the boat into the old dock, and we tied up, as the professor started taking notes. Then, like my Dalmatians after a bone, he rushed out of the boat toward the structure and surveyed it from every angle, taking photograph after photograph. He evidently knew a great deal about our lighthouse and was anxious to tell us all the facts, whether we had heard them before or not:

"The first lighthouse in South Carolina was constructed here between 1799 and 1801," he began. It was as high as a seven-story building and built out of wood, but it collapsed in a storm in 1806. The second lighthouse was build on this site in 1812, just in time for the war against the British in that same year. This second lighthouse was fifteen feet taller than the first, equivalent to an eight-story building. With repairs, this is the same structure that stands here today."

The professor explained about the Fresnel lens which was installed here in 1857. Fresnel, a French physicist, had been commissioned in 1822 to develop a better lighting system for French lighthouses. Fresnel thought that it made more sense to develop an efficient method of amplifying the light, rather than creating a brighter source. Using prisms, Fresnel was able to focus the light lost above and below the source back into a single beam. He had lens pieces precisely cut and the highly polished glass assembled like a puzzle into the shape of a lens that was held together with brass fittings. When the ten inch diameter lens was installed here in 1857, its light could be seen up to twelve miles away.

All was well until 1867 when Union forces shelled the lighthouse, causing extensive damage. It was repaired and this light, amplified through this Fresnel lens, shone for seventy more years. Unlike the ancient lighthouse at Alexandria, this one never fell into the hands of a junk dealer; it was converted to electricity, and the Fresnel lens went to the Coast Guard Museum. The beacon was placed on a timer but remained the last one to be manned in South Carolina. It continues to welcome ships into the Winyah Bay.

Dr. Alston and I sat there soaking up all this information, but the tide was falling and it was time to go back to Georgetown. We boarded the boat as the professor took more photographs, then we headed back westward through the bay.

THE *HARVEST MOON*

$\mathcal{I}$t was late April and time to make a trip out to Pumpkin Seed Island to see the nesting shorebirds. Dick Crayton said he would take

me there. When I called to remind him, it didn't take much to persua-
sion, since he was enthusiastic about nature, or about almost anything
that would get him out of his joggling board construction shop.

We decided to set off at high tide. When Dick cranked up the outboard on his old Jon boat and we eased out of Georgetown, I didn't
realize that I would see anything more interesting than shorebirds and
their chicks. Dick brought along his dog, Homelite, who curled up in
the bow of the boat and appeared either bored or asleep. As we made
our way across Winyah Bay, Dick cautiously avoided a rusty hunk of
metal, barely visible beneath the bay's surface. I was curious about it.
Dick told me it was the smokestack from a submerged Union boat and
that on the way back, when the tide was lower, he would tell me how it
got there.

When we got to within a few hundred yards of Pumpkin Seed
Island, its five-acre surface appeared like a mirage of snow. As we got
closer it became apparent that this expanse of white was made up of
many thousands of shore birds nesting their young. Side by side, within
inches of each other, were glossy ibis, snowy egrets, great blue herons,
great egrets, and Louisiana herons. There were little blue herons beside
yellow-crowned night herons in nests made of sticks, either on the
ground or in the branches of short scrub bushes. All seemed to be nesting happily together with their young, paying no attention to their
neighbors. Our intrusion did not seem to bother them as the parent
birds brought the catch of the day—small fish, frogs, eels and minnows—in regurgitated form to feed their down-covered chicks, babies
who all looked alike. Dick didn't want this nursery disturbed, so we only
lingered a short while before wading back to join Homelite aboard the
Jon boat.

We made our way westward around noon. The tide was ebbing and
several yards ahead we could see that two cormorants were sunning
themselves on the now easily-visible smokestack. Homelite awoke, sat
up, and yawned. Dick dropped anchor and told the dog and me to make
ourselves comfortable while he told the story of this rusty hunk of metal.

After hearing this "tall tale," I went to the library in Georgetown to do some research and found out that it was all true.

It was Wednesday, March 1, 1865, when the Union Navy flagship, *Harvest Moon*, met its watery doom in Georgetown harbor, just a month before General Robert E. Lee surrendered the Army of Northern Virginia. Adm. John A. Dahlgren, one of the Union Navy's ranking officers, commanded the *Harvest Moon*, and had been sent to accept the surrender of Georgetown. The day before, he had walked down Front Street in Georgetown to oversee this transaction and had placed a New York Colored Regiment in charge, a move which did not greatly please the local residents. A few days earlier, a local Confederate officer, Capt. Thomas West Daggett had arrived back in town. He recruited some of his local buddies to assist in the plan. They spent two days in his back yard on Queen Street preparing a "surprise" for the admiral and his ship. Their surprise was something the admiral would not forget: a torpedo containing a hundred pounds of black dynamite.

Admiral Dahlgren's *Harvest Moon* was no ordinary vessel. This was a federal flagship which had cost the Union $100,000 only two years earlier. This ship, with two large sidewheels, had been built and launched in Portsmouth, Maine, and carried over a hundred sailors, some of whom manned the four 24-pound howitzers on board. The *Harvest Moon* had served as a key ship for the Union in the South Atlantic. It blocked squadrons from interrupting shipping vessels sailing in and out of Southern ports.

After an outstanding career in Washington, old Admiral Dahlgren had participated in the bombardment of Fort Wagner and then was involved in the two-year siege of Charleston. Captain Daggett was not after a novice. He and the boys from Georgetown knew this.

During the night, the captain and his pals brought their torpedo from Queen Street to the river behind the Clock Tower. They placed it carefully in a small boat and waited for the tide to recede. Then they quietly rowed out near Frazier Point and deposited the bomb just beneath the water's surface at a place in the channel they were reasonably sure the *Harvest Moon* would sail over the next morning.

A little after 7:00 A.M., a great explosion was heard across Winyah Bay. As Captain Daggett and his friends watched from a tamarisk thicket on the shore, the *Harvest Moon* sank rapidly in twelve feet of water.

That evening, Admiral Dahlgren wrote in his diary, "It was a dull looking morning. A little after seven, the *Harvest Moon* was under way to go down the harbor and then to Charleston. I was pacing about the cabin waiting for breakfast, occasionally taking a squint with the glass at objects along the shore. Suddenly without warning, came a crashing sound, a heavy shock. The partition between the cabin and the wardroom was shattered and driven in toward me." The Admiral wrote that the water was coming in rapidly through a great gap in the bottom of the boat. The main deck was "blown through," and everybody scrambled aboard the Union ferry, the *Nipsic*, which was following them. He added, "And in this way I took leave of the *Harvest Moon*."

Only one person was killed, wardroom steward, John Hazard. Union soldiers soon took most items of value, such as furniture and rigging, from the sunken boat. Two months later, a court of inquiry determined that the ship's loss was not the fault of Admiral Dahlgren, as he had been informed that the channel had been swept clear of explosives. Captain Daggett and the boys of Georgetown had planted their "surprise" after the sweeping.

Homelite had long since lost interest and returned to his place in the bow. Dick pulled up the anchor and, with the outboard sputtering, we headed back toward the clock tower, the place where, one hundred and twenty-five years ago, Captain Daggett and the boys of Georgetown had gone with their torpedo. It had been a memorable morning, and I had seen something more than a white mirage on Pumpkin Seed Island. No doubt old Admiral Dahlgren would have greatly preferred a mirage to what he saw that morning as he awaited breakfast aboard the *Harvest Moon*.[3]

---

3. Dick Crayton died at the age of eighty-seven just before this manuscript was completed. The last words he said were, "Heaven is a beautiful place."

THAT AWFUL GRASS IN THE CREEK

$\mathscr{I}$t was early June, and the morning sun, even between seven and nine, did its best to bake me. I adjourned across the road to the crabbing dock with a visiting friend. We took cups of coffee to assist waking us, as last night we stayed up until after midnight so that I might show a guest the moons around Jupiter.

It was just above low tide on the creek and everything was relatively calm except for a bald eagle who had ventured out from across the marsh—a sight that I see most days lately since it has taken up residence there. The eagle flew down low over the creek and attempted to pluck a fish from a shallow pool, but it missed the catch and flew on southward toward the Bird's Nest end of the island. It has a favorite spot in a dead tree just across from the Johnstone's house on the west side of the marsh where the creek narrows. A snowy egret waded nearby, then stopped and stood petrified holding one foot up. Finally it took off in its graceful flight to another hunting ground. A laughing gull swooped down as if aggravated that it didn't have a chance at a mullet that jumped. As things quieted, my guest fixated her stare onto the saltmarsh cordgrass, the *Spartina alterniflora*. Finally she asked, "Why doesn't the town keep all that awful grass in the creek cut down?"

Where does one start to give a civilized answer to such a question? How does one explain that this is not "awful" grass? How does one answer that this *Spartina* is the basis of the creek? I sat for a minute, then tried to explain about these endless islands of *Spartina*.

I told her that we don't need a cutter. I explained that this grass has just turned green although it is already June. By autumn it will turn a chocolate brown as the temperature lowers and then the wind will cut it down. All across the creek there will be a mat of "wrack" as it is called. Some dead stalks will make it through the winter, but these gradually become a part of this "wrack," a creek product that is virtually unmatched on this planet for its nutrients. It becomes the nursery of the marsh, the spawning ground for grouper, flounder, and even some of the ocean fish such as trout.

She sat fixated, ignoring her coffee, as I told her about the particles which break off and find their way down the creek and into the ocean, helping to sustain fish life and even shell life along the coastal waters.

My visitor became more interested now. An adventurous type, she asked if she might take her sandals off and wade out to pluck a small sample. She buried up to her ankles in the gray mud but was successful in her attempt to take a stalk and its roots. She pitched the sample back on the dock and I helped her up. Like some detective, she sat pulling the roots apart, looking closely and smelling, paying no attention to the mire covering her feet. The guest had discovered *Spartina*!

I told her that there is evidence that this plant has adapted from dry land and now not only lives in this brackish water but also thrives in it. It is able, by osmosis, to filter out the salt—a process only one or two other plants can accomplish. At low tide a myriad of creatures burrow in its roots, either feeding or escaping predators. Here these creatures may find safety for a few minutes until, like clockwork, the current refills the creek.

I told my guest that I had recently attended a seminar at the Marine Laboratory at Hobcaw Barony and learned how vital the dissolved element of iron is to *Spartina*. Iron is filtered down from the upland creeks after it is dissolved from dying vegetation, trees, and even remains of birds and animals. There is evidence now that in some areas the *Spartina* is dying because of the lack of this vital element.

As our world becomes paved with strip malls, superstores, auto dealerships, and roads, I wonder how long it will take for this depletion of iron to have its effect here. Will our descendants eventually look out over a marsh without grass? They may not see the snowy egret, the laughing gulls, or the bald eagle. Will they drink their coffee in desolation?

By now it was just after eight o'clock and the breakfast bell at the Sea View Inn was ringing. We had been invited there for breakfast. My guest and I walked down the boardwalk toward the inn. Her feet were still muddy, but she clutched her *Spartina alterniflora*.

PART TWO

Life in England

AGONY IN THE GARDEN

*I*t was the fault of the director of Christies Fine Arts of London, who agreed to accept me into their school. I was the oldest student in the history of the institution, and with their quota system, I was one of the few Americans there for that academic year. The school took me as I was, a retired physician with little background in the visual arts.

Pietro Rafello, a brilliant Italian professor, but also a drunkard, was the teacher assigned to my tutorial group. During sober, and not-so-sober, moments in the afternoon, he reigned over us six students, his victims. How he was assigned is another story.

The students in this tutorial group, except for me, had outstanding backgrounds in the visual arts. There was Tessa Quigley from Trinity University in Dublin, Victoria Marie La Bruce from the University of Vancouver in Canada, William Morris from Bristol University, Brigita Hartmut from the University of Hanover, Emanuele Grozzi from Milano, and then there was me, from the University of Tennessee Medical School. With the exception of Emanuele, who had just finished secondary school in Italy, my fellow students held degrees and advanced degrees in fine arts and art history.

William Morris knew that he would fit into some glass niche in the art world, for his knowledge of this subject was superior to any glass historian in Murano, Italy. He had already become a consultant for Christies, but he appeared as fragile and delicate as any ancient piece of *latticemo*, which made it difficult for us to get near him at morning coffee or at afternoon seminars for fear that he might shatter. It was not easy to ignore his stuttering, not Etonian but of northwest England, so we tried to change the subject to glass when conversing with him.

William didn't stutter when he talked about glass. William and Tessa became inseparable; they bonded like two pieces of applied glass. This was strange because she was large and authoritative, bossy, and could have swallowed him. Tessa spent her spare time at the Victoria and Albert Museum studying a collection down in the bowels of the museum. She was writing a thesis on medieval English bronzes for Trinity. On rare occasions after a seminar, we could entice her to the pub for a lager, but she wouldn't linger. We thought this unusual since she was Irish. On one occasion, when she had left for the museum, Brigita, who could hold her own with any beer drinker, belched and then declared that Tessa was a direct descendant of Queen Boadicea. I disagreed because I was sure that I had seen her in Green Bay, Wisconsin, a few years ago when she was a linebacker for the Packers. A descendant of Boadicea in Wisconsin? Not likely. Tessa was bright and opinionated, and it was inevitable that she and Professor Rafello would clash. We suspected that she could handle his end runs, so we awaited a collision of the Irishwoman and the Italian.

Brigita Hartmut, the beer-drinking German from Bad Pyrmont, held a degree from Hanover University in Art Economics. Her Germanic sense of humor was presented with a heavy accent, and this frequently got her into trouble with Professor Rafello when we made our recitals in class. We felt that she accentuated it so that nobody would know exactly what she was saying. The professor would tell her to speak English and would say it in German: *"Sprechen zie Englisch."* Although she had a degree in art economics, some of her knowledge was elsewhere. She knew South German wood carvings intimately and apparently owned a significant collection, but her real love was the Deutsch Mark and how money related to her collection. At morning coffee, Brigita devoured the *Financial Times,* and we suspected that she knew the precise value of each worm in those carvings.

Victoria Marie La Bruce, the Canadian, was the delicate one, who had gone through Vancouver University with perfect grades while obtaining a masters degree in mannerist art history. She had her own tactics. In order to command sympathy, she exhibited fragility. She could weep on cue, the cue being Professor Rafello's tone of voice. We paid little attention to the crying and sniffing when the professor disagreed with her opinions. We could predict on which sniff she would disappear into the bathroom for a bulimic episode. However, these episodes did not appear to affect her weight, which stood at about six and a half stone, about ninety pounds.

The youngest, at age eighteen, and the brightest was Emanuaele Grozzi, the son of an antiquarian from Milano. Emanuaele, as handsome as Valentino, was just out of secondary school and had grown up surrounded by Renaissance antiques—significant objects with important provenances. They were acquired from old Italian families, according to Professor Rafello, who had gone to Milano to recruit him. Emanuaele's first love was football—European football—and at this young age he had turned down an offer to play in a professional league. It became evident that Emanuaele was to become a favorite of the professor. Sometimes their banter would switch from English to Italian, but serious conversation was always in English, with an occasional Italian word thrown in for emphasis.

Almost at once, we became close friends and, although I was old enough to be his father, we developed a unique *camaraderie*. We studied and partied together, as he was in London for a year of pleasure. He told me that he would be going back to Italy to law school. It did not take me long to tell him that he belonged to the world of art, not law, but several times he reminded me that for this year the young ladies of London belonged to him. *"La raggazze de Londra sono mio."*

Then there was me, the oldest student in this class of sixty-seven. I was the same age as Professor Rafello, and I knew from the beginning that we would have our battles, perhaps over an object that he might ask me to describe as if I was a cataloguer. But I also knew that I would approach these battles as I had in medical school, with common sense. I suspected that I could successfully compete with Bristol, Trinity, Vancouver, and Hanover. I also thought that I could hang in there with

Professor Rafello, and I became more confident as time went on. A pathology professor in medical school had taught me to be assertive and to have an answer even when I was not sure of myself. Following this advice had been effective in twenty-five years of medical practice.

Each morning there were classes in a building on Old Brompton Road, behind Christies South Kensington branch. In the afternoons, once a week, we boarded a bus for a trip to the country to visit a stately home—Blenheim, Broughton Castle, Hardwick Hall, Waddeston Manor—where we might be assigned a room. We were given ten minutes in which to survey its contents before giving the class a tour, talking about furniture, silver, paintings, and other works of art. Twice weekly, in the afternoons, we belonged to Professor Pietro Rafello. The six students in my study group were like dangling pieces of meat waiting to be devoured by this lion in seminars and recitals at some museum or collection in London. Security guards at the National Gallery, Soames Museum in Lincolns Inn Field, and at the Wallace Collection eventually knew us by name. On a rare occasion the professor took us to "Big" Christies on King Street for a preview or an auction. We felt that school officials did not want us to know too much about the value of auction pieces, for reasons unknown. Money, it seemed, was only of interest when it came to our tuition. It was a slight compensation that we students received a 10 percent discount on items bought at their auctions. At that time the dollar and pound were almost equal in value so my collection grew and grew.

In September, two weeks after our arrival at the school, Professor Rafello met this tutorial group at the South Kensington tube station, and we took a Piccadilly Line train to Leicester Square station, from whence we walked the short distance to the National Gallery in Trafalgar Square. It became evident on this walk that the professor had probably drunk a bottle of Chianti during the lunch hour. He bobbled along with us up the steps into the Gallery and then into Room 123, which housed some of the early Renaissance collection. We stood in silence as he lectured on three paintings by Andrea Montegna; his Italian accent becoming more pronounced as he approached each successive painting. He paused, looked at us, and said that he would expect us, by the following week, to have in-depth knowledge of every painting in the room. I couldn't even pronounce the names of some of the artists: Pollaiuolo, Pontormo, Piero della Francesca. There was some shuffling about as we had a good look round. This was interrupted as we were called into the adjoining gallery where the professor gave us our assignments for the following week. He told us that he would assign a painting from this area to each of us, and that the following week we would be expected to stand in front of it and lecture for ten minutes. We were told to ignore the tourists, as they would assume we were authorities. He added that he expected our recitals to be precise and worthy of his tutorial group. Then he gave the assignments.

Brigita was given a Palma Vecchio, Victoria the del Piombo, William a Carpaccio, and so on. I was the last to be sentenced. He hesitated, looked keenly around the room, and finally indicated a Giovanni Bellini that would be mine. "Minton, since you're the old man of this group, you will recite about the Bellini. You will recite about his *Agony in the Garden*. Next week you will be expected to tell us why this is the most important painting in this room. The name is appropriate as I may add to the agony for you." Professor Rafello excused himself and left. I took a closer look at the Bellini painting and then asked Emanuaele to go with me to The White Pig pub behind the Coliseum. I needed a tall lager to finish off this afternoon. On the way to the pub, I commented to Emanuaele that I could have been lying on the beach at Pawleys Island instead of jump starting my brain for a go at *Agony in the Garden*.

The week passed too quickly as I tried to complete all the other Christie assignments, our first written examination and an oriental auction at Phillips, but I crammed in three more visits to the National Gallery—to Bellini and my "Agony."

I studied the painting from many directions. From what angle would I attack it? Was there an angle the professor had not thought of? Why was it the most important painting in the room? I stood in front of the Bellini and talked to myself about it. I thought of mundane things pertaining to Bellini. Giovanni Bellini had been the teacher for Giorgione and Titian; Montegna had married his sister; he was the foremost Venetian madonna painter. No, these tantalizing tidbits were too mundane for Professor Rafello, and he would stop me in mid-sentence if I regurgitated such facts. After a second visit my agonizing subsided. I decided to concentrate on the background landscape, which I had concluded was the feature which made it the most important painting in the room. Glancing around, I noted that this was the only work exhibiting landscape painting, which was just evolving during Bellini's time. I planned to throw in a southern metaphor or two, which the professor would not understand and neither would my fellow students from Dublin and Bad Pyrmont.

The dreaded day came, and I stood on the platform of the Piccadilly Line waiting for a train for what seemed like hours. I arrived at the National Gallery only a minute late to find my tutorial group sulking in a corner of Room 124 like St. Sebastians awaiting the arrows of the professor. He appeared twenty minutes late, saying that there had been an accident on the Underground, but we felt certain that he had been fortifying himself at the pub.

Tourists milled about. Some were really interested in the paintings in the room, but for others this seemed to be something forced upon them by a tour leader or a teacher from Dulwich. The Professor took a piece of paper from his briefcase and marched around the room for a final review. Each of us hid behind a tourist or a fellow student. Victoria Marie disappeared into the bathroom. All was quiet when Brigita was called on to recite about the Francesco Parmigianino *St. Jerome*. She talked in a more pronounced accent than usual, which under these circumstances was to be expected. Rambling on for five minutes, she said that the artist was from Parma. We knew this because of his name, so no stars in her crown for this comment. As the professor started to load an arrow, Brigita said that he had painted *The Madonna with the Long Neck*, and that he was captured in the sack of Rome. The professor shot his arrow when she said that he was a Mannerist painter. He stopped her and asked her to explain this word, adding that she had said nothing about *St. Jerome*, her assigned painting. As she fumbled for words, the professor walked about the room, seemingly paying no more attention to what she said. He stood in front of del Piombo's *Raising of Lazarus*, loading another arrow. It was shot when Brigita mentioned that a painting from the circle of Parmigianino had sold in Munich the year before for the equivalent of two million pounds. A third arrow flew when she added that this sum did not include the commission nor the German sales tax. Professor Rafello finally said, "Brigita, we have had enough. Victoria, would you discuss *The Raising of Lazarus?* Brigita disgustedly crammed her notes into a Christies plastic bag and marched out of the room.

Like another St. Sebastian, Victoria received her share of arrows. The professor apparently had no sympathy for her bulimia. He allowed her to finish only about six minutes of her planned recitation.

I was called next, and I realized that the time had come to make an auspicious debut on the London art scene. Generally, I lost some of my southern accent when I came to London, but on this afternoon it resurfaced. I knew that I was on dangerous ground, but I commenced my recital by saying that the name Bellini, for some Americans, recalled a Hall of Fame quarterback from the Navy team at Annapolis, and that Giovanni could have been an ancestor because this American naval officer had become a recognized painter in retirement. No arrows flew, so I continued. I reminded my fellow students and the tourists that I was from the Bible Belt of the South and couldn't remember the first time that I had heard about the Garden of Gethsemane in Sunday School. I said I could recall that verse from St. Matthew about the flesh being weaker than the spirit. Only, being in a jittery state from the expectation of arrows, I said that the spirit was weaker than the flesh. Nobody noticed.

Realizing that I had to eventually get around to *Agony*, I threw in a metaphor, saying the Bellini had a wide row of cotton to hoe when he arrived in Venice in the mid 1400s, particularly when he decided to paint a biblical scene with a realistic landscape in the background. I challenged them to find another realistic landscape in that room. They were unknown in the early Renaissance due to a church edict, but Bellini dared to include one. I suggested that the diagonals made by the somnolent figures of Peter, James, and John were in contrast to the triangles of the mountainous landscape. Professor Rafello allowed me to talk on and on, but I could sense some unease when I glanced at him after mentioning the New World and how it had been discovered a few years before Bellini painted *Agony in the Garden*. I suggested that Bellini had probably heard conversations about this newly discovered land, as this was a prime topic of the day. Pointing to the worn down mountainous landscape, I said that these looked more like the Piedmont Mountains in western South Carolina than the peaked Alps of northern Italy. A lady tourist raised her hand as if to ask a question, so I stopped. She said, "Mercy, they look just like the mountains between Spartanburg and Asheville on Route 26." She had broken my train of thought. I hesitated and almost started comparing Bellini's mountains with those in Leonardo's background to his *Mona Lisa*, painted some years later. The professor was looking at his watch. Would I, too, become a St. Sebastian? I had talked for ten minutes and had said little of significance, but I had arrived at the National Gallery with a little Bible in my pocket. Like a southern preacher, I took it out and again reminded this audience of my Bible Belt background. I closed by saying that there wasn't time to read about the disciples in the Garden of Gethsemane, but that they could read about them for themselves in the gospels of St. Mark and St. Matthew, as most southern boys with a Sunday School background would do.

I left the National Gallery without an arrow and went to The Pig. Later Emanuaele joined me. He said that Professor Rafello was on his way.

DAME EVA TURNER

$\mathcal{I}$ first met Dame Eva Turner, the renowned English diva and that country's first international opera star, when she was eighty-eight years old, ten years before she died. I was a dinner guest of Col. James Laurie, her neighbor upstairs on Palace Place. She had just finished giving a private lesson, and it was late in the evening, a time when someone half her age would be thinking of sleep or else watching the *News at Ten* on the BBC, when Colonel Laurie invited her up for dessert. Always amenable to an invitation, she accepted. She wanted to meet me because we had a mutual friend, Francis Robinson, the public relations manager of the Metropolitan Opera and a fellow Tennessean.

She didn't bother with the elevator but walked up the two flights of steps. Colonel Laurie met her at the door. This rather large lady appeared as fresh as spring, dressed in a long dark blue crepe dress. She sat down beside me and apologized for her hair, which actually looked rather pleasing, wrapped in a pink silk turban—striking, as befitted a diva.

She asked our host for coffee rather than dessert and in a broad Lancashire accent, rolled every available *r*. She commented that it had been a long day and that she had just finished a coaching session for Gwyneth Jones studying *The Daughter of the Regiment*, her up-coming role at the Royal Opera House, although she really wanted to talk about America. She wanted to talk about Coach Bud Wilkinson and Oklahoma football. Over the years, she had become an Americophile, particularly during her five years as Artist-in-Residence at the University of Oklahoma. She had the football jargon down pat, the "end sweeps" and the "quarterback sneaks," and talked with authority on the subject. My host sat and listened, occasionally asking a question about Oklahoma, questions seemingly based on knowledge of that state acquired from the Broadway musical. We talked until after midnight, mostly about football and Oklahoma.

This conversation started a long friendship; musical conversations came later. In two years I was back in London to live, and I invited Dame Eva to my home at the Crown Equerry House to meet some of my fellow classmates at the Christie Fine Arts School. I remember that afternoon well because Dame Eva refused to drink the tea I had poured for her. She went straight to the point. I had made the mistake of pouring the tea into the cup *before* the milk. I had to start over. With properly poured tea, she freely discussed her life as an opera singer with these students, and told them that as a young person in Lancashire, she had almost become a painter, a visual artist.

Our friendship grew, and, during many evenings out together in London, we talked about music and her seventy years as a singer. I still have a mental image, and a photograph, of Dame Eva and the great Russian pianist, Shura Cherkassky, then eighty-two, sitting side by side. They were in the front row for an evening's entertainment I had arranged and named, "*Eine Kleine Nachtmusik,*" and they were listening to a nine-year-old violinist that I had included in the program. It must have been the sight of this pair of musical giants that made the young violinist forget her music. She stopped and all was silent for a minute or so, but she collected herself and completed the Bach piece. After the program had finished, Dame Eva gave the weeping child a warm hug.

Dame Eva was most radiant when talking of La Scala and of her friendship with Toscanini and Puccini. She talked of the conductor and composer as if they were the boys next door. She told the story of singing the leading role in *The Girl of the Golden West* at La Scala, with Toscanini conducting, when she stumbled and fell over a wagon wheel and landed face down. The audience, thinking that it was intended, gave her *bravos* for her acting ability. She talked about the heavy costume she wore at the same theatre when singing the role of the Princess in *Turandot* and how the crown weighed nearly a stone.

She presented me with an autographed photograph of herself in this costume and wrote on it: "To Dr. Lee Minton from Eva Turner, in memory of our mutual friend, Francis Robinson." This photograph hangs on the wall of my bedroom between photographs of Robinson and of another Tennessean, Secretary of State Cordell Hull.

Another story she told was of being placed in the back row of the chorus at the Royal Albert Hall even though she was singing the title role in a concert version of *Aida*. She was placed there because her voice overpowered the entire chorus. "But it was just natural and easy for me to sing loudly," she added, enunciating every syllable and rolling every *r*.

Once, Dame Joan Sutherland presented the aging diva with two tickets for *Norma* at the Royal Opera House, and Dame Eva asked me to escort her. After the performance, we immediately went backstage but not by the usual way of the stage door. She took me though an obscure doorway and across the stage from whence we made our way to Dame Joan's dressing room. Dame Eva did not bother to knock. She simply opened the door and invited me into the great soprano's inner sanctum. There stood Dame Joan, in her underwear. Neither of the Dames seemed the least concerned and neither blinked an eye as we stood and drank the champagne that some admirer had left at her door.

When Dame Eva was in her ninety-seventh year, she was invited to the Coliseum by the *Evening Standard* to present the annual opera Singer-of-the-Year Award and for dinner afterwards. I escorted her for this occasion also. I took a taxi to Palace Place to pick her up, and we headed in the direction of the Coliseum, going northward from Notting Hill Gate. Without warning, we found ourselves in a monumental and immoveable traffic jam. Dame Eva turned to me and said, "I must start limiting my nights out to three a week. After all, I'm nearly a hundred years old."

We twice drove down to Glyndebourne together to hear *Porgy and Bess*. After hearing it there in 1986, she wanted to go back again in 1987, and she arranged for these scarce tickets. On the second occasion, we left London in the early afternoon for the leisurely drive through the countryside of East Sussex. Dame Eva was in the mood to reminisce. She talked first about Toscanini.

"After my first audition with him, he said '*Bella voce, bella pronuncia—e bella figura'* (Beautiful voice, beautiful pronunciation—and beautiful body). I first sang the role of Freia in *Das Rheingold* at La Scala with Toscanini conducting."

I asked her if it was a frightening experience.

"Oh no." she answered. "I was taught back in Oldham that you need be afraid of nothing if you have the proper technique and have been blessed with God's gift of singing." She went on, "I was told that Puccini was writing an opera with my voice in mind. He had almost finished it when he died. His friend, Alfano, finished it. This was *Turandot,* and I first sang that role at Brescia in 1926, before you were born, I suspect."

We were driving along the South Downs, but Dame Eva's mind was still in the twenties and thirties. I asked her if she had ever sung with the great Italian tenor, Giovanni Martinelli, realizing that they must have been contemporaries.

"It was in 1937, the Coronation Year. I sang with Martinelli at the Royal Opera House. We did *Turandot,* and I actually sang '*In questa reggia*' as an encore. Then I sang it again. It must have been a success because we recorded it, but the record was not released until forty years later. I'll put it on my gramophone for you when you next come to Palace Place."

We were too early for the performance, so I drove up to the top of the Downs where we parked and sat looking out towards the sea. Dame Eva was still reminiscing and talked of an experience at Chicago's Lyric Opera. She was singing the title role in *Aida* when the tenor lost his voice and could not continue.

"I whispered to him to remain on stage and act his part and I would sing it for him. So I sang his part as well as mine. My experiences in America are among my fondest memories. I didn't know exactly where Oklahoma was when the university invited me to come there as Artist-in-Residence, and it surprised me that they were not all driving horses and carriages with fringes on top. I think my success there had something to do with a typographical error in the university newspaper which heralded me as the new 'Professor of Vice.'" She giggled, like the girl from Lancashire she still was at heart.

I turned the car, and we drove off towards Glynde. I asked her about a rc-rclcascd recording I had just heard on Radio 2.

"Oh yes, that's a recent EMI record of performances between 1926 and 1933, when my voice could be heard across Lake Lugano. I was singing '*Dich teurer Halle*' from *Tannhauser*, '*In questa reggia*' from *Turandot*, and '*Suicidio*' from *La Gioconda*. On that recording I also sang 'Because' and then Tosti's 'Goodbye!' EMI wanted to prove that I could sing something other than grand opera. And I could."

I dropped her off at the door of the opera house, just north of Glynde, and drove to park the car. When I returned she was still in the same place—signing autographs. At the intermission she was again besieged and couldn't leave her seat. With great patience she sat there and signed programs. During the long supper intermission, I carried our picnic basket and a folding chair out to the meadow behind the house, but Dame Eva refused the chair, preferring to sit on the grass with the cows standing about, chewing their cud and staring.

Occasionally, I took Dame Eva down to Reigate to see her former secretary and companion, who had shared a home with her. This lady had developed Alzheimer's Disease and was a patient in a rest home there. During these visits I read while Dame Eva and her old friend conversed in her sparsely appointed room. Sometimes I was invited to join in the disconnected conversation. This lady, now in her mid-eighties, always seemed to confuse me with some former friend or business acquaintance, often calling me "Tommy." This was Thomas Shipman, Dame Eva's manager of many years ago.

"Now, Tommy, Eva and I have discussed it, and she's ready to sing Donna Elvira. I want you to get her that role at La Scala." We would nod approvingly, and I would say something like, "It's in the works for next year." Another time she might give me a lecture on how well Dame Eva could sing the title role in *Aida* and suggest that I contact the opera house in Rio, or she would push me for *Norma*.

Upon our leaving the rest home, she always wanted to go with us. Sadly, we would leave her waving from the doorway. Even more touching was Dame Eva's weeping on the drive back to London. When her friend finally died, it was the beginning of the end for Dame Eva.

Most vividly I remember visiting her in mid-June when she was ninety-nine years old. I went to Palace Place late in the afternoon, soon after I had returned from South Carolina. She was alone and sat in a darkened room under a silk-shaded floor lamp. Not unlike some Strauss opera set, it reminded me of a scene from *Der Rosenkavalier* or *Arabella*. She was in a talkative but rather melancholy mood, telling me that she had no great desire to live any longer. She rubbed her eyes and looked down at the floor.

"I can't see. No longer can I hear. My companion has died, and I just sit here. I'm ready to go." I tried to encourage her but was at a loss for words. Finally, I said goodbye and left her alone. Late the next morning a call came from Jean Archibald, her friend and part-time nurse. Dame Eva had died during the night.

Her unforgettable memorial service at Westminster Abbey began with a recording of that familiar voice. It was the recording she had given me earlier on which she gives a spoken introduction. Then her voice was heard singing *"In questa reggia."* This was followed by one of the most noteworthy musical memorials ever held in the Abbey. The Royal Opera Orchestra and Chorus performed the *Kyrie* from Franz Schubert's Mass in A flat. The tenor, Denis O'Neil, sang Ceasar Franck's *"Panis Angelicus,"* and Dame Gwyneth Jones, her student, closed the service with the orchestra and chorus singing Haydn's "The Heavens are Telling."

I left the Abbey that grey, rainy afternoon, and walked to a little cafe on Buckingham Place. I ordered a pot of tea but was careful to pour the milk into the cup before the tea. Dame Eva would have been pleased.

THE MARRIAGE

OF

HIS ROYAL HIGHNESS
THE PRINCE ANDREW

WITH

MISS SARAH FERGUSON

ON

Wednesday, 23rd July, 1986

Order of

Carriage Processions

to

Westminster Abbey and Return

THE QUEEN'S CARRIAGE PROCESSION

Leaving Buckingham Palace at 10.57 a.m.

Mounted Police

Advance Points
1st Division of the Sovereign's Escort
2nd Division of the Sovereign's Escort
Two Outriders on Grey Horses

SEMI-STATE LANDAU

With Four Grey Horses

THE QUEEN

The Duke of Edinburgh

Escort Commander   Field Officer of the Escort

Standard Party
Silver Stick Adjutant   Silver Stick in Waiting
(Major Richard Morrisey-Paine   (Colonel James Emson
The Life Guards)   The Life Guards)

SECOND CARRIAGE

State Landau with Two Bay Horses

Queen Elizabeth The Queen Mother
The Princess Margaret, Countess of Snowdon
Viscount Linley
Lady Sarah Armstrong-Jones

Standard Party
3rd Division of the Sovereign's Escort

THIRD CARRIAGE
State Landau with Two Bay Horses

The Prince of Wales
The Princess of Wales

FOURTH CARRIAGE
State Landau with Two Bay Horses

The Princess Anne, Mrs. Mark Phillips
Captain Mark Phillips
The Earl of Westmorland
(Master of the Horse)

FIFTH CARRRIAGE
State Landau with Two Bay Horses

The Duchess of Grafton
(Mistress of the Robes)
The Dowager Duchess of Abercorn
(Mistress of the Robes to Queen Elizabeth The Queen Mother)
The Rt. Hon. Sir William Heseltine
(Private Secretary to The Queen)
Lieutenant-Colonel Blair Stewart-Wilson
(Equerry in Waiting to The Queen)

4th Division of the Sovereign's Escort

Motor Car

Motor Car (Metropolitan Police)

Rear Points

Mounted Police

THE BRIDEGROOM'S CARRIAGE PROCESSION

Leaving Buckingham Palace at 11.05 a.m.

Mounted Police
Advance Points

1st Division of the Escort
Two Outriders on Grey Horses

1902 STATE LANDEAU

With Four Grey Horses

HIS ROYAL HIGHNESS THE BRIDEGROOM

The Prince Edward

2nd Division of the Escort

Motor Car

Wing Commander Adam Wise

Motor Car (Metropolitan Police)

Rear Points

THE BRIDE'S CARRIAGE PROCESSION
Leaving Clarence House at 11.15 a.m.

Mounted Police

Two Outriders on Bay Horses

THE GLASS COACH
With Two Bay Horses

THE BRIDE
Major Ronald Ferguson

Escort of The Life Guards

Motor Car

Motor Car (Metropolitan Police)

Mounted Police

BEAN DIP

The July morning in London bloomed fresh and bright. It was one of those warm midsummer mornings when there were pleasing things to do, positive things to accomplish, like going to Christies auction house on King's Street for the Oriental Sale, and then to Queen's Club for tennis in the afternoon. I read *The Times* until I heard the doorman plop the morning's mail on the table by the entrance.

I fumbled through a bank statement, a travel card from Rex, who was visiting Dresden, and the usual bills and circulars. On the bottom of the stack was an unstamped envelope with only my name on it, no address. I recognized the clear handwriting of Sir John Miller, my host at the Crown Equerry House for the past three years. The envelope had Her Majesty's coat of arms imprinted in the left upper corner. Inside was an unimposing "At Home" invitation for 22nd July 1986. Imprinted across the top it read, "Lt. Col. Sir John Miller, M.C., K.C.V.O., The Crown Equerry House, The Royal Mews, Buckingham Palace." The date was recognizable — the day before the Royal Wedding of Prince Andrew and Sarah Ferguson. My host was having a few friends in downstairs for a drinks party. Nothing more, I thought. As is the English custom, I placed the invitation on the mantle with several other outdated reminders and two Glyndebourne tickets.

I left for Christies by taxi where I spent a most satisfactory morning. I met a friend there and we both bid successfully on the lots we had an eye on. We adjourned to the Bag of Nails pub for a ploughman's lunch, and I returned to the mews in a mood to match the weather.

Back home, I encountered Sir John in the courtyard of the mews. I showed him my newly-acquired rare chloromelanite tea pot, which he admired, and I thanked him for the invitation and asked how his plans for the royal wedding were proceeding. I knew he was responsible for getting the royal family to Westminster Cathedral that morning, and I knew that one of the "greys," which had been scheduled to draw Prince

Andrew's carriage, was injured. He assured me that the head coachman had a replacement if necessary. I was about to walk into the house when he called out, "Can you wait a moment?" He came towards me and said, "The palace chef's staff will prepare the food for my party, but I think that the guests would enjoy some of your bean spread. You know, the mixture you served at your gathering last week with sour cream and mashed up beans. 'Dip,' you called it. I had the same sort of thing in San Antonio early this spring, 'Texas bean dip.'" I was in a hurry, so I agreed to make some dip without giving it much thought. I entered the house and then hastily went back to Sir John to ask how many guests he was expecting. He anwered calmly, "About three hundred." Completely taken aback, I asked, "But won't it be terribly crowded with that many people in your drawing room?"

"Oh no, the party will be in the courtyard and the stables. The queen has asked me to host the official bachelor's party for Prince Andrew."

I was speechless. But as I walked up the stairs to my apartment I was muttering to myself, "He said three hundred! Bean dip for three hundred!" I gathered up my tennis things and left in a daze. Stuck in a traffic jam on Cromwell Road, on my way to Queen's Club, my thoughts oscillated dizzily up and down between the rare Chinese tea pot and bean dip for three hundred. When I finally got to the Club, needless to say, my tennis game suffered and several double faults resulted from my mind being elsewhere. The tea pot offered no problem at all. It would rest comfortably and safely on the shelf with other Chinese objects. But making Texas bean dip for *three hundred* was another story. Mashing beans and chopping onions for that many, another story indeed! After all, I was not a catering chef and making anything for more than ten guests could easily blow my gasket.

Two mornings later, Ivy Banks arrived to do the weekly cleaning and laundry. She was a true London Cockney who lived back in the mews and whose husband was the carriage painter. She had worked for me for two years and was good at the odd culinary job—she was my "secret weapon." We had a conference in the kitchen concerning bean dip for three hundred. As Ivy mopped, I sat down and calculated that we needed twenty-eight 8-ounce cans of pinto beans, sixty-three medium size sweet onions, thirty pints of sour cream, several heads of lettuce, plus enough Cheddar cheese for all the layers. Ivy finished her mopping, sat down with me, and looked at my list. In her cheerful Cockney she said, "Ow well, I'll just tyke me shopping cart over to Tesco's on Warwick W'y and fetch all this 'ere stuff. Then I'll get on wiv the mashin' an' choppin'. Tesco's 'as it all." She got up from the table and presently was on her hands and knees waxing the floor. "Over in the East End I grew up on beans from Tesco's. You just give me some money on the di and I'll go to Tesco's."

What a relief!

On July 20th, another envelope arrived. Again from Sir John. Inside was a note and seven typewritten pages. He wrote, "I thought you might like to know who will be attending my party on the 22nd. Here is the guest list."

I perused it with great interest. I was curious to see who would be exposed to my dip. The list was headed by the queen and the Duke of Edinburgh. I counted seven more dukes, nine duchesses, innumerable princes and princesses, including Princes Andrew and Edward and Princess Anne, barons, viscounts, marquesses and marchionesses, a maharajah and a maharanee, five ambassadors, eight generals, and an admiral of the fleet. There were quite a few European titled personages, such as Princess Louise of Hesse and the Rhine and the Prince and Princess of Hohenlohe-Langenburg and the Margrave and Margravine of Baden. The House of Hesse was well represented with their Prince Karl, Prince Christopher, and Princess Irina. The list seemed endless. Even Denis Thatcher was included among the less exalted.

Prince Charles and Princess Diana would miss the dip. Their names were not on the list. Perhaps they would be keeping an eye on Sarah, the bride-to-be, at Kensington Palace or maybe they would be at Clarence House with the Queen Mother or perhaps they had not returned from a skiing trip.

On the morning of the 22nd, Ivy appeared with the culinary supplies and *two* of her neighbors, each carrying several bowls and dishes. A
cacophony of Cockney chatter sounded from the kitchen as they
mashed, chopped, and grated, working like soldiers on bivouac. I tried
to help by chopping onions but tears started streaming down my face
from the juice. I rubbed my eyes with a wet paper towel, and they stung.
Ivy came over to look at the pile I had tried to chop. She said, "Ow,
your choppin' is not nearly fine enuff." I fled the place, walking the
short distance to Green Park where I lay thankfully on the grass, knowing that the dip was in good hands.

Alas, all too soon it was time to get ready. I put on a blue pin-
striped suit and tried to look as if I had never heard of bean dip. At 6:15
on this July evening London was like mid-day, a cloudless time just right
for a party. Limousines drove through the entrance gates to the mews
and deposited their elegant occupants in front of the Crown Equerry
House from whence they walked the short distance to the party venue.
This whole complex was designed by John Nash and handsomely laid
out. A friend, Sir Edward Ford, arrived, and together we walked
through the archway into the spacious courtyard flanked by stables and
the carriage houses where the royal coaches, broughams, and such are
kept. For this occasion, space had been made in one section to accommodate most of the furniture from Sir John's first floor. Tables were set
about in the carriage house and out in the courtyard laden with the
usual British party fare—none of it very exciting. I could see bowls of
the bean dip here and there. Sir Edward and I chatted while he quaffed
a warm whiskey. I drank a Pimms, and we watched the arrival of the
cream of Britain's high society. Sir Edward, as a former private secretary
to the queen, was no stranger to such gatherings. Etonian and European accents mingled in pleasing cadenzas as the guests filled up the
courtyard.

The queen entered from the palace gardens through the back gate of
the mews and from there directly into the stables. Guests paid little attention to her, and there was no gawking as she greeted the impeccably

dressed grooms standing at their assigned places next to their equine charges. Her Majesty had not forgotten her sugar lumps, which she presented to each horse. Afterwards she joined the Duke of Edinburgh, Prince Andrew, and Sir John standing at one of the tables. The royals drank champagne, Sir John sipped whiskey, and between them they finished off the remains of bean dip from a bowl with only scrapings left.

Eight o'clock was approaching as I visited with Arthur Showell, the head coachman, and his wife, Yvonne. I said goodbyes and then walked back through Nash's archway to the Crown Equerry House. Once again, I encountered Sir Edward Ford.

"It's too early to go home." he said. "Let's walk over to The Mall and have dinner at the Atheneum Club."

Thinking that bean dip would definitely not be on the menu as they probably had never even heard of Texas bean dip at the Atheneum, I accepted, and we strolled off together along Buckingham Palace Road.

The following morning I was up early for a "Command Performance." The Lord Chamberlain had sent a request to the mew's superintendent that he recruit residents to come to the courtyard in front of the palace and act as "wavers" to see Prince Andrew off on his way to Westminster Abbey for his wedding and for the return with Sarah. This was a task I knew I could perform; it was a lot easier one than making bean dip for three hundred.

In my blue pin striped uniform, I walked to the side door of the palace, where Sgt. John Dudley was on guard. He had the check list of "wavers" and told me where I was to stand. I joined Patricia Ellison, the Royal Mews' official hostess, and her daughter, Rose. We chatted as the others arrived, among them Wendy, Alice, and Samantha, the wives of the grooms who would be riding in the procession. Of course, none of them would be recognized in their white wigs and crimson and gold uniforms, looking like toy soldiers. They were quite ordinary appearing people under other circumstances, particularly Toby Evans, who without this paraphernalia might be mistaken for Ichabod Crane.

Michael Rosemon, an official we all knew from the mews, came down the line telling us that the procession would start in eight minutes. He whispered instructions: "Wave with your right hand only. Do not fully extend your arm. This should not look like a 'heil.' You are not to cheer, and you are not to wave too enthusiastically." Ivy, standing near me, said, "Bloody 'ell! What am I supposed to do? This ain't nobody's funeral. They say Prince Andrew was a fighter pilot in the Falklands or somewhere, so he ain't afraid of noise. He's heard navy farts in the showers!" Various ladies looked the other way, pretending not to have heard.

I did a practice wave at about the four minute mark. Patricia asked, "Who are you waving at? I don't see anybody except us." I said, "I'm practicing. I want to do this right" She waved both arms and I said, "No, no, Patricia! They'll think you're a born-again Christian. Wave only one arm, and bend it at the elbow." I showed her how. Three people, pressed against the fence outside, waved back.

Then she whispered, "Do you think we'll be seen on television?"

"Heavens yes. It'll be on BBC 1 and 2, and on ITN, too, honey. We'll be seen everywhere on this planet, including America, if they're tuned in to CNN at 4:30 in the morning."

With just two minutes to go, I reminded Patricia to save some energy for the *return* of the prince. She said, "Oh, I almost forgot that."

Suddenly, at 11:01, there were Her Majesty and the Duke of Edinburgh coming through the archway in the state landau, pulled by four grey horses. I recognized Rio, the horse I had held in the palace garden during the recent bomb scare, ridden by Steve Matthews. The other greys were Sydney, Cardiff, and Santiago, all alert and beautifully groomed. The queen nodded and raised her arm slightly. Prince Philip looked bored. Steve, riding postillion, seemed welded to Rio and looked straight ahead. Samantha, his wife, waved toward him as cheering erupted at the Palace fence. Another state landau followed closely behind carrying the Queen Mother, who was waving towards us with one arm and clutching several strands of pearls with the other. Patricia whispered to me, "I had tea with her last week."

There was enthusiastic applause and cheering for the next state landau pulled by two bays. I recognized Honey Buzzard ridden by Nigel
Day. This was the Prince and Princess of Wales' carriage. Princess Diana
appeared radiant, with her characteristic head tilt and bashful expression.
Prince Charles looked subdued and, perhaps like his father, he was having thoughts of what his brother was impaling himself upon.

A fourth state landau carried Princess Anne, Captain Mark Phillips,
and the Master of the Horse. Alphie Oates rode Monaco, one of the two
greys pulling the carriage. It seemed contrary and bucked, but Alphie
soon had it under control. His wife, Lorna, stood to my left. She cupped
both hands over her face and looked down.

At 11:05, the Bridegroom's carriage came through the archway.
Prince Andrew grinned and waved, as did his brother, Prince Edward.
This state landau was also pulled by four greys and was greeted with
loud cheers.

Sir John Miller and Head Coachman Arthur Showell followed close
behind in a long black Rolls-Royce. They headed into The Mall and
would pause a few yards down to welcome into the procession the
bride, Sarah Ferguson, in the Glass Coach pulled by two bays with two
outriders.

As the cheering subsided, Michael herded us into the pub on the
second floor of the palace's south wing where we sat at small round
tables. A barmaid, dressed in black with a white starched collar, served
coffee as we watched the proceedings on BBC 1. There they went,
through the Admiralty Arch, around Trafalgar Square, then towards the
Abbey. I sat with Patricia, Rose, and Samantha and could hear Ivy in the
background. Occasionally she cackled with glee, not being accustomed
to being served anything within the confines of the palace.

Michael brought in a second television set so that we could watch
on both BBC 1 and BBC 2. The camerman focused briefly on Sir John
and Arthur alighting from the Rolls. Yvonne smiled proudly and
remarked in her Jersey accent that last night's gin did not seem to have
affected him. Neither had the bean dip, I thought.

We watched the other arrivals at Westminster Abbey, the ceremony, and some of the return procession. Then it was time for us to finish the "Command Performance." Michael shepherded us back to our place in the courtyard. Caffeine-laden, we were ready to wave to the newlyweds.

Ivy was still chattering as Prince Andrew's carriage arrived. Sarah, now Princess Sarah, with her toothy grin, looked like an alligator that has just swallowed a very tasty frog. A few minutes later, to the background cheers of the crowds at the fence, the family appeared in front of the central doorway of the gallery above us. A flight of six Royal Navy fighter planes swooped low over the palace and disappeared to the west. Some of the "wavers" went back to the pub, for lager this time. Others went home to watch themselves on the BBC News. Ivy went home to watch *Coronation Street.*

Epilogue

A few weeks later, Princess Sarah presented both Sir John and myself with a signed photograph taken as he assisted her out of the Glass Coach at Westminster Abbey. It was a handsome photograph and worthy of the memorabilia photographic collection in a sitting room of my home.

But I took it off the wall when, some time later, a London newspaper printed a photograph of the princess lying nearly nude by a swimming pool with a man sucking her toe. According to the caption he was her "Texas agent." Perhaps he had dipped her toe in Texas bean dip. The photograph now catches dust in the attic.

A PARTY IN THE GARDEN

*D*aphne's invitation arrived in the Royal Mail. My invitation arrived in an 1896 two-horse carriage which runs each day between Buckingham Palace and the Crown Equerry House in the Royal Mews. My invitation came directly from Her Majesty on an engraved card. Daphne's came from the office of Prime Minister Margaret Thatcher because she designed Mrs. Thatcher's dresses.

Realizing that, as an American, I would need some guidance, Daphne explained that being asked to the Queen's Garden Party was not an invitation to sit across a table from Her Majesty and sip tea while exchanging pleasantries about the latest matches at Wimbledon. She told me that tennis is not a topic to discuss with the queen because if it does not involve horses, she isn't interested. More importantly, she reminded me that there would be ten thousand guests at this garden party, and we would be lucky to see the queen, even if we were allowed to bring binoculars.

Daphne called back to say that she had received a big windshield car sticker with a large blue *X* inscribed on it, indicating that she had permission to park her 'chauffeur-driven or owner-driven' car on The Mall directly in front of Buckingham Palace. I interrupted her.

"Honey, don't worry about parking. You just come to the gate of the Royal Mews. Michael, the guard, will allow you to park right beside my Rover in the courtyard, and we'll walk to the party."

"But I'm coming by Tube from Islington to Victoria Station."

"Daphne, that's OK. It's OK. You just come out of the station, walk two blocks down Buckingham Palace Road, and zip, you'll be at the Crown Equerry House. We'll walk through the back gate to the garden. We'll miss standing in line with nine thousand other people and we'll be at the tea tent in no time."

"But I'm not wearing a thirty-one pound number from Peter Jones. I'm wearing a new silk dress that I designed for this party, and I'll be in Gucci high heels. Maybe I should take a taxi from Victoria."

"No, no, Daphne. Wear a pair of flats and bring your Guccis in your purse. Don't worry, there'll be other ladies and gentlemen walking from the station dressed to the nines. And besides, if you take a taxi, the driver will be upset that you're only going two blocks. He'll expect a double tip, maybe triple. Also, the taxi can't come in the gate if the Garden Party is on. You just walk."

She called me a third time.

"You're an American, and if I'm going with you, I want to make sure that you know how to dress."

"Look, my invitation clearly states that 'Gentlemen are to wear morning dress, uniform, national dress, or lounge suit.' I couldn't squeeze into my uniform even if I starved for a year, the national dress in America is a T-shirt and Levi's, and I don't intend to lounge in the queen's garden, so I'll wear morning dress. It's already at the cleaners. It got all sweaty at Ascot. Too much champagne in the afternoon, remember? Yeah, if I'm going with you, I'll make sure that I look civilized. Don't worry." Morning dress is an essential part of the British social scene much favored for weddings and day-time formal events: A modified penguin suit, with a long black cut-away jacket worn over grey pin-striped pants.

The day of the Garden Party arrived, and by 2 P.M. I could see from my third floor sitting-room window party-goers walking toward the palace. They were not due until 3:15 P.M., but, as I reminded myself, the English don't mind waiting. There was a catch to this scene. A monsoon had descended on London. From my third-floor flat in the Crown Equerry House I looked down onto a sea of umbrellas. A patchwork of sober colors, black, dark blue, and gray with an occasional dash of red or green.

Daphne arrived just before three on the arm of the gate keeper, Michael Shillabeer. Michael, dressed in Welsh Guards uniform, was cheerfully optimistic and insisted that he saw clearing skies to the west. Knowing that I'm not much at carrying an umbrella, he had brought along a rather large black one from Sir John's supply on the first floor. Daphne inspected me, tugged at my tie and brushed my back. Michael followed us down the steps and into the pouring rain. We marched through the great John Nash archway of the mews toward the back gate to the palace garden. We stood in a small queue awaiting the opening of the gate with five men in morning suits, and their ladies. As we bumped umbrellas, I recognized Capt. John Smith who had just retired as super-intendent of the mews. Daphne and I walked in with him. He explained that there might be three hundred or so VIPs coming to the party. Cabinet ministers, exiled kings, ambassadors, sheikhs and other notables, who would take tea in the royal tent to the right, where they would have waitress service. Her Majesty and party, including Princess Di, the Duke and Duchess of Kent, Prince Edward, and the Duchess of Gloucestershire would be in that tent also but roped off in their own little cocoon. He told us that on the left would be the rest of us: lord mayors from towns in counties from Northumberland to East Sussex, hospital matrons, rear admirals, presidents of various chapters of Aid to Distressed Gentlefolk, bishops, actors, and many others, who would queue up for tea and cucumber sandwiches.

We bumped umbrellas again and walked on through the deluge. The captain stopped and asked me to hold his umbrella while he rolled up his pant legs. Daphne held my umbrella while I did the same.

I had been in this garden once before when I had been asked to hold a horse here for two hours when a bomb was planted in the Rubens Hotel just across from the Crown Equerry House. Not just any horse but the venerable Rio, the oldest and wisest of the queen's carriage horses.

We had been heading towards the line up for tea on the left, but I stopped.

"Daphne, we need a plan." She suggested that we walk by the lake and see the flamingos. We strolled along the gravel walkway, now a sea of mud and water, behind three bishops, two with purple umbrellas and the other with a bright red one. Each one had their trousers rolled up nearly to their knees. Daphne thought she spotted a flamingo but it was a tall young woman in pink stockings carrying her white shoes and escorted by the defense minister.

We walked on by the lake and tipped back our umbrellas to admire a gorgeous climbing rose. I almost stepped on a bishop who had squatted down to admire the herbaceous border. He inspected the wet lavender astors and commented that lavender astors are impossible to grow in his vestry garden. The bishop with the red umbrella had also squatted, and we walked carefully around their Right Reverences.

We turned back towards the palace as the band played "God save the Queen." It was now 4:10 P.M., and Her Majesty and the royal party had formed a receiving line to greet the appointed guests who were to be introduced. We got closer and could see that drenched Irish Guards were holding umbrellas over the royals. The bishops joined us, and we watched the proceedings. The bishop with the red umbrella folded it up, yielded to the downpour, and commented to Daphne that the southeast needed the rain. As we watched, I spotted a tennis buddy from Queen's Club, the under secretary for Costa Rica, standing with his wife in the queue to meet Her Majesty.

Next to Daphne stood a middle-aged lady in a wilted lilac chiffon hat. She was explaining to her lounge-suited gentleman friend that she was the president of the Greater Cheshire Humane Society and had arrived in London that morning on the Manchester Express. She told him that she had met Her Majesty two years ago when she had come up north to cut the ribbon for a new building. She said she was surprised that she had not been included in the group to meet Her Majesty again. The gentleman in the lounge suit commented that he had never met the queen. The rain had slackened, and Daphne reminded me that we were observing the English on their best behavior.

"We're not seeing the Great and Good, but the Small and Worthy. We're seeing the backbone of our local communities, so let them make small talk about cricket, the weather, and Wimbledon. They're at the most prestigious tea party in the world, and they are enjoying it, even in this monsoon."

Standing there, Daphne was stuck. Her Gucci heels had sunk deep into the muddy gravel walkway. She took my arm and managed to work them free while a military band in the distance played something from *Cats.* Then we noticed that Her Majesty and entourage were making their way towards the royal tent, so we turned and joined the throng of groupies lining her path.

Gentlemen ushers, recognizable from their military uniforms, armbands and bossy manner, parted the onlookers courteously and created something like a royal shipping lane. Her Majesty occasionally stopped to have a word with an unsuspecting guest. I heard a lady with a Yorkshire accent lecturing her husband in a loud whisper, "Ian, remember to bow from the neck if she picks you out. And don't say 'Ma'am,' say 'Your

Majesty.'" But Her Majesty passed Ian by, so he didn't have a chance to bow from the neck. The queen was on her way to tea.

The graveled path became more and more boggy, and I stopped to roll up my trouser legs one more notch. I asked Daphne if I might take my shoes off, and she said 'No.' She said I couldn't have tea in Her Majesty's garden in my socks. She said we had to be proper. We finally got out of the rain and into a tent guarded by two Beefeaters. Waiting for tea, we stood behind a lady in a white linen dress, wrinkled beyond definition. She was with a short Oriental man in a bowler hat. They were talking about the impending turnover of Hong Kong to the Chinese and both agreed that it was a bloody shame.

Daphne and I were now within striking distance of the tea and sandwiches. She took a small plate and placed two cucumber sandwiches and a cookie on it while a young waitress, dressed in a white-trimmed black dress, poured two cups of tea. She appeared bored and probably couldn't wait to take the number 29 bus back home to Watford. No tea for her. She would have a Beck's beer later. Carefully holding our tray, I searched for a place to sit. We found a partially occupied table for six and sat down gratefully with our three bishops—three bishops in their purple shirts and their trouser legs rolled up. We all had our trouser legs rolled up. Except Daphne.

THE VILLAGE HAMPDEN

A few months after establishing a residence in London, I found that I had American "friends" whom I hardly knew. But when real friends wrote to say they were "coming over," I frequently asked them to be my guests in my apartment on the third floor of the Crown Equerry House in the Royal Mews of Buckingham Palace, a beautiful house designed by the renowned eighteenth-century architect, John Nash. My guests enjoyed the delights of its excellent location, the services of the gateman, who would carry their luggage up to my quarters (there was no elevator), and the smug pleasure they could derive from telling their taxi driver, "Take me to the Crown Equerry House in the Royal Mews. Buckingham Palace that is." One such taxi driver told some visiting friends, "I've been driving a taxi in London for twenty-two years, and I've never driven through these gates before."

One of my "coming over" friends, visiting from Nashville, ws a professor of English Literature at Vanderbilt University, who was writing a book on Thomas Gray. She came to England to do final research in the British Museum Library. Alice's only request during this visit waas that I should drive her to Poke Stoges Church in Oxfordshire to visit the graveyard where Gray wrote Elegy Written in a Country Church Yard. On the way to Oxfordshire she read to me from a Gray anthology she had brought along. Nearing Poke Stoges she finally got to Gray's Elegy. Mist and rain added to the atmosphere as we parked near the church and Alice read, "The curfew tolls the knell of parting day." I looked toward the tilted tombstones in the church yard and was lulled by her voice and the sound of the rain. On and on she read as Gray reminded us how unimportant we are:

> Full many a flower is born to blush unseen,
> And waste its sweetness on the desert air.

But then came,

> Some Village-Hampden that with dauntless breat,
> The little tyrant of his fields withstood.

This line, this "Village-Hampden" line, jogged my memory and I interrupted Alice to tell about my encounter with real life Hampdens.

The previous September I had become a student in the Christie Fine Arts School, my reason for living in London. In my class of seventy students, I was the oldest along with Clara, Viscountess Hampden, and as a result we "hung out" together and bonded. I was frequently invited down to Glynde Place in East Sussex, the Hampdens' Tudor stately home, where Clara, as pretty as a new dime, was the lady of the manor and where she looked after her Etonian husband Antony, Viscount Hampden, and their three children. Our friendship grew even closer when they purchased a London residence on Warwick Square in Pimlico, near the neighborhood where I lived.

For a long time I had been curious about the "village-Hampden" mentioned in Gray's Elegy, and wondered if there was a connection with the Hampdens I knew. I finally brought up the subject one Saturday afternoon during tea-time at Glynde Place. The slightly built Viscount is not a person given to visible enthusiasm, but my query seemed to galvanize him. He took a deep breath, as if reviewing in his mind what he would say, then, struggling with his stutter, told me that John Hampden was a seventeenth-century member of Parliament representing Buckinghamshire. He said, "I have always been proud of 'Uncle John.' In 1635, he simply refused to pay the thirty-one shillings and six pence ship money tax which King Charles I demanded. His refusal led others to follow suit and the ship tax issue became the final straw which forced Charles to retreat from Westminster to Hampton Court, where he lived before being taken back to London and the Guildhall to face execution." After a pause, the Viscount added, "Uncle John indeed became notable and was well-remembered even in Thomas Gray's time, a hundred years later."

Alice seemed transfixed as we gazed at the graveyard through the rain. I had another little story to tell her about Viscount Hampden. On a visit to Glynde Place, Antony and I had gone into Lewes to the market to do the weekly shopping and on the way back we passed by the adjoining estate, Glyndebourne. While attending the opera there, in my mind I had often compared Glyndebourne and Glynde Place and wondered which was the oldest. On this occasion I posed the question to Antony. He told me, "Well, Glyndebourne goes back a long way. I think my family, the Richard Hampdens, gave it away as a wedding present in 1523."

The rain finally stopped. I glanced at the notes Alice was taking. These notes were not about Gray or the cemetery. They were about the Village-Hampden.

One spring, the Hampdens accepted an invitation to visit me in South Carolina. Once settled into the Duck's Nest, Antony established a most unusual morning routine. After morning tea on the lower porch, he selected one of my baseball caps, walked southward and crossed the causeway over to the mainland and to the intersection of the island road and Route 17. On this corner there was an abandoned building which still had its sign, "Saloon." This place, with its graffiti, broken windows, empty beer cans, and moulded board advertising "Fresh Corn For Sale," became Antony's domain. Most mornings he could be found there, sitting on the ground leaning against the building, watching the passing traffic. I wondered if he could be imagining himself as the proprietor of this saloon rather that the lordof the manor of a Tudor estate in the South Downs.

SIR HAROLD ACTON AESTHETE AND ENGLISH EXPATRIATE

I first met Sir Harold at a dinner party at the East India Club in London where he was visiting from his home, Villa La Pietra, near Florence. He had lived there for forty years after inheriting the estate from his parents. Sir Harold was in his mid-eighties, well preserved, dignified, and handsome. He spoke proper English with a slight Italian accent. Every word seemed chosen, but he spoke without effort or affectation. I shall not forget the small dinner party, and that one of the guests was Donald Sindon, whom I did not recognize as the well-known actor. During the course of the evening I said, "You must have had experience as an actor," to which he replied, "Yes, I am Donald Sindon."

That evening Sir Harold presented each of us with his reprinted book, *Memories of an Aesthete*. As we gathered our coats, he told me that if I came to Italy, I must come to La Pietra for a visit. On the way home on the Tube I read the introduction to this book:

> The label "aesthete" had clung to Sir Harold Acton ever since he left school. Although aware of the late Victorian connotations, which have parodied its meaning, he is unrepentant in applying it to himself, since his

is one in the proper meaning of the word. His book is witty and a lively record of an era in which the "aesthete" still held his ground against the specialist and the politician, and in which it was still possible to be a true citizen of the world.

Later that year I saw the film, *Brideshead Revisited*, a story about Sir Harold and his set while they were in school at Oxford and afterwards. Sir Harold was played by the handsome young actor, Anthony Andrews, whose portrayal was more appealing than that of anyone else in the film.

My chance to get to know Sir Harold came while I was a student at the British Institute of Florence. He owned the fourteenth-century building where their offices and library were housed and was on the board of directors of the institute. Soon after my arrival in Florence, he invited Dr. Dick Howland, a visiting American classics scholar, and myself to lunch at La Pietra. His car and driver picked us up for the short trip to the estate that was situated north of Florence on the road to Bologna. We turned right into the villa's driveway and on the left could glimpse Fiesole and San Dominico across the valley. A long avenue of cypresses led toward La Pietra standing in the middle of Montieghi Hill. The ocher-colored house with imposing green wooden shutters had belonged to the Capponi family for three centuries before Sir Harold's father purchased it. It was considered to be one of the finest villas of Tuscany.

Four other guests joined us for lunch. Sir Harold was not having his best day. We sat, surrounded by Donatello bronzes and enamels by Lucia della Robbia and Tuscan primitives, while he openly criticized the white-gloved waiter and sent derogatory messages to the chef. The guest to my right was Contessa Lucrezia Formoni. I suspected that he had invited her so that he might have someone to disagree with, and this he did as often as possible. The guests thought it a perfectly delightful lunch and seemed to ignore Sir Harold's contrariness. I soon learned that this was only a façade. Afterwards he was affable and congenial. He apparently had kind words for the white-gloved waiter, speaking to him in Italian with a mellow voice, as cappuccino was served. Perhaps Sir

Harold was trying subconsciously to rid himself of the "aesthete" title, even after he had entitled his book, *Memories of an Aesthete*.

Sir Harold's eighty-fifth birthday was coming up soon, and Frank Woodhouse, director of the British Institute, had asked me to do a David Hockney–like montage photograph of him to hang in their library. Sir Harold agreed that I might return to La Pietra the following week when he would pose in the garden.

I arrived early to survey the garden and select the most appropriate place for his posing for the many photographs I needed for the montage. Standing on the terrace, I looked across the valley to The Villa Palmiere where Boccaccio wrote *Decameron*.

From this viewpoint the garden revealed its architectural refinement with several broad terraces, each like a separate garden. A staircase on either side flanked the first, a long platform enclosed by a balustrade, which defined a place for a row of ancient statues. On the lowest terrace there were four fountains with circular basins surrounded by stone benches. A mossy staircase descended downward toward a peristyle of Corinthian columns, where a statue of Hercules stood vigorously in the center. I walked through this garden then went back to the second ter-race to a Roman sculpted *cassone*, where on the background wall were mosaics of shells and pebbles in festoons and garlands. Here Sir Harold patiently posed for the long photographic session. Afterwards we went back inside for tea.

I returned Sir Harold's hospitality by inviting him one Sunday afternoon to attend a concert by the Maggio Musicale Fiorentino when Maestro Zubin Metha conducted a program of music by Gustav Mahler. After the program, he returned with me to my residence where he climbed the five flights of steps with ease. He proceeded directly to the terrace balcony where, at dusk, we sat and observed the festival-like atmosphere in the Piazza Santa Croce below. As the sunlight sank lower on Michelangelo's old city wall across the Arno, he asked for a whiskey, then another and another. We discussed the decade of the thirties, when he lived in Shanghai, and his association with our mutual friend, Laurence Sickman, who at that time was acquiring the nucleus of the Oriental collection now in the Kansas City Museum of Art. I made a simple dinner, and during the meal we talked about his mentor, Bernard Berenson, who had owned Villa Tahiti near La Pietra. We discussed diverse subjects from Tuscan primitive paintings to his time in London during the Blitz and then finally his frank dislike for his father. These confidences were eased by many glasses of Chianti and port afterwards. Finally at 11:30 P.M. he called for his driver then walked down the 186 steps in seemingly perfect sobriety.

I saw Sir Harold once more when he sat on the front row for my lecture on nineteenth-century American paintings given at the British Institute. Afterwards we went out for dinner. He died three months later. But he didn't rest in peace for long, for alas, a half-sister appeared in Rome. Previously unknown to Sir Harold, she claimed to be an illegitimate daughter of his father. She laid claim to half of the estate, which he had left to Columbia University. The situation is still in litigation, while caretakers enjoy the Tuscan primitives, the Della Robbias, and the Donnatellos.

RUGBY THE "NEW JERUSALEM"

I grew up near Rugby, Tennessee where in the late nineteenth century the English writer, Thomas Hughes established a utopian community in the foothills of the Cumberland Mountains. Relics of such communities were scattered over the eastern part of America, and I never paid much attention to this quaint place. When I went to live in London the subject of Rugby, Tennessee, came up. Hughes, who had been a headmaster at Rugby in England, a reformer and author of such books as *Tom Brown's School Days,* called his settlement in Tennessee "The New Jerusalem."

During my years in London I belonged to England's oldest tennis club, Queen's Club, and frequently played tennis and socialized there. On Saturday afternoons the games manager arranged what we referred to as S.A.M.D.—Saturday Afternoon Mixed Doubles, when a lady and a gentleman were paired against whomever came along. However, the main excuse for playing seemed to be to get finished and have tea. It was a social event each Saturday afternoon.

Memories of those afternoons linger, particularly one afternoon when, making conversation while having tea, I asked a gentleman opponent, who had an accent that I didn't recognize, what he *did* in London. He answered that he was the king of Greece.

It was also during tea at Queen's Club that I met Basil Robinson, who was a graduate of Rugby School in Warwickshire and who knew of Rugby in Tennessee, as his grandfather had been a settler there in the 1880s. He told me that his grandfather had qualified to go to Hughes' new town because he was a second son who wanted to learn agriculture and the manual arts, the exact reason for which Hughes had established this colony. Like Basil, his grandfather had been a tennis player and probably played on the famous tennis court at Rugby, one of the first in America. My friendship with Basil bloomed from that afternoon tea at Queen's —not for his tennis abilities but for the Rugby connection.

Eventually, I invited him to come to Nashville during one of my sojourns back in America. Once over his jet lag, I packed a picnic, and we drove eastward the eight miles through my home town and on to visit the restored community of Rugby. Besides Basil, there was a good reason to go there as the editor of *Classic America*, the Victorian Society's official publication, had asked me to write an article on the settlement. During this visit I went to Rugby's library where we viewed its extensive collection of nineteenth-century photographs of Rugby, and where I collected research material. Basil was delighted when we located a photograph of his grandfather, identified with a group of settlers with his handlebar mustache, wearing a suit and wide-brimmed hat. This visit to Rugby, Tennessee, with Basil inspired me to complete the article for *Classic America*. Here it is as it appeared four months later in that magazine:

RUGBY, TENNESSEE: THOMAS HUGHES'S "NEW JERUSALEM"

THOMAS HUGHES'S Rugby was not on the Avon in Warwickshire, but situated distantly on the Clear Fork in Mor-
gan County, Tennessee. Rugby is a monument representing
what Thomas Hughes (1822-1896) called his "New
Jerusalem," England's last colonial enterprise in America. This utopian community has been remarkably preserved in a cocoon of anonymity for nearly a hundred
years. Now, during the centennial of its most eventful
year, signs are seen of the revitalization of its Victorian spirit.

Along Rugby's old Central Avenue the occasional visitor
is impressed with the buildings that stand as reminders
of the utopian dream that failed in the wilderness.
Christ Church Episcopal, a carpenter gothic building in
continuous use since 1887, has been restored and
repainted in its original colors—burgundy, pastel pink,
and blue. Nearby, the Hughes Public Library of 1882,
containing 7,000 volumes, is among the finest representative collections of Victorian literature in the United
States. Down the avenue is the cottage Kingstone Lisle,
built for Rugby's founder, Thomas Hughes. The many-
gabled Uffington House where the founder's mother,
Madame Margaret Hughes, lived the last years of her long
life stands I good repair. North of it and down a ravine
is the "gentlemen's swimming hole."

At Rugby School in England, Hughes was influenced by
the philosophy of its headmaster, Dr. Thomas Arnold. The
headmaster molded the characters of schoolboys and would
develop in them the "souls of saints and the bodies of
Vikings." Hughes became concerned about the medieval
legacy of primogeniture, the system is which the younger
sons of "gentryfolk" received little monetary inheri-
tance and were relegated to the only respectable professions: law, divinity, medicine, or the military. If
gentry class Will Wimbles or middle class Tom Browns did
not care for these professions then they could "starve

like gentleman." By 1870 English public schools as Wellington, Eton, and Clifton had produces a surplus of Wills and Toms. Hughes determined to establish a colony where these younger sons could earn honest livings in agriculture and the manual arts. He appealed to his countrymen and to Americans to join the venture of Rugby in the New World.

The colony was zealously launched with the publication of a sophisticated town plan which emphasized aesthetic consideration more than the American norm of the period. The new Rugby would use the natural, scenic characteristics of its site, running roads along ridges, locating parks in scenic spots, and allowing views from public places. Advertising and promotion was intense in England and America. Bulletins were issued describing the beauty of plateau, its location and accessibility. The nascent colony attracted worldwide attention and became the pet subject of press and conversation. Hughes impressions of the colony were recorded in letters he wrote for London Spectator when he first visited the colony in 1880, and later published in his book, Rugby, Tennessee.

On the journey from Sedgemoor Station to the settlement Hughes noted the strange spectacle of English public schoolmen in the wilderness. He wrote in this book:

"A lighter-hearted party has seldom scrambled though the Tennessee mountain roads on to this plateau. We were led by a Etonian and also six feet and upwards in his stockings, whose Panama straw hat and white corduroys gleamed like a beacon through the deep shadows cast by the tall pine trees and white oaks. The geologists brought up the rear and between rode the rest of us . . . all public school-men, I think, another Etonian, two from Rugby, one Harrow, one Wellington—through deep gullies, through four streams . . . and so up through more open ground till we reached this city of the future."

The colony was renamed Rugby following a tennis match. Hughes thought the original name "Plateau" was neither good English or Yankee usage:

"You may be startled by the address at the head of
this letter. It was adopted unanimously on our
return in the twilight from the tennis ground…It was
sharp practice thus to steal a match on the three
Etonians, still far away in the forest. Had they
been present, possible Thames might have prevailed
over Avon."

Hughes recorded his early doubts:

"The thought occurs, are our swans—our visions,
already so bright, of splendid crops, and simple
life, to be raised and lived in this fairyland —to
prove geese? I hope not. It would be the downfall of
the last castle in Spain I am ever likely to build."

Rugby was dedicated on October 5, 1880 on the verandah
of the newly completed Tabard Inn. Dignitaries from
across the country and most of the 175 settlers
attended. The Episcopal Bishop of Tennessee celebrated
Holy Communion in the vestibule of the inn. At the end
of the day, a vestry of nine colonists had founded
Christ Church.

Soon Hughes returned to England and the colony bustled
with activity although few private residences were
built. Titles to the land were not cleared. Some
colonists temporarily lived in tents. Socializing,
games, afternoon tea, and intellectual pursuits were the
order of the day. Little land was cleared. The gentlemen
settlers participated in the Dramatic Club, the Library
and Reading Room Society, the Tennis Club, and the Coronet Band. Deprived of their liquor in the settlement,
the young colonists jaunted the eight miles to Glen
Mary, where they bent an elbow with mountain boys drinking local sour mash whiskey. Hoes and rakes were dropped
early for tennis or croquet. A plateau newspaper
remarked on the terrible agony about the exhausted supply of Worcestershire sauce. Even worse, was the failure
of London Punch to arrive on time.

An imposing hotel to attract colonists and visitors was
the first significant building undertaken. The Tabard

Inn was the name selected from Chaucer's ancient inn in Southwark. The three-story Mansard-roofed structure, situated on an elevation overlooking the gorge of the Clear Fork, featured wide verandahs on both upper and lower floors. The impeccable nine acre oval grounds were complete with gravel walks, a tennis court and a deer park. Finely manicured lawns and flower gardens set the standard for the cultured Victorian landscape so often the point of great praise at Rugby. Board and lodging was advertised at $2.50 per day. Dinner partied were festive as were holiday celebrations with dancing and music. The Coronet Band regaled the Rugby community from the roofed balcony of the third floor. The uncertain history of the Tabard reflected that of the colony. This focal point of community social life suffered a disastrous fire in 1884 and burned completely. It was rebuilt in 1886 and then in a declining year of the community, 1900, it burned again. Only the foundations remain.

The year 1881 was significant for both the glory and sad demise of the settlement. In January, the colony's press issued the awaited newspaper called The Rugbeian. During the same month construction of the Hughes Public Library and Reading Room was scheduled to begin immediately. Publishers had promised to donate 4,000 volumes. A few weeks later, Macmillan Press in London published Hughes' book, Rugby Tennessee. Numerous Articles in the English press discussed Rugby. Travel to the colony became fashionable as steamship lined devised and advertises excursions to Rugby from Liverpool via Philadelphia, Cincinnati, and Sedgemoor Station.

A crowning glory for the community was the arrival of Hughes' eighty-three year old mother in May 1881, along with her 18 year old granddaughter, Emily, and a retinue of retainers. Madame Margaret Hughes soon moved into Uffington House, in sight of Tabard Inn. The magnificent matron inspired the settlement as she entered wholeheartedly into the promotion and gaiety of the community. Her stately presence gave visible support and stability for the 300 member colony.

All the while, litigation over land titles haunted the
settlement. Drought withered the few crops being raised
and internal dissension over management lowered the
colonists' morale. The typhoid epidemic of 1881 cost the
lives of eight settlers. The epidemic was traced to con-
taminated water at the Tabard Inn well, and it closed
for several months.   By 1882, many new settlers had
arrived, the library was open, and school was in session. The Tabard Inn again welcomed guests. The saw-mill
cut lumber for new buildings and a canning factory was
also evidence of new industry. Hughes returned to the
colony each year and saw the census grow to 450 residents. Buildings numbered more than fifty. Numbers, however, were insufficient to eclipse the failure that
loomed on the horizon.

Except for a few, the Tom Browns at Rugby were not con-
stituted for labors under wilderness conditions. By
1887, the year of Queen Victoria's Jubilee Celebration,
the colony had entered its twilight. Madame Hughes died,
the library had financial problems, The Rugbeian ceased
publication, and settlers were leaving the colony for
England or resettlement in the United States. The gov-
erning board was reorganized in 1892 too late to save
the colony. Only memories remained of enthusiastic settlers arriving at the Sedgemoor Station, of afternoon
teas at Uffington House, of the buzz of the sawmill and
of music from the Coronet Band. Rugby's twilight became
its night.

Today seventeen original buildings of rugby colony
stand. The Rugby Restoration Association owns or main-
tains eight structures,—four of which are open to the
public. Most of the other buildings are private summer
homes or year round residences. These are open to the
public during the annual pilgrimage each August.

Printed descriptions of the grounds of most Rugby cottages suggest a "Gardenesque Romantic" landscape style.
These descriptions refer to paisley shaped plant beds,
vined arbors, and exotic local plantings of yucca, spirea,
and forsythia—all pleasing to Victorian sensibility.

Approaching Christ Church on a Sunday morning today, a
visitor might hear music from the same 1849 English
rosewood reed organ heard by the colonist a century
ago. The church stands as a perfect example of carpenter gothic architecture, virtually unchanged since
1887. Cornelius Onderdonk, a talented cabinet maker,
architect, and builder superintended the construction.
The simple designed church was built of native virgin
timber.

Across Central Avenue is the clapboard building, Hughes
Public Library. When the large jack-knife key unbolts
the lock, the visitor is treated to a kaleidoscope of
colors and textures of thousands of book bindings reaching from the floor to a decorative wall papered ceiling.
As a tribute to the founder, publishers donated the
Library's books between 1880-1885. The single room is
simply furnished with two heavy walnut tables. Four modified Windsor cane-bottom chairs and ten captain chairs.
The room is replete with the atmosphere of its history.
A German Librarian, Edward Bertz, organized and classi-
fied the library, and started the book catalogue.

A commentary of the fate of Rugby can be read from the
library's circulation cards. Cards for novels were worn,
while cards for books on agriculture and technical subjects were unused. The library has remained available to
students and visitors since its beginning in 1882.

Strolling across the school yard from the library,
through the gate of the white picket fence the visitor
comes to the verandah of Kingstone Lisle, the house
built for Thomas Hughes. The English rural cottage,
built from a design by Cornelius Onderdonk, reveals the
finest decorative detail of any Rugby building. Down
Central Avenue to the west is Uffington House, the seven
gabled house of Madame Margaret Hughes. The apparently
unplanned building is the result of several small structures moved to the site and assembled to create an
intriguing house with gables of many variations and
slopes. Some of its English garden continues to flower
with plants in the gardener brought from Madame Hughes'

home. In the Spring, her primroses and lilies-of-the-valley bloom near a spacious lawn where croquet and tennis were played. In September, the lavender Michaelmas daisy blooms and resembled the native wild astor. Inside the verandah house is the drawing room where Madame Hughes held court, poured afternoon tea and welcomed homesick settlers with hospitality. Here she presided over the Women's Church Working Society. Emily Margaret, her young granddaughter, wrote from Uffington: ". . . its not at all dull, in fact, I am not likely to be nearly as dull here as I was in London."

The colony remains a remote Victorian monument to man's eternal struggle to improve society. Some of Rugby's swans did become geese. Hughes' "last castle in Spain" failed as a colony. But there is renewed hope for this settlement in the wilderness as it is restored for tourists, scholars, and the merely curious.

A MONTH IN THE COUNTRY

INTRODUCTION

*E*ventually I realized that I needed to live completely on one side of the Atlantic or the other. Having a home I loved on the coast of South Carolina was the enticement I needed to buy a home in Georgetown, D.C. The residence in Belgravia, London was sold. Finally, after years, I experienced my first summer in the United States, and I found that my body's thermostat had a British setting. I had difficulty coping with the heat and humidity.

I had visited Shotover House near Oxford many times as a guest of Sir John Miller. He invited me to come there and spend a part of each summer, utilizing one of the Victorian wings that had been added to this 1710 house during the late nineteenth century. I gladly accepted this invitation as Shotover Estate covered thousands of acres of land with the natural beauty of lakes and ponds, plus two man-made lakes between the house and the long vista toward a Gothic temple façade. Many think this to be one of the most breathtaking views in England. On the other side of Shotover House is an equally impressive view of William Kent Temple and Obelisk, marking the site of Queen Elizabeth I's visit in 1590. There were formal gardens, cutting gardens, an aviary, and picturesque paths in every direction.

Inside the seventy-room house the scene was equally impressive with three drawing rooms, a grand dining room, and a smaller dining room. Paintings, works of art, and furniture matched the overall grandeur. The house is thought to have been designed by William Kent just before he designed the temple and obelisk.

Shotover House proved to be a wonderful interlude from my life in South Carolina and Georgetown, D.C., during the summers. Here are some excerpts from my diary during one July spent at Shotover House.

Arrival—Oxfordshire
29 June—Oxfordshire

*A*rrived early yesterday, Sunday, at London's Heathrow Airport. After leaving the hot and humid early South Carolina summer, this morning damp and coolness were welcome in my bones. Can it be thirty years ago that I first came to this island? Can't be!

But still there is that identifying atmosphere—a particular smell, a characteristic sound. The whining of the buses, the clink-clank of the underground trains when they are above the ground, and the accented enunciation of the mysterious Englishmen and their foreign counterparts who have learned English from God-knows-who.

I understand these Englishmen even less than I did years ago when I first visited here. I understand their language—their English—but I find the meaning of what they say hidden. But this no longer bothers me, as my genetics are here. My DNA is here. It lies buried a thousand years ago on a knoll in Lancashire. No doubt, some of my English is hidden. It's subconsciously hidden.

Jet fatigue left me too tired to think much about genetics or hidden meanings. On the bus—Oxtube—traveling toward Oxford, I tried to read some of *The Times* and *The Mail* on Sunday. I thought, "if I could just stay awake, reading the newspapers might help the re-entry process. I might recapture the lingo." The usual roadwork's detour off A40 took the bus onto a country road and down into a slight valley where the fog thickened, reminding me of some Dickens scene from *Bleak House*, as the fog hung to everything. Finally, we went up an incline where it cleared leaving a mist hanging over the rolling hills, onto the yellow fields of rape blossoms. The mist, like some old ghost, clung to the hedgerow fences as they curved outward and onward.

Passing by a centuries-old church, its yard encased in tilted mossed tombstones, I was reminded of Thomas Gray's *Elegy Written in a Country Churchyard*. I thought, "wasn't there a curfew tolling the knell of parting day? Lowing herds winding o'er some lea? Plowmen doing something— plodding a weary way? Are they leaving the world? Are they leaving the world to darkness—and to me?" Half asleep, the words were not easy to recall. I dozed, then mentally slapped my face, woke up, and tried to recall other lines, lines less known. "The paths of glory lead but to the grave. But, can flattery soothe the dull cold ear of death?"

I arrived at Shotover House and was greeted at the door by Juliet, the Irish housekeeper. In the midmorning, Sir John was still asleep. So I claimed my familiar quarters in the north Victorian wing. I was welcomed by faded maroon-colored roses in the hall, by dusty dried hydrangeas on the landing of the staircase, but by fresh yellow roses in the bedroom. Without unpacking I fell into bed and tried to sleep, snuggled and content for the moment. Or was I? I counted sheep from Grey's lowing herd—"Far from the maddening crowd's ignoble strive," and "flowers born to blush unseen." Unseen. Unseen. Sweetness wasted on some desert air. Rain beat onto the lead windowsill. And now to sleep. Sleep, sleep, one of the few pleasures I have left.

Juliet rapped on the door and awakened me at 4:30 to come down for tea. For an instant I thought it was some character from Poe's *The Raven*, then I realized it was Juliet. I got up, and, somewhat awake, I gazed through the rain across the lake toward the Gothic temple façade in the distant. It appeared forlorn and like some hovering apparition. I staggered down the winding staircase toward a sitting room, the military room that Sir John had chosen for Sunday tea.

Sir John was asleep and slumped in his overstuffed, weary chair, its velvet long faded but still red. Even the flames of the fire seemed sleepy. He awakened transiently to greet me, then went back to sleep, clutching the latest *Horse and Hound* magazine. I tried to eat the toast, now cold, spread with Marmite, then some leftover birthday cake. This was low tea in Oxfordshire. Sir John awoke and asked how things were at the Duck's Nest, but before I could answer, he went back to sleep. So I ate the cold toast and Marmite and watched the afternoon rain.

Sleepy and rainy, that was England on my first day back.

REX'S CODA
30 June—Oxfordshire at Shotover House

Soon after arriving at Shotover House, John Hoban called from London informing me that our mutual friend, dear old Rex Britcher, had died.

On Thursday, the death notice arrived in the mail: "Dr. Rupert (Rex) Jesse Britcher, aged 88 died suddenly on 23rd June." What a dear friend, what a gentleman, what a raconteur. I never even knew his name was Rupert Jesse. I never knew he was eighty-eight—he was more like sixty-eight. What a collection of art works he had amassed, and yet he was still collecting. What a collection of friends he had! What a superb host who could prepare a supper in an instant. I am pleased he had his last birthday, just a year ago, in my garden when his little Italian friend Fredrico was visiting. So pleased that he had his last Christmas dinner in my home—his last three.

Sad that he did not write his memoirs. We had encouraged him to. He was too busy being a friend.

Yesterday I took an early bus into London and a taxi to the Brompton Oratory where A. B. awaited me outside the church. The long Black Death carriage arrived moments later, and we went inside to claim a seat. Four stout young men carried Rex's casket on their shoulders; a retinue of Roman Catholic clergy followed. The casket appeared terribly small, and I thought, "Rex can't possibly be in that." Faure's *Requiem* was sung as Rex had planned. He would have been pleased but possibly amused at the fuss.

I looked across the Oratory and noted the empty pew where he usually sat on the aisle. I was more than saddened and would have shed a tear—had I been capable. But then I recalled one of Rex's favorite sayings, "Dismiss it from your mind." I knew I would try.

While leaving the Oratory, petite Elma Dangerfield greeted me. Seventy-pound Elma had introduced Rex to me some fifteen years ago, at a Byron Society meeting. Elma was being escorted out of the sanctuary by equally petite, ninety-two pound Fredrico who had come to London from Milano for the funeral. Little Fredrico, not much larger than a Chianti cork, as a captured Italian soldier, had been Col. Dr. Britcher's valet and "batman" during World War II. The relationship was never ending as he was frequently in London, speaking practically no English, and continuing his "batman" services. On one occasion after several glasses of port, Rex had whispered some of these "batman" services, the old scoundrel!

We stood on the Oratory steps and watched the hearse leave toward Rex's birthplace in Kent to his final resting place near Canterbury. Elma and Fredrico's little heads could just be seen in the back of the imposing limousine following the hearse.

A. B. and I walked down Knightsbridge Road toward the V. & A. The splendid new silver exhibition was on display. Nearing the museum I stopped and asked A. B., "I wonder, why did I ever go to that Byron lecture fifteen years ago?" It must have been intended that I meet Rex.

EPILOGUE—REX
22 October—Pawleys Island

A. B. writes to South Carolina: "I went today to Rex's memorial service. It was in the Little Oratory, a very pretty chapel beautifully decorated with cupids next to the Oratory. Rex's great-nephew, dressed in a short-sleeved shirt, read the lesson. Mrs. McGarry, his niece, was dressed in bright red. Lady Torphicon was there dressed all in black. Patricia Ellison, in a big hat, was perfectly charming as usual. Elma Dangerfield was in royal purple and her little head was wrapped in a black turban. Fredrico was not there. I met the American lady who paid a million pounds for Rex's house. She is from Nebraska. Her husband's family lives in Warwickshire. She is tall and not well dressed. Is Nebraska in the Midwest?"

He enclosed an obituary dating from sometime in July. Rex's estate amounted to about £5,000,000 ($7,000,000). He left money to the Georgian-Irish Society, The Royal Opera, Distressed Gentlefolk, but most went to the niece who later was dressed in red at his memorial service.

I clearly remember that Rex would usually take the bus when he came to Belgravia to visit. I also remember that I never saw Rex without a necktie. Maybe Fredrico did.

ANOTHER LUNCHEON INVITATION FROM ARMIDA
2 July—Oxfordshire and Bath

A lady friend with the memorable name of Armida Colt (of the revolver family) is a nearby neighbor in London and in Georgetown, D.C. Armida showers me with invitations on both sides of the Atlantic— I accept an occasional one. Her invitations are always written on index cards in her own small calligraphy. On the reverse side there will be an amusing little picture she has cut from a magazine and glued on. She slips these invitations through the mail slot, never mailed. Armida oversees two homes on each side of the Atlantic. Armida is not on welfare. Armida is eighty-seven years old.

The latest invitation was to the thirtieth anniversary celebration and luncheon at the American Museum at Bath. She insisted that I come to London and go with her by train to Bath. She added, "We will be met and escorted. I am on their board." But I had a houseguest at Shotover and decided to drive to Bath, as it would be much closer.

We parked near Queen's Square, I took a taxi to the museum, and A. B. vanished toward the antique stores. Bath, that wonderful Georgian town, which I had not visited in years, is now being tarnished with carbuncles called modern architecture. It is surprising that the planning commission, strange English organizations, would allow it. But they have, as I observed on the way to the outskirts where the museum is located on a hill overlooking valleys to the east.

I arrived early—Armida was not in sight—and was greeted warmly by the staff before taking a walk through the galleries. After the second gallery I decided that it would be appropriate to give my Currier & Ives print, *Midnight Race on the Mississippi,* to the collection. I had new thoughts when, in the last gallery, this print hung above a Windsor chair. Might give them Alfred J. Miller's *Lost Greenhorn.* I wonder if they would know it is a fake?

Outside on the lawn the three hundred guests were arriving. I spied Armida holding court, beautifully dressed and wearing yellow sunshades. We drank Pimms and toasted Winston Churchill, who gave his first political speech in this house seventy-five years ago.

Armida and I claimed our seats at the imposing board table. As usual for me, on my left was a talkative New York lady who said she headed the Ukrainian-American Society. Across the table was another guest whose loud talking might have been heard at Land's End, so there was little conversation with Armida. I excused myself to go pee, and there in the WC next to me was Admiral Schultz, the American Ambassador. I was not surprised that his pee sounded like mine. I was not surprised that he seemed relieved. I was not surprised that two security men stood behind him.

Back with the ladies, a superb lunch was served. At the next table there was M. P. Winston Churchill, the grandson, and Mary Soames, the daughter. There was David Frost. And there was the peed American ambassador.

But for some reason I was restless, not interested. Had the noon-time Pimms dulled my senses? I wondered why everybody seemed to be having such a grand time and thought to myself, "Why have I come all the way to Bath to eat and listen to loud-talking, luncheon guests?" By now it was three o'clock. Just as Mary Soames got up to make her speech, I whispered to Armida, "My car is arriving." I silently disappeared, wondering if I would ever accept another luncheon invitation; wondering if I would donate the Alfred J. Miller; wondering how many more years Armida can continue this pace.

"GOD" IS DEAD!
3 July—Oxfordshire

I shouldn't read the morning newspapers. This morning I glanced at the second page of *The Times*, and there was a photograph of a hefty, shaven-headed smiling man who I immediately recognized as the actor Brian Glover. The first thought was that Brian was starring in another movie or play, but then I read and realized that he had just died of a brain tumor.

Brian and I first met in 1984 on a Tuesday morning. I know it was Tuesday because that was always the day at Christies, South Kensington, for the preview of Oriental works of art sales. We always seemed to be examining the same things. After several Tuesdays, we introduced ourselves, and I asked, "Are you an art dealer?" He answered in a broad Yorkshire accent, "Bloody nowt me!" I fumbled at a piece of jade, and asked, "Then what do you do?" Brian answered, "I work at the theatre over there on the bloody South Bank." Before I could even think that he might be a janitor, he said, "Come on over tonight, and I'll have a ticket waiting for you. I'm a crazy bloody king in *St. Joan*." I did go that evening, and it remains a highlight of my theatre-going in London.

A jolly giant of a man, always with a shaven head, Brian had started his early career as a wrestler in Yorkshire, following his father's path. He was asked to assist in the direction of a wrestling film scene. The director ended up giving him the part. The rest is history: from Sheffield to London to the BBC to Hollywood, for a film with John Wayne, then back to the National, where a memorable part was his portrayal of God in the mystery play, *The Passion.*

Brian and I became friends. Once I attended the Comedy Theatre where he was playing the part of the miller in the naughty *Canterbury Tales,* belching and farting throughout. I was seated on the aisle on the second row where he spotted me. He instantly ad-libbed and changed his lines to something like, "The bloody knave had stopped off in South-walk, resting on his way to Canterbury—from South Carolina—with narry a dime," all done in a rather perfect southern accent. His lines over, he belched again, left the stage, and came to sit in the aisle next to me. He told me about a little bargain painting he had purchased that morning, then whispered, "Let's have a bloody lager when this bloody thing is over." And we did.

When available, he would always accept an invitation to a party and nearly always stayed in character as a Yorkshireman. But I always introduced him as "God." And I think he liked that.

I can just see him up there now. Holding court. "Nowt bad, but where do I get this bloody head shaved?"

Keep me a warm seat, Brian.

NIGEL DEMPSTER, COLUMNIST OF ROYALTY
4 July—Oxfordshire

*Y*esterday morning I drove to the village of Wheatly, near Shotover House. I did the grocery shopping, then had a friendly chat with the butcher, Ian Hoban. This place also serves as the post office, so his wife sold me stamps as Ian cut thick pork chops. From there I walked down the pavement to the chemist and newsstand. I bought two London newspapers, the *Guardian* and the *Telegraph,* then returned to get a *Daily Mail.* I drove back to Shotover and sat in the garden to catch up on what was going on beyond this cocoon.

It was Thursday, the day Nigel Dempster's column was published in the *Daily Mail*. Realizing this, I was reminded of something. When I first arrived in London several years ago, I never read this newspaper, not until Dempster wrote an article pertaining to me. It was entitled "Is there a Doctor in the House?" Since he is a columnist who devotes his life to investigating and writing about anything remotely involving Royalty and its peripheral scene in London, I was fair game, since I lived as a permanent guest on the top floor of the Crown Equerry House of the Royal Mews. Since this article, I have occasionally read the *Daily Mail*, sometimes to see what he has written about my host, Sir John Miller, a proper Englishman and military figure whom he seems to dislike. The article written about me had not been intended to be complimentary, and I didn't appreciate it. But as time passed, I saw it more objectively. He had asked "Why is this American retired surgeon living at the best address in the world?" But this article didn't answer the question he posed, and it left his readers confused.

AMERICAN INDEPENDENCE DAY IN ENGLAND
5 July—Oxfordshire

*I*t's unusual and a bit sad to be in England and not to have a garden party at my residence on Independence Day. But here I am in Oxfordshire on July 4th at Shotover House having a supper party for six, which includes Sir John's houseguests and my two guests, Maj. and Mrs. John Mole, a completely civilized couple I met in Burma last year. Sir John's guests were former Ambassador Leslie Johnson and his wife, Jane—"diplomatic" people. John and I looked Leslie up in the Who's Who prior to drinks—Ambassador to the Czech Republic, Panama, and Zambia, or was it Tanzania? He was married three years to this younger Jane, who seemed in Who's Who, to have several names, some hyphenated.

Things were congenial during drinks in my sitting room. I gave Jane several strong, warm gin and tonics, managed conversation about the rain at Wimbledon, the new Court 1, and about the Summer Exhibition at the Royal Academy, which I had not seen but pretended I had. One needs only, in this company, to say, "It's not like it used to be. Too abstract." Leslie looked tired but managed to talk to Maj. Mole about his command of the Gurkhas in Burma. Sir John drank warm whiskey and water, then walked about impatiently stopping to gaze at the swans swimming near the Gothic temple façade. Anne Mole admired some of the broken Meissen on the mantle, drank another sherry, then complimented Sir John's relatively new portrait. I knew what his comment would be, "I appear too old, for heaven's sake. I look terribly old."

I had prepared the dinner for this Independence Day in England, and Juliet would serve it. She had put lots of Georgian silver and a fair sprinkling of American flags in the flower arrangement. We finally sat down at 9:15, and I placed Jane between the two Johns. My cold beet-clam-tomato soup had to be extended at the last minute—the soup bowls were too big. Then Jane was treated to barbecue pork—Robby's pork from South Carolina—Kentucky Wonder green beans, garlic mashed potatoes, and, of course, coleslaw. At dessert she devoured the pecan pie, ice cream, and then a champagne glass of sinful créme de cocoa. There seemed to be a good conversation all along—Prague, Panama, the proposed banning of fox hunting, the death of the eagle owl on the dome of St. Paul's, the hand-over of Hong Kong, and how awful Robin Cook looked at the ceremony.

Then we dispersed over the house—Leslie and Jane to separate bedrooms, of course. The Moles couldn't be separated. The next morning John and Anne had breakfast with me. They had detected something I hadn't. With good military antennas, it was clear to them that we were not grand enough for Jane. A major and a doctor could not relax her stiff upper lip. After breakfast we walked in the garden to the William Kent temple. Leslie and Jane were also in the garden. They pretended not to notice us.

Today John—wearing tweeds in July—and Anne were returning to their home near Windsor, and I saw them to their car. We chatted about his upcoming watercolor exhibition on Cork Street in London and about their proposed visit to South Carolina and about our meeting up in Rangoon later in the year.

I waved good-bye and returned toward the house, wondering why Jane had allowed Leslie to wear maroon polyester trousers at dinner last evening; wondering how Leslie ever became an ambassador.

IS THAT YOU IN THE MIRROR DR. MINTON?
6 July—Oxfordshire

Even in July the early mornings are cool and misty in Oxfordshire. It matched the fog in my mind at that hour. It was a good atmosphere to talk to myself while shaving. I looked in the mirror. "Hello. Good morning there. Is your cerebral cortex attached today? Are you on line? Is that really you in the mirror, Dr. Minton? Couldn't be you. Looks more like your father. But no, your hair is whiter. Oh, I do see a black one remaining. But goodness, it's growing out of your ear. Several out of your nose."

The monologue continued as the water warmed. "Oh, is that a new pigmented nevus on your temple? Could it even be a senile keratosis blackened by the Carolina sun? Get a few more scattered around that area and your temple will appear like Cassiopeia! Oh sir, on the other side there are some new ones. Looks like a little Pleiades is arranging itself. Beginning to look like the autumn night sky from your back verandah at the Duck's Nest. Didn't Dr. Sayler freeze all these off just last year?"

I dipped the Gillette, gave it a shaking, tapped it on the edge of the sink, and observed my naked chest. "Sir, your mammary glands and tits are appearing more and more like Dolly. Homeresque, aren't they? I can't even see your heart surgery scar. Too many white hairs. But why are those hairs less curly now? Must be missing your testosterone. Anything else missing?"

The shaving deed done, the monologue continued. "Oh Dr. Minton, dear knave, goest to fair scales and do weigh thyself. How much? Not fourteen stones! Is that not two centuries of pounds in thy colony? My boy, you are not the nimble Mercury who ran noble races in thy youth."

"Shall thy day start? Fair swans await thee."

ANOTHER DAY
7 July—Oxfordshire

I'm hopeless. Can't adjust the margins of this typewriter. Takes a morning to get a new ribbon in. Can never replace the erasure ribbon. Only with great difficulty can I get a cassette to play in the car radio. No ideas about making the microwave oven function as I want it to. Can't record a TV program on video. Too many buttons on the remote TV control. Too many buttons on the telephone. When I dial the cell phone it rings me back. It's a major puzzle to set the clock in the leased car. The rear window wiper won't turn off. Had to get assistance from a fellow customer to get the petrol lid open, and trust that I shall not have to open the hood. Otherwise, I do well with gadgets.

* * *

I drove Sir John's Rover into nearby Headington this morning. Sketchleys were able to clean my woven silk coat and trousers for ten pounds, about seventeen dollars. I tried to leave them on a side street where I had parked near a small dry cleaning establishment. The sour young man, appearing much like the labor leader Neil Kinnock, estimated about thirty-eight pounds for the job. That was sixty-five dollars.

I went to the stationery store for index cards, typewriter ribbon, and ink cartridges. They supplied neither, but the wonderful fruit and vegetable market next door compensated—fresh peaches, raspberries, melon, mangos, watercress, and other things I did not recognize. Went back to the Rover so pleased that I tried to get in on the wrong side.

* * *

Exactly when does one erase from the address book the name of a deceased friend? I've delayed three times erasing dear old Rex Britcher's name. I did the deed late yesterday afternoon. Each time I look through the *M* section I can see through the erased named of Jack Muir and

Lady Nina Martin; in the *A* section, Fred Akel; in *C*, Jeff Cousins; and I could go on. Perhaps I should erase better, but if I did I might forget these friends. I wonder if a friend or so will have the same problem in their *M* sections in the not too distant future. Perhaps some are ink writers in their tattered address books.

OF CRAZY DREAMS AND TESTOSTERONE
10 July—Oxfordshire

The article in the *Daily Telegraph* and yesterday's recollections apparently stimulated a crazy, scrambled dream last night. A silly dream. As a young man in Washington I seemed to have been driving a new Dodge convertible onto the frozen Potomac River in the middle of the night, having with me the Tennessee congressman's daughter, Jane Evins, whom I was dating during the Korean War years. We skidded across the frozen river, back and forth with hilarity, waving at other frolickers on the ice. Actually, now I do remember a similar incident that really happened on Sixteenth Street in front of The White House, but the ice was on the street, and not the Potomac. As a blooming "G-Man," I could get away with such nonsense.

The recollections of yesterday apparently reactivated a neuron synapse in the cerebral cortex dealing with the days in the F.B.I. and in the Korean War. This reminded me that the problem with being young is being a youth.

Yes, to be young again. No, not young, not necessarily young, but to have testosterone. Now I can only dream of it. I realize now and without question that the effect of the absence of testosterone breaks one of the most basic laws of the universe: "For every action there is an equal and opposite reaction." This translates into a kindred fact, "For every valley there is a peak." Not so if a man is without this juice of life. Now for me, there are no peaks, only the status quo and the valleys. What do I mean? Some simple daily examples: a Savigny-Les-Beaune, 1990, might as well be a Fetzer Sundial Chardonnay squeezed yesterday; "Regnava nel Silencio" from *Lucia* might as well be a Berg dissonant phrase from *Lulu*; a basketball move by Michael Jordan is as uninteresting as a joke by Bill Cosby; seared marinated scallops Brioche Croutes might as well be catfish and hushpuppies. Everything is the same. No spice remains.

Without the stimulus of testosterone, the catalyst and the fuel, a man is not really a part of the world. He is an observer of life, not in the ball game. He is on the bench, in the stands. As the game clock ticks, he waits. And he waits. But then I rationalize its sweet lemons, as I recall the proverb, "He also serves who only stands and waits." I am becoming awfully good at waiting, and sometimes I wonder just when that spring in the clock will break. When will it become too loose to make the clock tick?

SAMUEL FARRAND WADDINGTON, MY GREAT-GREAT-GREAT-GRANDFATHER
12 July

*A*lthough there is no dictionary here, Shotover House is blessed with an extensive library. During one of the many rainy days here I took the time to read in the 1899 *Dictionary of National Biography* about my direct ancestor, Samuel Waddington, known in his day as "Little Waddington." He was the grandfather of my maternal great-grandmother, born in 1759 in Walkeringham where his father was the vicar. He was one of eleven children, not unusual in the eighteenth century for a vicar.

Knowledge gained through family records and this extensive entry in the *Dictionary of National Biography* whetted my appetite to learn more about "Little Waddington." I called a French cousin, Claude Waddington, in Paris, who owned a book entitled *The Waddington Pedigree*. It was compiled during the nineteenth century by John Waddington of Waddington Old Hall in Lancashire. Claude, the grandnephew of the first Protestant French Prime Minister, William Henry Waddington, allowed me to borrow this book so that I might complete the picture of

"Little Waddington." Most Waddingtons in this book had one paragraph "Little Waddington" had six pages.

Immediately, I could see my own restless nature in this ancestor. Almost without exception Waddingtons had been educated at Trinity College in Cambridge, but this Waddington, as a late teenager, joined his older brothers William and Benjamin in New York, selling linen. This was New York during the American Revolution—the action was there. He stayed two years before going back across the Atlantic to attend a German university. Indeed, the rebel instinct was expressing itself early. He returned to England and married Sara Jarvis, then proceeded to sire ten children during spare time. But there seemed to be few spare moments in this man's life.

In the early nineteenth century in England, there was a liberal movement in vogue—Radicalism—which championed the cause of the labor classes, and Samuel Waddington was soon on board. Not known for sartorial splendor, he appeared in court not dressed as a radical. In December 1823, the *London Times* wrote, "The Lord Mayor's Court at Mansion House was hilariously astonished because a Radical appeared before it in a clean shirt." The following day this newspaper described his costume closely. "Not only was the Radical's shirt clean, his cravat was clean; it is implied that his face was clean. His hat was not a Radical's hat—the white hat which Henry Hunt had recently made a badge of political opinion. It was a high-crowned hat such as would become a swell of first water. His coat was cut in the first style of fashion." His business that day at Mansion House was to prosecute a beadle for assaulting two of his hands, according to the *Times*.

Although remaining a Radical, he made an effort to become respectable. While siring children he joined his brother William as a banker in Clapham, a suburb of London. But he had other irons on the fire, such as trading in hops. In 1798, he sensed that there would be a poor season for hop growing. He *walked* over the counties of Kent, Sussex, Herefordshire, and Worcestershire and bought up all futures in hops. His prediction was correct, and when he resold these hops he made a fortune. But this came at a price. Back at Mansion House he was convicted of gaining a monopoly on hops and served a six-month term in King's Bench Prison at Ilchester in Somerset.

Prison in England during this period was an adventure. Inmates were allowed to bring their own servants and lived a life of luxury—if they could afford it, and Samuel could. It happened that his rooms were directly above another well-known prisoner, Henry Hunt, the celebrated radical. Hunt, the popular, quarrelsome, stubborn politician had been a member of Parliament and had been imprisoned after a trial of doubtful legality. Hunt wrote his memoirs while in jail. He said, "As I lay in my bed, thinking of my new situation in which I was placed, I lamented that I had not overnight made some inquiries about Mr. Waddington, as I still felt anxious to become acquainted, when my hostess knocked on the door to say that Mr. Waddington sent his compliments and wished that I could favor him with my company for breakfast that morning. Having dressed myself, I was shown to his rooms above. Having read a great deal about him in the papers, I had formed myself an idea of Mr. Waddington, but instead of meeting a tall, stout, athletic person, I found him a short, thin gentleman, who approached me with the air of a foreigner . . ."

From that time onward they were like toast and Marmite, inseparable. Samuel stayed busy, and on a furlough conceived a son, John Jarvis, my direct ancestor. He finished a book, *The Critical Moment*, to add to others he had written on diverse subjects. He wrote not only in English but in German under the pen name Algernon Sudney. This book was called *The Metaphysical Man*. He also wrote a collection of letters entitled *Letters to the Greatest of Political Apostates*. Other publications included "An Appeal to British Hop Planters" published in the *Times*, written while in prison. He wrote a treatise on the Oriental Exposition advocating open trade with China and India. He frequently wrote under an English pen name, Esculapius, possibly trying to escape his reputation of being a radical.

He and Henry Hunt remained close friends, and he assisted in

Hunt's reelection as a member of Parliament. Neither ever gave up their fight for the working class—even while in prison Hunt wrote that each week they gave a ton of Irish potatoes to the prison's kitchen so that inmates would have enough food.

"Little Waddington" continued a busy life as a banker, businessman, politician, and author and finally died at seventy years of age in Brixton, a London suburb. He was buried in St. Marks, Newington.

I planned a trip to visit my ancestor's grave.

A HOT DOG "ALL THE WAY"
13 July

Sir John invited me down for dinner last evening. We ate stuffed Cornish hens, fennel, mashed parsnips, and marinated fresh plums in the loggia under the front, or is it the back, of the house facing the lake. Surprisingly, he was on time and we ate at 9 o'clock. Juliet's supper was still warm. He was chatty and in good form, and more so after a few glasses of Beaujolais.

We discussed in detail a dinner he was giving on Sunday evening at a restaurant at Bray on the Thames. I was surprised as I could only recall his going to a restaurant once—except when I took him to Robby's Place on the roadside at Pawleys. We sat at the counter, the only place to sit, and each ordered a hot dog. He didn't know how to respond when Robby asked, "all the way?" He didn't recognize what the iced tea was. He tasted it and drank no more.

After discussing the proposed menu at Bray, I inquired as to why he was not having the dinner for eight in his grand dining room here at Shotover—particularly since he had indicated the meal would cost the equivalent of seventeen hundred dollars. He answered, "Well, the queen and the duke live only sixteen minutes away from Bray, at Windsor Castle, much closer than Shotover. The Corgies wouldn't like such a long drive up here."

We ate dessert, had port and cheese, then went upstairs to watch a television special on our mutual friend, Monte Roberts, a Californian who breaks horses by talking to them.

I didn't ask what the Corgies would be fed. I didn't ask if the chef at Bray would be serving anything "all the way."

GARDENS, BEES, BIRDS
14 July—Oxfordshire

*B*ill and L. P. drove up, or is it down, from London yesterday morning. We immediately drove over to Waterperry Gardens where I had taken Bill last week; he's back to buy plants for his garden near Kew. I thought it unusual that he comes here to get plants with Kew next door. But Waterperry dates from 1088 A.D., and the plants have a long provenance, I suppose. Kew Gardens are only two hundred years old.

Bill and L. P. knew the names of most everything, but they quickly corrected each other if the slightest error was made. Statements like, "No, it is not a Do Dad. You must see that there are no bees on it. It is a Do Dad if its leaf has two ribs." The observations go on and on, and they smell everything: the petals and the leaves. The English walk very slowly through gardens, always with their hands behind their backs, so that they do not pose a threat to the plants, I suppose. And even on the warmest day, as yesterday was, they wear a Jersey—a sweater. Garden-goers have rosy cheeks, agreeable expressions, as if they had just had tea. It is particularly pleasing that few of the women have beige shoulder bags in tow. The mustached men all appear to be characters out of the World War II movie *Mrs. Miniver.* These garden-loving men, most in their seventies, were at Dunkirk or El Alemain but now so benign-looking that one cannot imagine that they would shoot anything. Yes, I find these strolling garden lovers as interesting as the flowers and plants.

We observed few honey bees around Waterperry. There seems to be an Asian virus that is taking its toll of the hives, and the beekeepers have to supply honey to their bees. There is an equal lack of butterflies, apparently due to the late spring, with some not yet arriving from the continent. An occasional white admiral glides in a wide circle and finally settles on a bramble blossom.

My guests seem unaware of the sounds from above—the birds; perhaps I am apt to look up more than down. A blackbird is stationed on a leafless limb of a tall chestnut tree singing its heart out, reminding me of Carolina as it mocks every bird in the county. It is unusual for this bird to sing in July for its mate has gone until next winter. In February, he will be singing in my London garden at 4 A.M. I ask Bill to find and to identify the singer. He looked, fumbled a bit, then went back to the flowers.

So we left the flowers, bees, birds, and garden lovers and came back to Shotover House. We spread a picnic overlooking the lake, the swans, the coots, and the mallards. The feast ended with peach schnapps drowning fresh peaches.

It was a civilized day.

THE NEWS
16 July—Oxfordshire

It was an early morning and "all at sea" again. The house was too quiet and prison-like. Juliet had not yet opened the heavy eighteenth-century wooden shutters. She had not released the imposing rods that keep the night vandals out. So I did the task that morning. Then I sat in the garden and drank coffee, freshly squeezed orange juice, and ate grapefruit soaked in grenadine. I watched forty-some rabbits between here and the Kent obelisk. Magpies mingled, rocks flew over, all on the alert for a fox, which could have sprang out at any instant. The papers had not been delivered yet, so I re-read yesterday's *Times* and *Telegraph*.

The news: "Versace murdered in gay slaying in Miami." "Age of consent for homosexuals lowered from eighteen to sixteen." "The synod meets and decides that gays may be ordained." "Oxford don charged in 'molesting' a boy." (The article didn't suggest that the boy probably instigated the "molestation" and thoroughly enjoyed it.) Lesbian golfer makes hole-in-one at Gay Pride Golf Tournament. But then there was an article about more killings in Belfast and the latest killings in Cambodia, with a photograph of a bridge I had crossed in Siem Reap last year. But without the daily "gay" articles and killings, there would possibly be nothing to print or perhaps nothing of interest to some of the British readers. Photographically, there seems to be a rage for photographs of young people with their mouths stretched open. Perhaps they want us to see the silver rings clipped into their tongues. It's a strange world!

Enough. So I watched the rabbits and rooks. The butler, with the memorable name, Barry Brookbank, came out dressed in a blue pin-striped suit. We talked about the weather and Versace. He seemed more than pleased that I would prepare dinner for Sir John and a guest this evening. He would be able to watch *Coronation Street* on the telly, I suppose.

Then I went upstairs to PP—that is, peaches and pills, the telephone, and the morning post. I even took my little white "Lorry," that is *Lorazepam*. At least a half one. "Lorry" doesn't replace my prostate, nor the testosterone, but it helps to bring me in from the sea.

G-MAN
17 July—Oxfordshire

$\mathcal{I}$ recalled F.B.I. experiences of many years ago because of an article I read in yesterday's *Daily Telegraph* concerning the fiftieth anniversary of Sen. McCarthy's committee objective to rid the government of Communists—The Great Communist Chase, Washington 1948. I was eighteen years old and worked for the Bureau.

Professor Constance Hill's English literature classes were not interrupted. But I remember it well—I remember the day it was interrupted. I remember that knock on her classroom door. Some terrified classmate was trying to read from Milton's *Paradise Lost*, or was it Keats? Prof. Hill dropped her book on the desk and answered the intrusion. She called me out. Slamming the door, she left me alone with a tall imposing man wearing a brown brimmed hat. He flashed a card, then I recognized this intruder was a "G-Man"—an agent of the F.B.I. I quickly learned that I was not wanted for some crime. I was wanted for something else. How he found me I was to learn later.

That knock on Prof. Hill's door changed a life.

As a result of that knock on the door, which interrupted Milton, I became a part of that chase. Two months later, as an eighteen year old, I walked through those great brass doors of the Justice Department on Pennsylvania Avenue in Washington. Along with two other uneasy recruits, we were directed to the office of Mr. Hoover, who had a policy of meeting every new F.B.I. employee on the day of arrival. We sat in his reception room, shaking. This bull-dog-of-a-man called us into his inner sanctum and gave us a short lecture while seemingly jotting some notes beside our names. Mr. Hoover never smiled.

As late teenagers, scared and with little formal education, we had no choice concerning our assignment—to the Identification Division, perhaps where we could do least harm if we were not the "right stuff." Here they could size us up for assignments more interesting. So, in the beginning, I was designated to a fifth floor classroom where whorls, loops, arches, and tented arches greeted me—fingerprints! I was disappointed, then realized that a G-Man had to start somewhere.

As I remember, I spent considerable time gazing at peasants and tourists down on Pennsylvania Avenue, then toward the gleaming dome of our capitol, wondering if I really wanted to be a G-Man. There was enough learning and testing until our class was carted off to the F.B.I. Identification Building, down south of the Smithsonian. In this maze, in these acres of tombstone grey file cabinets, I alighted in the arch section—to be more specific, the "Garden of Tented Arches," as we called it. Not ordinary arches but tented—on the right index finger. I thought in the beginning, "I shall catch every Communist in America, if he has a tented arch on his right index finger."

Although this section housed the fingerprints of known criminals—wanted men, subversives, and Communists. Within a few days, the job became mundane. Occasionally, there was a productive hour, when one got to march—very slowly—up to the supervisor's desk and plonk down a "hit," thinking "G-Men, I shall join you soon."

But there was a curious diversion within the catacombs of tented arches. I was frequently the host for fellow employees who had nothing more to do than come to this section to see the prints and photograph of the actor, Robert Mitchum, who was in his heyday just then. Mitchum's tented arch in that right index finger placed him squarely on file row M666, my domain. Picked up in Birmingham for pot, his expression on the mug shot was as expected—cocky and arrogant. But we seemed to have struck up a friendship since that face was flipped across several times a day.

There were mundane days with Mitchum and friends, but the excitement of nightlife awaited. Could it be fifty years ago that I first saw those bright lights—the bright lights of "K" Street, of Fouteenth and Sixteenth Streets, of Mass. Avenue and Georgetown? Lights dim by today's standards were bright to a young country Tennessean.

But alas, it had to end. Paradoxically, it ended because of another Communist theme, this one not in Washington but in North Korea. G-Men and knowledge of tented arches were not needed in Korea, so I went back to school, feeling that I would prefer to fight Koreans with an education rather than an M-1 rifle.

Four years later, with a degree and commission, Washington was clearly in sight, and I was back there again where I found the lights even brighter. As an Army Signal Officer, and with the Korean War angrily on, the authorities somewhere thought that if I had learned about fingerprints and had that top secret clearance from the FBI, why not have a go at cryptoanalysis. They taught me a bit about the Russian language —military stuff—a bit about code deciphering, and I did have a go at it. Then suddenly, the Army Signal Corps loaned me to The National Security Agency. So I found myself at the secretive Arlington Hall, a former girls prep school, just across the Potomac River in Virginia. There, I didn't have anything as exciting as Robert Mitchum, but I was given a more tantalizing assignment than someone's tented arch—this one Russian. Handed to me, as I admired my new lieutenant's bars, was a coded message system originating in Odessa. This didn't seem too terribly complicated until I learned that the Russian cryptographer was using a captured German system with messages scrambled into numbers, which was sent by radio to Kwangchow, where the Chinese recoded it into Korean. But enough about that!

Rather suddenly, the war was over and a release from the military was offered. I said, "Yes!" and drove the new Dodge to enroll in premedical studies. Somewhere along the line I had decided that if it was possible to decipher fingerprints, if it was possible to decipher scrambled Russian codes, that it might be possible to decipher the human body. How wrong I was! I didn't know what I was getting myself into.

Anyhow, thank you *Daily Telegraph*. Thank you for reminding me. Thank you for bringing on the recollections of fifty years ago. Now it might be interesting if I could remember what happened last week, what happened only yesterday.

NIGEL DEMPSTER
18 July—Oxfordshire

Sitting in the garden yesterday, I flipped through the pages of the *Daily Mail* to Dempster's column, and to my surprise, after all this time, his computer had pulled me up again. The article involved the resignation of Maj. Ian Kelly, who was on a ten-year contract "to run the Queen's Royal Mews." According to Dempster, he was forced to give up the job as a cost-cutting part of the palace's budget. He added that the queen is a notoriously "parsimonious employer."

Dempster went on, "The mews, the elegant Nash quadrangle behind the palace, houses the sovereign's ceremonial carriages, including the historic golden State Coach and the 1902 State Landau (used to carry the Prince and Princess of Wales after their wedding)."

Then he added, in the last paragraph, "Staff changes at the Royal Mews are rare. Former Crown Equerry Sir John Miller left in 1987, just months after I revealed that the confirmed bachelor had been allowing a retired American surgeon to use his grace-and-favor house."

I felt an obligation to reply to Dempster, and I sent him a fax complimenting his computer on being able to "pull me up" after all these years. Then I reminded him that his previous article concerning the "retired American surgeon" had nothing to do with Sir John Miller's retirement, since he was already three years overdue to retire at the time the article was published. I added that two months after this article appeared the queen had given Sir John a second knighthood, the highest. I then suggested that this article might have inspired the queen to bestow the second knighthood.

I told Dempster that I was visiting Sir John at his stately home for the month of July, away from the heat of South Carolina. Then, with full southern hospitality, I invited him to come over to Pawleys Island. I invited him to come and have a sunset mint julep on the verandah. I told him that the fish were jumping and the cotton was high. I told him that it was the perfect time to come to South Carolina.

* * *

Today, I read in the *Telegraph* that Mr. Dempster had been arrested on the M25 highway for driving under the influence while on his way home to Surrey. I promptly sent him another fax and suggested that rather than a mint julep we would drink cranberry juice in South Carolina. I told Mr. Dempster that we would munch toasted pecans. I didn't tell him about Deputy Sheriff Claude Roundtree.

I LOVE ENGLISH WOMEN
19 July

I just love English women! Like Benjamin Franklin, I would have married one, had there been a chance.

They don't answer for their husbands when you ask them a question. When they're called and asked to dinner, she is apt to say, "That would be lovely, but I'll have to ask Ian. He'll be in late this evening, and I'll call you at nine in the morning." At the end of the conversation her voice goes up into a sweet little "Cheerio!" At the car door, they don't stand like a duchess with a broken arm. These English women slowly reach for the door, and will open it themselves, if necessary.

On a cold and rainy day, they hum a little tune while putting on their wellies and raincoat. Then they use civilized umbrellas, as big as a tent, and offer to keep you dry.

Back at home, they're great with nursing babies, changing diapers and spit-ups. And when the children are older, these English ladies impart the exact amount of discipline to keep order in the house. There's no fight about the "telly," and the children look at it sparingly. Even their pets fit into this scheme and know their place, except for the independent cat who hides in some bookcase.

In a whiff, these English women will serve you with a meal if you happen to drop in at that hour. It might be ground meat and mash and green peas or brussel sprouts, but after a glass of Bristol cream sherry, it'll be appetizing. Give them a little time and they will prepare Yorkshire pudding with the batter made just right. After this, there will be some ingenious dessert—"puddings" as the English call it—maybe a treacle tart. But if you want pie for dessert, you'll have to bring it, for they don't know about the pecan variety.

WELLY LADY
20 July—Oxfordshire

Sir John's nearly royal sister, Mrs. Barksdale, arrived from Badminton yesterday afternoon at teatime. I knew she was here because her poodleish dog bounded up the stairs, into my kitchen, and emptied the garbage can onto the floor. Mrs. Barksdale is into horses. Mrs. Barksdale is into hunting. Mrs. Barksdale rides to the hounds every day. She is into horses as her little dog is into my garbage can. She rides sidesaddle. Mrs. Barksdale is eighty-six.

Mrs. Barksdale and I got on quite well in the past. Generally, I had to ignore the fact that she could converse on only one subject—hunting and conversation about those who were equally addicted. Generally, we got on well until one afternoon at tea I forgot and called a hound a *dog*, and that was it. Mrs. Barksdale nearly blew a gasket.

Mrs. Barksdale arrived at Shotover House to be escorted by her brother to Bray in Berkshire for supper with Her Majesty and the Duke. For some reason this makes me think of an occasion at the Royal Mews where I lived between 1984 and 1987. In mid-December 1984, I attended the Royal Mews annual Christmas party which was held in the open enclosure of the mews and in the Royal Stables. I shall not forget that evening—a Yankee in King Arthur's Court. I had a roasted chestnut then went into the stables to talk to Arthur Showell, the head coachman, who had invited me for drinks after the party. In the semi-darkness I noted Sir John standing over in the corner in front of the stall of the well-known ceremonial horse, Burmese. He was talking with a hired-help-appearing woman wearing a moss green scarf, a somber green well-worn long coat, and wellies. He seemed to whisper something to the Welly Lady, then motioned for me to come over. With some hesitation I excused myself from Arthur and joined the two. He mumbled something to me, which could not be heard because of the carol singing outside. In retrospect, the whisper to the Welly Lady was that I was an American eye doctor, and the mumble to me was an introduction to her. This date was two or three days after the Union Carbide explosion in India, an accident causing untold eye burns to many Indians. Welly Lady plied me with questions about these eye problems and their consequences. While listening to *Silent Night* and trying to answer ophthalmic questions, I suddenly discovered that the Welly Lady was actually the queen. I am not sure how the conversation ended. I do remember the drinks afterward at Arthur's.

The next spring S. J. invited me to join him and his brother-in-law to go to Saville Gardens in Windsor Park to admire the early flowers. His relative, Gen. Sir Alex Stanier, was an authority on daffodils. By chance, there in the gardens, was the Welly Lady doing a walk-about. We all met up and had a chat. She said, "Oh, you are the oculist. Welcome back to England."

Obviously S. J. had never told her that I occupied the top floor of her Crown Equerry House. She only learned that three years later when

Nigel Dempster wrote one of his gossip columns for the *Daily Mail* entitled "Is There A Doctor In The House?" Three weeks after the article she gave S. J. his second knighthood, the highest, the George. Even now she doesn't know that he lost that medal in the palace gardens while walking back to the mews after the ceremony. That is one of our secrets.

Anyhow, early that evening, the former crown equerry, S. J. came into my sitting room. He held an open can of dog food. "Would you please give 'Twigs' four tablespoons of this at 8:30. She's in the billiard room." S. J. was dressed formally. He was wearing a ribbon with a rather large gold medal dangling from it. It appeared to be the K.C.V.O.—the Knight Commander One, but I don't know; it might have been the George.

Barry, the batman, waited at the door then escorted him toward his purple Rover. Mrs. Barksdale was in the back seat. She stared straight ahead. Mrs. Barksdale was wearing her tiara. They were off to Berkshire to have dinner with the Welly Lady. I was alone with "Twigs."

OF BEETHOVEN, MOZART, AND ELGAR
21 July—Oxfordshire

I watched the telly last night—a snowy picture of the opening of the Proms at Royal Albert Hall from London, which compares to the interest in America of watching the Super Bowl, a necessity. The performance was Beethoven's *Missa Solemnis*, which was beautifully performed by the London Philharmonic and their choir. It's sad that its composer, poor deaf Beethoven, never heard it performed. He was not even in St. Petersburg on the occasion of the first performance of this noble work.

As for me, these days, I have gravitated to listening to some of the more melodic masses, sometimes referred to as "operatic sweet sins," such as Puccini's Mass in G written when he was only twenty-one. It's interesting that so many themes and melodies of later operas are apparent in this early work, this *Messa de Gloria*. The inspiration and melodies of Gounod's *St. Cecilia*, and Mozart's *Coronation* mass linger in my head. I have seen to it that they have been performed on "my" festival—also Schubert's Mass in G. These masses have a certain sensual quality, as does Faure's *Messa Brevis*. But most great music has a sensual quality, none more than Dvorak cello works and Bruch's cello concerto, *Kol Negri*.

I find Elgar's *Variations* of particular interest—variations in which he describes some of his friends musically. But it would be more than interesting if an Elgar composed "variations" on some of my friends. What would M. P. sound like? And B. C. I suspect that Homer would be a jig. And Daphne? Dick? None of these would be dissonant!

Have just seen a rerun of "The Three Tenors" in concert at the World Cup in Italy. I am now determined to put three young tenors together for such a program and call them "The Three Young Tenors," led by Jason Balla of the Chicago Lyric Opera, with two of his young buddies. The premier of this must be this spring at some venue at Pawleys Island. Might add the Met coloratura Jennifer Welch for some real spice—three tenors and a soprano?

Let there be music![1]

SWANS, BUTTERFLIES, AND FOXES
22 July—Oxfordshire

I took pieces of bread to the swans on the lake this afternoon after the rain, which had not bothered them. Like a cat, these swans will swim the other way if you want them—if you do not want them, they will follow you. They are particularly into bread, any old bread. The six swans here are from a refuge for injured swans—all have broken wings except the Pa Pa. Apparently he has a proclivity for ladies with broken appendages. The queen owns half the swans in England, so I wonder if this arrogant male realizes that he is half-owned by the Welly Lady.

There were more butterflies about today. In the cutting garden this morning there was a great blue—wonderful markings it has, with

---

[1.] This took place at Pawleys later in the year, and in Chicago later.

iridescence like the grackles in South Carolina. It is difficult to think that a few days ago it was a "worm" parasite feeding off the juices of a grub's larva in a den where it had been deposited as an egg.

At coffee time this morning, I observed a fox chasing a young rabbit into its hole by the great oak out in front. In an instant the fox was back with the baby. It squealed but only gently; the fox ran with its breakfast across the old grass tennis court and vanished into the undergrowth.

I turned in the other direction and noted a great blue heron plucking a goldfish from the pond.

Life seems to be all about eating, surviving, and procreating.

THE MAN WHO CAME TO LUNCH
23 July—Oxfordshire

We ate supper in the loggia by the lake. S. J. updated me about the anniversary dinner with Her Majesty and the Duke, which he had hosted at a riverside restaurant near Bray. The only hitch, other than the bill, was the fact that Juliet had failed to send a clutch of Georgian candlesticks along for the table setting. At the last minute a taxi had to be hired for the forty-mile trip. He might have to sell a picture to pay for the taxi—and for the meal.

After an appropriate amount of port, he spoke of Prince Charles. He talked candidly of Camilla Parker-Bowles. He expressed a rare opinion about the Royal Family, saying that Charles should not be king if he marries this common and unattractive woman. We both agreed that Her Majesty would live to be 110. Charles would be eighty-five then. Even William would not be young—and probably into some royal disgrace. We wondered what Camilla would look like at eighty-three. He mentioned Maj. Parker-Bowles. I reminded him that I was at the Crown Equerry House for lunch on the day we first met, when Maj. Parker-Bowles was the only other invited guest. I admitted that I had accepted this invitation with some fear—fear of going to have lunch with the equerry to the queen as a guest of someone I did not know. He chuckled when I told him that I had worn a blue pin striped suit, then noted that the stripes on Maj. Parker-Bowles were farther apart than mine, more "county." (A sign I grew to recognize.)

He became more serious, took a sip of port and talked of Maj. Parker-Bowles, and why he was at lunch that day. It seemed that the major was being considered as his replacement as the Crown Equerry. He said, "That invitation was only a formality. He would not get the position because both the queen and I knew that Charles was having an affair with Camilla, the major's wife. And both were married. We knew that the major should not have the position because of this. We were also aware of Princess Diana's emotional problems and could foresee no solution. We realized that the family was in for some public disgrace when they learned this. The queen was already philosophic about the whole matter, including the potential problem with Sarah."

We finished dinner then walked down by the lake to watch the full moon. We sat on a rose arbor bench and all was quiet. Then Sir John said, "Yes, I remember. I remember that I invited you to lunch and you stayed four years."

THE DAY I RECEIVED A GOO GOO
24 July—Oxfordshire

A. B. and I went to Oxford last Sunday to visit the Ashmolian Museum. Great problems parking. We had to walk several blocks on High Street toward the museum, stumbling over clusters and gaggles of sixteen-year-old LEPs. This is a term I have applied to them, meaning Levis, Earrings, and Pimples. It could be BLEPs if we add the backpack. They have been carted off to Oxford to see history, but they stand in front of the McDonald's and talk. They yell, usually in some foreign language.

Of course, the museum was closed. We drove back home and drank champagne. It was A. B.'s birthday.

On Tuesday Patricia Ellison came from London for lunch, bringing with her a houseguest, Rosemary Ingram. Rosemary is a delightful "southern lady" who is doing research at the British Museum Library on children's literature, of course. We walked around the gardens; Rosemary fed the swans a piece of stale crumpet, then we sat down for lunch in the loggia. Afterwards we walked up to the William Kent temple then back by the fishponds. Before leaving, Patricia gave me a small cake she had baked. Rosemary presented me with a box of Goo Goos. She thanked me graciously and said that this was her first visit to a castle. Rosemary is from Nashville. Rosemary teaches children's literature at Belmont University. Rosemary didn't drink the Bristol cream sherry before lunch. Rosemary is a Baptist.

Speaking of Nashville—yesterday's post brought a large manila envelope postmarked from this Tennessee capitol city. It was from the writer, critic, and socializer, John Bridges, a friend of many years. I have greatly admired his "Keeping Up" articles published weekly in the *Nashville Scene*, and he periodically sends a bundle of these pearls cast before Nashvillians. John is originally from Slap Out, Alabama, and his best writing is based on his childhood memories of growing up in the rural south—in a fundamentalist Church of Christ-Bible-Belt-Straight-Family. I can identify with this writing, and at night I ration these to myself like rare Belgian chocolates. Last night I read "Out of Respect," based on his memories of a passing funeral procession in Alabama. What a sensitive and astute young boy! What insight and how well expressed. I breathed the dust made by the procession.

John enclosed a short note: "I hear that you have had surgery." Yesterday afternoon I wrote him a five-sentence letter. "Thanks for the goody poke which arrived in the Royal Mail. Yes, John, I have had surgery. When I was ten years old I took the Tennessee Central to Cookeville. Dr. Terry cut my tonsils out. I got to chew Aspergum that evening."

Years ago John, a Vanderbilt University graduate, ventured to New York to make his fortune. That stay lasted two weeks. He would have been a big hit as a writer and southern socializer, but he could not tolerate the glare of the bright lights in the Big Apple. Too much Slap Out in that boy's veins!

MESSIAH?
25 July—Oxfordshire

*T*he newspapers are still spilling ink concerning the murder of Versace. As I have been thinking, some writers such as the columnist of the *Times*, Boris Johnson, are now asking, "Was he the great Messiah, who liberated women,"—so that they might wear outfits pinned together with large silver safety pins rather than being sewn? They paid five thousand pounds to be liberated with safety pins and leather—frocks which showed their tits and see-through, which showed other things. The silly masses who admired such things might have a different opinion if they had attended a genito-urinary clinic at John Gaston Hospital in Memphis on a blistering July day before the clinic was air-conditioned. Their admiration might not have been the same had they delivered a baby from a breach position when everything split apart and had to be sewed back together. Silver safety pins would not have solved this problem.

No, he was not the Messiah; he was not a genius; he was not a great artist. Getting tanned in Miami Beach and taking the waters at Como, he probably never even saw these frocks until he flew to Paris to peck Liz Hurley on the cheek and tell her how smashing she looked in one of his pinned little numbers. If I could crack this code of what is beauty, I might have ecstasy while looking at some gold threads and silver pins. But in the meantime I shall be a Philistine and an intellectual snob.

Diana, Princess of Wales, announced that she was "devastated" over his death. I had rather be a Philistine.

TO SLEEP—PER CHANCE TO DREAM
26 July—Oxfordshire

*Y*esterday, dear old Dennis Bardens, the eighty-two-year-old author, came up from London by bus to spend the day and evening. I am always pleased when he comes as he can keep the conversation going with Sir John while I relax and think of other things; my computer tuned into the conversation if need be—on automatic pilot.

I drove down and met him at the Oxfordlink bus stop; he was already wound up and ready to "cast his pearls." Juliet's afternoon tea awaited us. Sir John awaited us. Barry awaited us to take Dennis's bag upstairs to the green room. A pleasing feeling of someone else in the seventy-room house awaited us. Small talk and gossip awaited us— Camilla Parker-Bowles, Princess Diana. (Around Sir John, we never say Princess Di.) But of course Sir John was soon sound asleep, and we might call her whatever and his eyes would barely open. Dennis disappeared for a rest. I went out and fed the broken-wing swans, then sat alone in the rose arbor by the lake.

Dinner conversation centered around the proposed banning of fox hunting. My brain went onto automatic pilot, but then finally I changed the conversation to eighty-two-year-old Dennis's poetry quoting. He quoted Tennyson and Gray. It was now about eleven o'clock and the port was taking its toll; there was stillness. The candles dripped as tears and I mentioned Hamlet. Very slowly Dennis quoted this Shakespeare:

To sleep—per chance to dream; ay, there's the rub!
For in that sleep of death, what dreams may come
When we have shuffled off this mortal coil,
Must give us pause.
What is he whose grief
Bears such an emphasis? . . .
I will fight with him upon this theme
Until my eyelids will no longer wag
The undiscover'd country, from those whose bourn
No traveller returns—puzzles the will,
And makes us rather bear those ills we have
Than fly to others that we know not of?
I will win for him if I can; if not, I will gain
Nothing but my shame and the odd hits.

Candle wax dripped onto the linen, the ports a drop. Dennis was now quiet and looked sleepily at me. Sir John was asleep.

SUNSET AND EVENING STAR
28 July—Oxfordshire

I just returned from Winkfield in Berkshire. It was a pleasing barbecue lunch and afternoon with John and Anne Mole. After lunch in the garden, we drove to Ruscombe and had a boat ride on the Thames. John was the pilot. He pointed out a great crested grebe; it dived and was gone. We drank limeade and soda in the angled sunlight of the late afternoon; Henley was in the distance. River cottages and their gardens greeted us, and a lone fisherman waved.

Anne and Sir John sat in the stern. S. J. did not wear a tie.

S. J. and I returned to Shotover, and he insisted that we go up to the ponds to feed the carp and goldfish.

Juliet had a picnic supper waiting. We drove up to the picnic folly, drank Pouilly Fumé and watched the sunset, and the rooks going to roost. We were joined by the curious cows. I am not sure what we had for supper, except for a Scotch egg. Yes, there was cold chicken and green grapes.

After supper we watched Venus as it set. "Sunset and evening star. And one last call for thee. May there be no wailing at the bar, when I set out to sea." S. J. said that it was recited at his father's funeral. He requoted it—twice, I think.

As we walked toward the car, I pointed out the constellation, Cassiopeia, and the nearby position of our neighboring galaxy, Andromeda. S. J. said, "Yes it's always just above Shotover Hill."

Historical records, in fact, do indicate that in 1590, Queen Elizabeth I and her Oxford supporters met on this exact spot on Shotover Hill, the county's highest elevation. So I suppose the galaxy Andromeda came to rest then.

It is a notable site. Geographically, Shotover Hill is the highest point between the west coast of England and due eastward to the Ural Mountains—a fact.

MY CABINET OF CURIOSITIES
30 July—Oxfordshire

𝒯he long summer days at Shotover House had finally given me a chance to get to the task of assembling a catalogue of my artistic belongings, my "collection"—the "Cabinet of Curiosities," as the sixteenth-century Italians referred to it. This assortment of things contains nothing of great significance, only things of interest to an occasional friends and me.

Actually, the insurance company in Washington put me to this task, insisting with yet another letter that it must be done, along with photographs of most every object and picture. The work was revealing, as well as a pleasure. For years there had been in the filing cabinet an "Art Info" section into which documents, receipts, and clippings were thrown, then never disturbed, until they crossed the Atlantic with me.

To delve into this archive was like finding a lost treasure. There were 1937 letters from the University of Chicago archaeologist Professor Banks, who excavated a Babylonian site. He smuggled out two four thousand-year-old clay tablets, which he sold to the president of the high school from which I graduated. In 1970, they were given to me by this schoolmaster, along with Dr. Banks's translation. Forgetting that I had a translation, I took it to the British Museum where a Dr. Finkel rather quickly read it like the morning newspaper. He typed the text of these Ur of the Chaldees cornerstone tablets and gave it to me. Now the two translations—"I, Lipit-Ishtar, the humble shepherd of Nippur, etc."—can be compared. The tablets are virtually identical except that Banks dated them 2160 B.C. and Finkel dated them 1934–1924 B.C. (Now I have the pleasure of finding someone who might appreciate some four thousand-year-old mud.)

These clay tablets are not the only objects of curiosity. The two hundred or so eighteenth-century plaster impressions by the Italian Antonio Picler and their cobalt blue glass counterparts had to be dealt with and placed in the catalogue correctly. Trying to translate the marks on Chinese porcelain was another matter—are they "good" marks and of the period or are they nineteenth-century marks of an older period?

The eighteenth-century Kano—a Tosa School four-panel screen—
depicts tethered falcons as only a sensitive Japanese artist might paint. It
has had few owners, or keepers, in these 250 years. It is a museum piece
that has been seen by few of my friends. I added a new category: Travel
Art. It contains Paleka lacquered boxes—Russian—numbered, dated,
and signed; ancient bronze pots from Borneo; glazed terracotta brandy
flasks from nineteenth-century Hungary; a six-armed little bronze of a
Nepalese god.

Spelling all these objects was a problem since among Shotover's
thousands of books there was no dictionary. I had to guess at such
words as *applique*, or is it *aplique*? How do you spell *candelabra*? Is cloi-
sonné correct; it looks right? Then the Chinese dynasties were another
problem. Does one use the old or the new spelling? But I can't spell
either. Is it *Kangxhi* or *Kanhxi*? It's pronounced "Kang She," I think.
That eighteenth-century Chinese dynasty was also a puzzle. Chi'en Lung
or Chien' Lung? There's an apostrophe somewhere. I talked to myself,
wrote it out several times, and, still confused, occasionally I simply cata-
logued things as Ming—I could spell it and it sounded good.

It is a pleasure to know that an object has been broken and repaired.
Japanese and American collectors snarl at this, but I feel that these
repaired things are my special friends. After all, if I discarded all friends
who have a flaw or have been repaired, then there would be no remaining friends. So why should I expect a two hundred-year-old piece of
porcelain to be perfect?

The cataloguing process made me aware of just how many things
have been given to me by friends. I looked through the sheets and saw
friends, friends, friends. I trust that I have been as generous. The question remains, what will eventually happen to these things in this "Cabinet of Curiosities?" I trust that someone will keep the Kano falcons out
of too much sunlight. I hope that someone will dust off the impressions,
then take a magnifying glass and admire the work of that eighteenth-
century Italian artist. I hope that someone will occasionally fondle some
of the little pieces of jade—"Boy with Waterweed" would appreciate

that. I trust that someone will enjoy some of this collection as much as I have.

I just hope that they can get the spelling right.

AFTER THE BALL IS OVER
29 July—Oxfordshire

*Y*esterday was calm. Yesterday was a communication day—FAX, letter, and telephone. Yesterday was a social communication day. As the clock ticked, I had nothing else to do. Armida can come to dinner next week. Yan-Kit So can also. A. B and B. C. cannot. Princess Rama of Nepal can. Andrew Skarbek can. His girlfriend cannot. Cannot reach Daphne. Kay had gone to Persia. Lillie wants to bring a gentleman friend. S. J. was not invited and neither was Bill. Chelsea Pensioner Voller can come. Rosita canceled other plans to attend. Charlie is on duty at the palace. Sir Eduard is going to Scotland with the queen. Patricia will come early. And now I'm confused.

I must have two dinner parties.

I must have three dinner parties.

I must stop the ticking clock.

I must go into a cocoon.

After the dinner parties.

After the party is over.

After the ball is over.

PART THREE

Going Places

ARCHAEOLOGY

I was fortunate to be involved in four archaeological ventures. They were ventures because I was untrained for archaeology and wasn't certain about what I was getting involved in, but I took the chance and in general they were rewarding experiences. The archaeological trips involved a Copper Age site on Mallorca, a Minoan pottery project at Knossos on Crete, the excavation of Roman baths under the Piazza della Signoria in Florence, Italy, and Knossos again for the excavation of the Roman city adjacent to the Minoan city. These experiences gave me a slight knowledge of archaeology so that now, when I read articles in the *Archives of Archaeology*, I have some insight into the subject matter.

Mallorca

*I*n November, approaching the holiday season in London, it became obvious that I would not have guests during Christmas, so I found a place in the sun, as a paying volunteer for an archaeological excavation. This was with the American expatriate archaeologist, William Waldren, who for many years had been working on a Copper Age (2300 B.C.–1400 B.C.) and Beaker Culture (2000 B.C.–1200 B.C.) site near the Mallorcan village of Vallemosa in the Sierras of the Balearic Islands, off the coast of Spain.

Bill Waldren was a congenial and relaxed expatriate who went to Mallorca as an easel painter after World War II. At that time, Mallorca was the place to be for a person who had an interest in archaeology, for this island was honeycombed with caves that sheltered the early humans who migrated here from the Iberian peninsula some thirty thousand years ago. It was here perhaps that man first came out of caves to develop community settlements. Waldren was among the first to explore some of these caves. By accident, he made some rather astounding discoveries in one particular vertical cave—discoveries of human remains, artifacts, and bones of the now extinct myotragus deer, which set back the time table for human habitation in the Mediterranean thousands of years. Waldren was awarded a National Geographic grant and, for twenty-five years he continued his work there.

By the time I met Bill Waldren and came to Mallorca as a volunteer, it was years too late for any great discoveries in his excavations, but it would be a start. I arrived in Mallorca in December, during a rainy period, and lived in the dampness of the Deya Archaeological Research Center with other volunteers from the United States and England.

The first day consisted of finding how adept we were with pencil drawing of bones and artifacts—something certainly not planned on. The next day we were driven in a van to the excavation site through a monsoon-like storm. But instead of some exciting cave or Copper Age site, we were deposited at a more peripheral location to start the excavation of a Punic War settlement. Instead of a small trowel, I was handed gloves, a heavy pick, a crow bar, and a shovel. I had a choice of instruments. Instead of Mediterranean sunshine, I was in rain, wind, and fog. The weather seemed no obstacle to our "excavation" through clay and mud, through giant boulders placed here 2000 years ago. We went back to this site each morning. Even on Christmas morning the rain did not hinder the volunteers' digging.

Waldren seemed to have forgotten that it was Christmas until I stole away and cut down a cedar tree. I brought it back and deposited it on top of a pile of boulders. Without decoration it seemed appropriate for the occasion. During this period of digging at the Ferrandell-Oleza Prehistoric Settlement—FOPS—I came across only three shards of Punic pottery and a scapula of a small animal. I shall not forget that day because I rushed to Waldren, who was sitting on top of a heap of boulders. I yelled, "Myotragus, myotragus." He casually glanced at it expressionlessly, lit another cigarette, and said nothing. This was a typical reaction of Bill Waldren.

After days of rain and many Punic boulders, I developed influenza and took the next available flight back to London—with my scapula bone from a "Myotragus." On the flight back, I reflected on those days on Mallorca. I said to myself, "The world of archaeology has not seen the last of me." I knew that I could do better than Deya, Mallorca.

The Dump of Pyrgos

$\mathcal{S}$everal months later I received an introduction to Dr. Gerald Cadogan, chariman of the Bristish School of Athens. I had read his articles on archaeology in London's *Financial Times*. I took a train to Banbury in Oxfordshire and was met at the station. His American wife, Lucy, had prepared lunch and a pleasant afternoon followed. I learned that he had been on the archaeology faculty of the University of Cinncinati and that we had mutual friends. A few days later he called to invite me to join his small team who would be researching ancient pottery he had excavated at Pyrgos, a Minoan site off the southern coast of Crete. The excavated material had been brought to Knossos across the island. He reminded me that this would be during the wintertime, in February, and that Crete could be frigid. But he said that we would be living at the Taverina, the guesthouse of Sir Arthur Evans's Villa Ariadne. With this enticement, I accepted his invitation.

Knossos! Knossos! I thought of King Minos and the Minoan civilization of four thousand years ago. I thought of Heinreich Schliemann and Sir Arthur Evans, the noted archealogist. Knossos—I had been ther in 1969 as a tourist. I never imagined that I would return in any other capacity.

Usually when I fly to the Mediterranean there are complications—airline strikes or canceled flights or fog and a diverted plane. The god Icarus and his father have cast a curse on me.

On the flight to Herakleion, on the island of Crete, near Knossos, we flew for awhile above the city and then diverted to Athens. It was too windy to land on Crete, according to the pilot's announcement. I called Dr. Cadogan from Athens and told him of the revised time of arrival: 4:30 A.M. He was good natured and reminded me that, unlike Icarus, I wouldn't have to worry about the sun melting my wings at that hour.

Finally arriving in Herakleion, I handed the sleepy taxi driver a piece of paper with the address of my destination, thinking the impressive location would open his eyes. The note read in English and Greek: "Sir Arthur Evans' Villa Ariadne, Knossos." The Zorba just looked at the address and yawned. By 8:00 A.M. I was in the dining area of the Taverina having a breakfast of feta cheese, a hard roll, an apple, and black Greek coffee with Dr. Cadogan and his staff of five archealogists and conservators, including Dr. Vrony Hanky, the noted authority on ancient pottery whom I had met in Egypt on a Nile cruise. She had arranged my introduction to Dr. Cadogan.

I carried my duffel bag up to a Spartan room of the Taverina through a bare hallway on the second floor. I stood in the stark room viewing Fortesta across the valley. My cubicle contained an army cot, a chair, and a table with a goose neck lamp. These frugal surroundings seemed to exude a scholarly British energy conducive to study. Suddenly, I felt at home in the cool dampness. The overcast sky seemed appropriate.

That morning Vrony introduced me to the compound. We walked through the Taverina's bleak garden up the lane of pine trees toward Sir Arthur Evans's Villa Ariadne nestled in a thicket of olive and eucalyptus trees. Evans had built this structure eighty years ago while excavating at Knossos and had named the villa after the daughter of Minos, who gave Theseus the thread which enabled him to find his way out of the labyrinth after killing the Minotaur. Many years later it had served as the German headquarters for the occupation of Crete, and now it served the same purpose for the British School of Athens.

Facing the villa was the headless figure of the Roman sculpture of Hadrian, unearthed years ago from the vineyard back of the villa. But the building was locked, and it seemed dead and forsaken at this time of the year.

I was not in Knossos to sightsee, and I was reminded of this as

Vrony and I walked along a path through dead weeds toward Evans's laboratory building on a knoll overlooking the Minoan Palace. A tethered mongrel barked and rose on its hind legs realizing that I didn't belong here. It was chained to an Ionic capitol. We walked between other marble fragments, pieces of fluted columns, sections of capitols, and a pediment from the Roman temple that once stood near here. Like scattered litter, these artifacts lay near the entrance to Evans's laboratory as a testimony of a splendid past with nobody paying attention except the herds of goats, who nibbled on the weeds that surrounded these remains.

Vrony unlocked and slid open the great metal door, disarmed the alarm, unlocked another door, and we entered. On tables there were heaping mounds of Minoan pottery sherds, the world's largest jigsaw puzzle. A four-thousand-year-old puzzle composed of thin curving carnellian-colored pottery sherds decorated with red lined and faded black and white decorative motifs. There were tables of molded rims, thicker bases, and handled of lugs of innumerable shapes. This building would be my domain for the next several weeks.

It was an amazing sight. We sat down, and Vrony explained that I was being confronted with five hundred years of the town dump of Pygros, an early and middle Minoan settlement located across the island on the southern coast of Crete. This town dump, dating from 1800 B.C., had been brought to Knossos.

Vrony instructed me that my job would be very simple. She said, "A monkey could do it. You may select your table and then join pieces together which belong to each other, and finally reconstruct a pot." I stood looking out over these tables and thought, "A pot! Ten thousand pots, if enough monkeys like me could be recruited." Ten thousand Minoan pots or twenty thousand pots, if Dr. Cadogan could get enough monkeys in the next few years.

But I took a philosophical attitude, and later that morning, with great enthusiasm, I attacked a table of sherds. For two hours I attacked a pile, first from the top then from one side and then the other. Relentlessly I attacked, but more than an hour later I still had not found two pieces joined correctly. I developed a headache, a backache, and became dizzy, so I retreated outside and sat on a fluted Roman column in the weeds and gazed down across the valley toward Evans's reconstructed Palace of King Minos.

The goats stood chewing, looking at me. Feeling better I returned, sliding open that heavy door to start siege against another heap of sherds from Pyrgos's dump. It proved as stubborn and unyielding as the first. But I remained determined because I knew that I had come to Knossos to help on the advancement of man's knowledge of the past. I was in Crete to monkey with little pots, pots from the dump of Pyrgos.

During lunch Dr. Cadogan's staff were encouraging about this venture, convincing me that I would have several pots by the end of the day, so I returned to my battle with yet another table of sherds.

Standing over a table I though of Homer's writing in Odyssey, lines composed to his wife:

> Out in the dark blue sea there lies a land, washed by waves on every side,
> densely peopled and boasting ninety cities. . . . One of the ninety towns
> in a great city called Knossos and there, for nine years, King Minos ruled.

And then I thought of the mythology of Ariadne and her ball of twine fashioned for Theseus' escape from the Minotaur and from the labyrinth. Daydreaming, I could see the king's daughter and the Athenian youth sailing up and out of the palace flying westward. It was gradually dawning on me that I was standing in one of the archaeology's most sacred places, for through the heavy doors to the right and out of sight for the Pyrgos dump, there were shelves of thousands of objects unearthed by Sir Arthur Evans from King Minos' palace, lying as proof that Knossos was the site of Europe's earliest known civilization. But not only here, for some of the other ninety cities mentioned by Homer could still be visited on this island—or their encrusted remains, such as Phaestos, Mallia, and Zakro. Each in their heyday living in a peaceful society without walls or fortifications. These people had advanced writing systems, commmerce with Egypt and the Hittites, elegant city life, festivals and sports. But it all came to a sudden tragic halt when in about 1450 B.C. something, still unexplained, happened to end this society of bejeweled ladies, of sportsmen leaping and charging bulls, and, of course, of gods escaping with their lovers. This was Knossos in some yesteryear, and this was the same Knossos where I stood today.

During the next few days I managed to make some progress. As I learned to recognize subtle differences in the red and black decorative motifs, the tables of sherds gradually surrendered. An occasional pot was reconstructed, some with complex red designs of interlocking circles and guioche motifs, others with encircling black lines. Vrony, with her vast experience of studying ancient pottery, could readily identify the pot's age and its use. But I remained the monkey who had a headache each evening.

One Saturday, Dr. Cadogan drove us to Crete's southern coast to visit Pyrgos, where I developed an appreciation for this regional Minoan city and its dump. On that cold windy and overcast day we parked by the silted Myrtos River bed, then walked up a steep hill toward Pyrgos on one of Europe's oldest paved streets.

Halfway up, we sat and rested, we could hear sheep bells in the distance moving up the hill. The sound got louder, and then we were in the midst of the herd that formed and reformed, jostled and bleared, as it wound around the path embracing us. Finally the shepherd came by, paid no attention, and walked on, trudging on the same path that shepherds had troded for thousands of years.

We walked on to the summit high above the Mediterranean and looked out southward toward Egypt—a land which had traded with Pyrgos for a thousand years before a Pharaoh called Ramases existed. We stood on the site of a three-story country house, which Cadogan and his team had excavated ten years earlier. It had gypsum floors and staricases, with a courtyard paved in purple limestone. The house had been destroyed by a mysterious fire millenniums ago. At the rear of the remains I was shown a communal tomb with an ossuary pit which had housed great jars of bones surrounded by stacked skulls.

But I was awaiting our visit to the town dump with eager anticipation, and once I was there I experienced no disappointment. Pyrgos's dump had at one time been a 2000 B.C. water cistern situated on the rim of a hillside. Its twenty tons of wtaer had caused the collapse of one of its walls, and unrepaired, it became a despository of broken pots, pans, and dishes. Its innards had been carted off to Knossos where, for ten years, they had awaited a "monkey" like me.

We stood by the empty ancient cistern looking northward toward the bleak and arid Myrtos valley. The sun poked out between wet clouds, and Dr. Cadogan took my camera and photographed me standing by my dump with a double rainbow in the background.

Later that Saturday afternoon we walked back down the hill and into the village of Lentas, where we went to a *kentron*, a little eating place and a meeting place for townsmen. We drank—or I should say nipped—*tsikoushia*, a strong local brandy while Dr. Cadogan greeted locals who had worked for him on the excavation. He spoke to them in Greek. We were attended by a lean and rangy young woman with rook-black hair, a long bony face, and high cheek bones. She went about her work without expression. She seemed to doubt what a half drunk local was singing—*Samiotissa*, a love song promising roses and golden sails.

Back in Knossos, and after days and days of attack and counterattack with the dump sherds, Dr. Cadogan learned that I had served during the Korean conflict as a cryptanalyst of Russian and Chinese messages. I was promoted to the task of examining, describing, drawing, and indexing potter's marks which had been etched in handles and rims of certain pots and jugs. Much of this was done in the library of the Taverina where I worked alone, surrounded by memorabilia of Sir Arthur Evans—a photograph of his wife and of Evans as a young man holding an excavated vase. There were archaeology books, a replica of a soapstone head of a Minoan bull, a basket of sherds, and pieces of broken sculpture. I spent hours studying the *Journal of Hellenistic Studies*, Ventria's Documents in Mycenaean Greek, and Englishman John Pendlebury's *Archaeology of Crete*. I took an occasional break to look at names and entries in an eighty-year-old guest book for the villa.

Finally, I wrote an essay, now in the archives of the villa, on several hundred potters' marks, which were examined and analyzed. Some forty distinct marks were identified: a stylized double ax, an inverted *F*, an *M* with three peaks and so on. These were then compared to marks recorded at Mallia's excavations and were found to be similar. I concluded that these etched marks corresponded to old Linear A Minoan script, which had never been translated nor deciphered.

During this stay at Knossos I had the opportunity to visit the Minoan cities of Phaistos and Zakros, which helped prepare me for a considerable time spent in the Museum of Archaeology at Herakleion. In this museum I was greeted by its director, Dr. Charalampos Kritzas, who I had met at dinner at the villa. I had lengthy discussions with this eminent Greek scholar about the depiction of athletes in Minoan art. We discussed the possibility of an article on the subject for the upcoming Olympic Games in Barcelona, an idea that neither followed up on.

I had to leave Knossos two weeks early because I broke a tooth while chewing on the emaciated carcass of a Cretan rabbit at the local *kentron*. I tried to fly from Herakleion to London, but as the Greek gods would have, the winds swept across Crete too fiercely, so I took a bus westward to Kastelli where the wind had calmed and I got a flight to Athens. Like Icarus, I flew away—but not too near the sun—determined to return to the Mediterranean archaeology scene. Dr. Cadogan had invited me to join his team in the spring for a Bronze Age excavation at Paphos on the southern coast of Cyprus.

Roman Baths under Piazza Della Signoria

*D*uring a sojourn in Italy I attended the British Institute of Florence on Via Tornabuoni. Each morning I walked there from my residence on Donatello Piazza, down by the Duomo, and along Via Cavoir.

This route took me by the Piazza della Signoria, most of which was fenced as it was being excavated. This activity was watched by Michelango's David, Cellini's Perseus, Giambologna's equestrian statue of Cosima, and also hoards of tourists. Four or six people deep leaned against the fence and poked their noses through, peering past the scaffolding at the thirty archaeologists who were digging through a cross section of history from the Bronze Age to Medieval times. Periodically there were signs attached to the fence in Italian, English, French, German and of course, Japanese:

> Piazza della Signoria; one of the most beautiful squares in the world is alas, in a state of upheaval. We know that you will be disappointed and we would like to offer our apologies.
>
> —The Minister of Cultural Affairs

The truth is that Florence almost did not let the archaeologists excavate the site. The ruins were discovered in 1974, but the city fathers argued for a decade over courses of action. Finally, the archeologists won the debate and were allotted three years in which to complete the excavation.

I appeared in Florence toward the end of this three year period and met one of the project's archaeologists, Judith Bardgei, at the Café Revoir nearby. Judith was an American married to a Florentine and the only fluent English-speaking member of the team. I told Judith that I had become more interested in this excavation than in the British Institute, where I was supposes to be studying the Tuscan Renaissance. I told her that I had been involved in two previous archeology projects, adding that I had retired from a career as an eye surgeon and knew how to handle delicate things. Then I went right to the point, asking her to give me an introduction to Dr. Giuliano De Marinis and act as a translator. I wanted to go to work with those archaeologists. She agreed, and set a time for the meeting for late the next morning.

I went home and called Dr. Cadogan, who sent over night a letter of recommendation. With this letter in hand I went to the project office, realizing that I had nothing to lose if his reaction was negative. I found Dr. De Marinis to be a most congenial man, who looked more like a farmer than a doctor of archaeology, one of Italy's foremost classic scholars. Judith translated, and occasionally seemed to add remarks of her own. Finally, he asked me when I might be available to start, and we agreed that I would go back to London and return in ten days. I would

Excavation site, Pyrgos, Crete

Above: Excavation site, Knossos, Crete

Below: With Kosti Voskakis at excavation
site on Crete

Nepal with Annapurna Mountains in the background

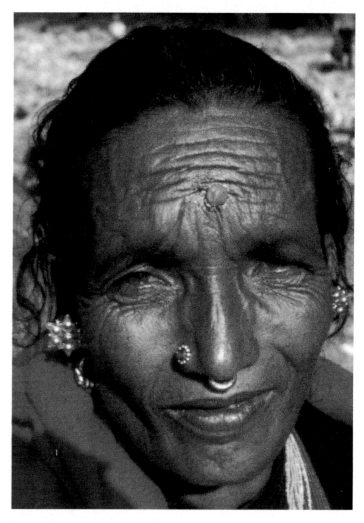

Nani, the porter in Nepal

Left: How to carry fourteen bricks in Prome, Burma

Below: A fisherman, duck farm, and footbridge, Pokokku, Burma

A young monk with his alms bowl, Rangoon, Burma

At the pyramids of Egypt

Our "felluca" on the Nile

Above: Squatting in his designer t-shirt, Tut appeared confident as he announced boiled eggs and chilled macaroni for
breakfast.

Below: A sphinx, Kmo Ombro, Egypt

At Angkor Wat, Cambodia

Left: A Blue-footed Boobie chick, Galapagos Islands

Below: Rafting the Tatshenshini River in Alaska

Above: With Sir Harold Acton at Villa La Pietra, Florence, Italy

Top left: In Leipzig with Renate Lehman, soprano

Bottom left: Conductor John Nelson at the door of the Gewandhaus Orchestra auditorium in Leipzig

Above: Elyas, a ship's mate on the "Kemal Reis"

Top right: On the "Kemal Reis,"
Turkish coast

Bottom right: With my friends on
a schooner (a "gulet") on
the coast of Turkey

Posing for the painting of a portrait at my home
in Washington

be assigned to Judith's team. As we left his office she said, "Nothing ventured, nothing gained. I'll see you in ten days."

That afternoon I leased a residence with a balcony and a view toward the Arno on the fifth floor of a fourteenth-century building on the Piazza Santa Croce. Farewells were said to my friends and teachers at the British Institute, and the next morning I boarded a train for Pisa and the flight back to London.

A week later I returned to Florence and moved in. I got accustomed to walking up the five flights of steps and discovered the farmers market in the neighborhood and two pleasing little trattarias around the corner. I even learned to read—at least getting the idea of what the writer was saying—the morning newspaper. There must have been a writer assigned to the excavation because almost every morning there was some kind of derogatory article about the project—clearly the Florentines were not amused by this digging and would be pleased when they could return to their piazza.

At last the day arrived when I would start to work in the deepest recesses of Piazza della Signoria, probably as Judith's slave. I walked down the 186 steps and stopped in the March drizzle to unfold a tangled umbrella. I stood for a moment on the Piazza Santa Croce to admire the stark Gothic church to my left, then I turned right, past the little *trattoria* to walk the short distance to Piazza della Signoria, a route which would become familiar and routine—Palazza Cocchi at the end of the square, then up narrow Bargo de Greci with its Palazzo Perugi, the green grocer, the fishmonger and the cheese shop. At Via Leoni a Sophia Loren look-alike allowed her Dalmatian to pee on a green and red fire hydrant. An old lady dressed in black swept water from the worn steps of Palazzo Vecchio. At the top of Bargo de Greci on the edge of caged Piazza della Signoria, Ammonetti's *Neptune* stood looking toward the piazza, his head crowned with a soaked pigeon and his wet buttocks protruding toward the temporary archaeological office. In front of Ammonetti's splashing fountain I opened the gray galvanized gate, and as if I belonged, I walked into the piazza. To my left Michelangelo's

towering *David* stood holding his smooth flat rock, then to the right the
equestrian statue of Cosima. I looked on.

I walked on but the umbrella had obstructed my view, and I proceeded rather directly into the obstacle. It was no ordinary "lion in the
path," for I looked up and was confronted by Donatello's *Judith*, holding the severed head of tyrant victim, Holofernes. I almost said "*Prego*,"
then quickly realized that Judith was innocently static for five hundred
years and had her bronze sword drawn.

Near the excavation site I looked down to avoid and walk around
what seemed to be a dark puddle of water, but the murky circle was not
liquid. It was the porphyry disc marking the spot where the heretic
Savonarola and his two companions were burned at the stake during the
fifteenth century. At the ladder that led down into the excavation stood
another Judith—Judith Bardgei, the archaeologist. Judith awaited her
slave. This Judith's bronze sword was a chrome trowel. With her crusted
glove she presented me with this trowel and a boar bristle brush. Judith
didn't stop to pass the time of the day. She ushered me by several wheel-
barrowed workmen and two young woman who were busy dissecting a
medieval skeleton, then to another ladder that extended even deeper
into the excavation. She invited me down into an area with a marble
floor twenty feet below pavement level. She took a seat on the floor, lit a
cigarette, and instructed me to go to work exposing more of the mosaic
in this Roman thermal bath.

Judith was not only pleased that I was doing her work, she was
delighted to have a chance to speak English, a language which she spoke
with no uncertain Bronx accent. That she might tower over me, she
brought in a ladder, placed it above me, and sat there to give me instructions—and to smoke. From this perch she explained that we were in
baths and that the adjoining room was the frigidarium in which there
was something like a cold swimming pool where the togaless visiting
officials bathed before proceeding to this room and a warmer bath.
Judith, practicing her English, continued her oral dissertation as I
stopped for a rest to look up at Cellini's Perseus. The eyes of Medusa

seemed to be gazing directly at me, daring me to take a rest, a pleasing distraction for any neophyte archaeologist. Judith continued her history lesson, saying that Caracella had commissioned these baths, and when finished he came to Florence in about 200 A.D. for a visit, not expecting that his empress would commit suicide and that he would be murdered a few months later.

By late morning the rain had ceased and sunlight was bathing the green plastic roof of the piazza compound. We climbed out of the frigidarium and walked through a wave of Japanese tourists on our way for a cappuccino interlude over on the west side of the piazza. It was no ordinary coffee house, for this was the fashionable Café Revoir, the only remaining great coffee house in the city. In spite of our damp and mud-stained archaeology garb, we were welcomed and given the best table. Enzio Innocenti, the project superintendent, joined us.

Enzio, a towering Italian of about sixty, doubled as a gentleman farmer a few miles out in Tuscany. Judith translated as he answered my questions about the finds down in the excavation. Enzio told me of the obsidian tools and pottery from Sardinia that had been unearthed. They were evidence that beneath this Renaissance Square there existed a Bronze Age settlement that pre-dated the Medicis and Ghibellines by four thousand years and a Greek and Etruscan settlement dating a thousand years before Savonarola met his doom here. Enzio explained that the excavation had been fruitful, and that now historians and archaeologist had to rethink the antiquity of old Florence. It has become obvious that even Renaissance Florentines were newcomers.

After several cups of cappuccino, we all returned to the excavation site—to the zoo and Judith's frigidarium. Before climbing down the ladder, I inquired about the unusual enclosure adjacent to the latrine. She told me that this was one of the rare features of this excavation—a fabric-dying facility utilizing waste and urea that flowed from the latrine to fix the pigment of dyes to textiles. But Judith was impatient to get me back to work, so we did not linger.

During the next month, morning after morning, I proceeded on this ritual walk up Bargo de Greci. I became familiar with the shopkeepers, and we talked in sign language as they tried to practice their English. The old lady in black, who was always there sweeping the steps of the Palazzo Vecchio, finally stopped to smile and try to speak to me.

Judith declared that I had become an expert at "refining" and left me alone with the task of brushing and cleaning for the final drawings and photography. A television crew came down to the bowels of the excavation, and that evening I saw myself on television, working as if I had been an archaeologist for years. They didn't realize that I was an American who had been taken in off the streets.

It was saddening to see sand and pebbles dumped into each section as it was finished, covering the work of the past three years. It reminded me of graveyard burial scenes. During the final week of the excavation, Judith and I were assigned to the last segment where the pavement stones had just been removed, a space in front of the doorway of the Café Revoir from which we were separated by the fence and sidewalk. Judith and I had the opportunity to start the excavation downward, as most of the archaeology team had gone to a new excavation site north of Florence. Only a few inches down my trowel hit an object that at first I thought was a strip of ivory but with careful examination, it proved to be the small rib of a child. For the next three days I excavated this little skeleton and one beside it. These bones were placed in a cardboard box and deposited in the artifact office. (I learned that through carbon dating it was determined these were probably the bones of Black Death victims from the fourteenth century.)

It was now late on the last Friday, and the excavation had to end. A dump truck loaded with sand was parked nearby and as we gathered our tools. The driver started the engine of the truck, almost dumping sand on us. We walked out from the excavation site and into the temporary office area where Enzio sat at his desk. I washed Judith's trowel until it shone like new, and then I washed the boar bristle brushes. I said goodbye to Enzio as he presented me with a half gallon of olive oil from his farm. Judith walked me to the gate. I hugged her and said goodbye, then walked out toward Bargo de Greci but stopped to look back. She was standing under the Donatello statue, lighting another cigarette.

Roman City at Knossos

*W*hen Roman legions defeated Crete two thousand years ago, the Minoan City of Knossos was already in ruins. But the Roman authorities knew that there had been a thriving city and palace here, so they proceeded to build their town in the vicinity, very near the Minoan Palace of 1750 B.C.

Sir Arthur Evans, the legendary English archaeologist, started his excavation of this palace a hundred years ago, and during this time had the Villa Aridene constructed as his Cretan home, with living quarters for some of the excavation staff. On a slope above, it faced the excavation site. Being a scholar interested only in the very ancient world, he paid little attention when his vineyard keeper unearthed a cuirassed statue of the Emperor Hadrian in his backyard. He simply moved it to the front lawn of the villa and didn't even speak of it. Neither was he impressed when the same vineyard keeper dug into a Roman mosaic floor while planting new grapevines. This mosaic floor proved to be one of the best in the ancient world, but Evans never bothered to go take a look. His interest was in the Minoan Palace, and this field behind the Villa Aridene lay virtually untouched until 1993.

I received an invitation to join an excavation called Knossos 2000, although seven years would pass before this date was reached—a date which would coincide with the one hundredth anniversary of Sir Arthur Evans starting his excavation of the Minoan Palace site. This invitation was extended by two archeologists of the British School of Athens, Dr. Kenneth Wardle and Dr. Gerald Cadogan. I would be the only non-archaeologist or student of the classics, a fact that bothered me. But I had been on three other archaeological ventures, had learned the lingo, and knew to stay quiet and do the job assigned to me. So I accepted and arrived at Knossos three days before the excavation was to start to photograph the site for the archives.

Within Sir Arthur Evans' compound I was housed in the Villa Aridene, a step upward from the noisy Taverina where I had stayed previously. It was midsummer, and the villa was musty; it reeked with a
peculiar unventilated odor, and the ghost of Evans seemed everywhere.

The unkept garden appeared thirsty. Dusty olive trees served as trel-
lises for pink bougainvillea, and a pomegranate here and there had put
out a parched flower. A turkey and her brood scratched at the feet of
Hadrian's statue. Fragments of antique statuary were strewn about
amidst struggling hollyhocks. Behind the villa, toward the slope to be
excavated, the pines had shed a dark slippery carpet of needles like some
worn Persian rug. The hillside appeared parched and bleached with rem-
nant of old grapevines gasping for water. Fringes of eucalyptus edged
toward the gradual hills and the village of Fortesa in the distance.

The following morning, with the photography finished, I sat in the
garden courtyard of the Taverna down the dusty lane toward the road
leading to Herakleion. Across the road and the ravine many gaunt-from-
travel tourists worked their way through the labyrinth of the reconstructed palace, as I had done thirty years ago. Dr. Cadogan joined me,
and we sat quietly in this garden. Morning glories swarmed over the wall
by the road, cicadas screeched mistily from the pine trees above, a distant dog barked, and the scent of jasmine filled the late morning air.

Members of the twenty-person team were arriving and greeting each
other with the enthusiasm reserved for youth. He introduced me to
Natasha and Cloe, young classicists from Athens, Laurence from Birmingham University, Hillary from Cambridge, and Steve and Sheilagh,
young archeology professors from Christ Church in Oxford. Each had
their own expertise, including chronology, pottery, plants and seeds,
metals, animal bones, and marble. They were all here to excavate but
were available for consultation in their own fields of interest. We drank
tea while Dr. Cadogan held court, answering questions and filling in
gaps for the new arrivals. He explained that there had been years of
negotiation and fund-raising to start this excavation, with the Greek
archaeological bureaucracy being the most difficult hurdle to overcome.
On the long picnic-like table Dr. Cadogan spread maps of the area to be

excavated, showing below-surface densities revealed by ground-sounding radar, indicating walls and pavement. The site would not be attacked blindly.

Late that afternoon, all twenty archaeologists had arrived, and we regathered under the pines along with eight Cretan workmen, all of whom had had extensive experience in excavations. At the last minute as we gathered, Sara Paton, a London friend arrived. She was a Roman architecture and mosaic expert who would be excavating the floor of villa Dionysus nearby, but would also be available for consultations. Sara was the person responsible for my being a part of this team. While Dr. Cadogan talked about plans for the excavation, Sara translated this into Greek.

After his talk, we all adjourned down the hill and into the village to the *kentron* while we drank Greek beer and listened to music by a local yelping rock band. I sat between Natasha and Cloe, who eventually proved to be among my best friends on this team. Cloe, a seed specialist, had lived near my residence in London prior to going to Greece to assist with excavation of the Athens forum. She was a trooper who knew her way around. Natasha, the quiet one, was an animal bone specialist who could tell the difference between the femur and ulna of a prehistoric rabbit. Greek beer flowed abundantly as Nikon-laden Japanese tourists giggled at us before boarding their bus.

Dr. Cadogan came to our table and warned us that we would be digging at 7 A.M. the following day. He told me that I could dig at whichever site I chose. He unrolled the sounding map, and after a consultation with Cloe, I selected a site that seemed to offer a possibility—a dense, shallow surface about three feet under ground.

On Monday morning after breakfast, I reintroduced myself to the young archaeology professor from Birmingham University, Laurence Crowley, who was in charge of this section. He had an assistant, a Greek workman, Kosti Voskakis, who proved to have the instinct for archaeology, sometimes found in shrewd and perceptive country people, but who spoke no English. After surveying and setting the corded lines north and south, we started the excavation with fifty meters separating us from the other two groups. We alternated rolling a wheelbarrow, digging through dense hard clay, and sifting. An hour after starting, Cloe yelled from the section to our north that they were already finding Roman coins. At the morning break for refreshments of Marmite spread on bread, we admired these coins, but then went back to our own digging. By the afternoon recess Cloe and her group had already excavated down to the Roman street pavement. We could only admire and continue to dig down to the solid surface which the sounding had indicated might be productive. On the fourth day we reached concrete, but it proved to be the foundation of a World War II German gun emplacement. We had become suspicious of this as we had discovered spent casings of machine gun shell on the way down. It was hardly surprising since this had been the site of a British paratrooper landing in 1943.

A week later we abandoned this spot and moved up the slope to open another section for excavation. The work progressed slowly at the beginning, but then our labors paid off. Near the partially excavated Villa Dionesius our group found what had become known as the Saromilos Mosaic, a blue and white inscription dating from 188 A.D. It depicted two male figures facing each other with outstretched arms, athletes perhaps. (Later, research indicated that these figures represented local athletes who won a victory at the Olympic Games of 188 A.D.)

We always looked forward to the morning rest period. I sat on an old truck tire with Kosti, the workman, as we ate grapes and figs. Kosti, a man in his mid fifties, had a face of some bronze Zeus, wrinkled and walnut colored from the sun and wind, with a lined and deeply furrowed forehead. He wore a handle bar mustache. Kosti was a contrast to Laurence, the prematurely white-headed Englishman with a white military mustache, always wielding an English kind of authority. Each morning we stopped before noon for lunch in the shade of the garden surrounded by plumbago and hibiscus flowers before dispersing for naps.

I took an afternoon off and rode the bus into Herakleion to call at the British Airways office. I walked in the market place, sat and smelled the roasting coffee beans, then strolled along the stalls of vegetables—beans, cucumbers, aubergines, and beetroot—and fruits—dark maroon cherries, apricots, and oranges. Further along, there were cheese hunks and raw meat dangling from hooks, a Horn of Plenty.

Back in the garden of the Taverina the air was cooling and soft. Already the owls were calling from the pines. During the following days we extended the excavation into an adjoining area, unearthing a hypocaust room (an ancient Roman heating system). We found lead-glazed pots, several of which had relief decoration in blue and amber. One morning I was assigned to sifting duty, and while daydreaming and thinking of the recess with grapes and Marmite, I discovered a glass intaglio, later identified as Artemis Ephesia. He was flanked by the sun, moon, and a pair of deer, a little treasure now in the Archeological Museum of Herakleion.

But alas, late August was approaching, and I had to return to South Carolina. That same Cretan Zorba taxi-driver, who a year earlier had brought me to Knossos, picked me up at daybreak. A sweet musky scent drifted from the slopes toward Fortesa brought by a light wind through the eucalyptus and pines. Morning glories were opening up on the walls, and pink oleanders glistened with dew. At this hour everything was sweet, cool, and gentle.

I took a last look toward the slope back of the villa then heard the voice of a frog from the little pool near the statue of Hadrian. We drove down the road that ran southwestward beside a ravine, past little houses and gardens, and between vineyards.

As I flew homeward from Knossos, I was thinking of Natasha and Cloe, of Kosti, and of Laurence. I was thinking of Marmite.

RAFTING THE TATSHENSHINI RIVER OF CANADA AND ALASKA

Eight Days in Primal Wilderness

There's a land where mountains are nameless,
and the rivers all run God knows where;

> *There are lives that are erring and aimless,*
> *and deaths that just hang by a hair;*
> *There are hardships that nobody reckons;*
> *there are valley unpeopled and still;*
> *There's a land—oh, it beckons and beckons,*
> *and I want to go back—and I will.*
>
> —Robert Service, "The Spell of the Yukon"

$\mathcal{B}$y late June the weather and humidity closed in on Pawleys Island like a vice. I was fed up. I snatched up the telephone and called Sierra Club's office in San Francisco and asked one question: "Where is the coldest place your club is taking a small group to in the next three months?" In late August, I joined a party of ten going to the Yukon and Alaska for a rafting expedition of the Tatshenshini River.

A few weeks later the following article was accepted for publication in *Diversion Magazine*:

Mention Tatshenshini and people may say: "Tat—WHAT?" And, that's it, confusing to pronounce and hidden from the world like a rare jewel encased in a wilderness vault. Regarded as one of the five great rafting rivers of the world, the Tatshenshini stretches like a winding serpent from Canada to Alaska, while being a premier river that has been rafted by only a few adventurers who have passed through its watery doors into incredible unspoiled beauty.

It has been listed in the elite company of these five great rafting rivers: the Omo of Ethiopia, the Bio-Bio of Chile, the Watut of New Guinea, and the Colorado of Utah and Arizona. There are plusses: the Tatshenshini is relatively accessible from the Yukon Territory north of Haines, Alaska, it has splendid wilderness beauty, the weather is usually bearable, its flow generates lively rapids, and wildlife is abundant.

Jack Dalton, of Gold Rush notoriety and Edward Glave were perhaps the first white men to explore this wilder-

ness when in the 1890s they made their way down from
Dalton Post in the Yukon along this river to join the
Alsek River and successfully reached the Gulf of Alaska
at Dry Bay. Since that time this pristine wilderness was
virtually untouched by man until 1976, when Sobek Expeditions scouted the Tatshenshini River by helicopter and
then by raft.

In the late summer, ten members of the Sierra Club,
including this writer, met Jim Slade and his crew from
Sobek Expeditions in Juneau, Alaska. He briefed the
group and the next morning we boarded a sleek Alaskan
state ferry for the six-hour cruise up Lynn Canal to
Haines, Alaska. With little imagination, we might have
been in Norway as the Chilkat Mountains rose from the
royal blue inlet waters edged by occasional fjords. During the crisp afternoon, we had a last briefing and soon
the town of Haines dotted a distant fjord. Stan Boor, an
expert boatman and photography graduate of Brigham Young
University, awaited us in a dusty, beaten, white tin-can
of a bus for the ride northward to the Canadian border
and the Yukon Territory.

We headed up Haines Highway between the Chilkat and
Chilkoot Rivers through a wide delta to Chilkat Pass by
Mosquito Lake; then we stopped at a gasoline station
where gasoline was pumped into the bus by hand. At
Pleasant Camp we crossed into British Columbia. The
road, now gravel and more narrow, warned us that we were
leaving civilization behind. Jim handed me a map—we were
passing locations which sounded nostalgic and ghostlike.
We went through Rainy Hollow, then ascended to Three
Guardsmen Pass, to Chilkat Pass, and onto Mosquito
Flats, Bear Camp—sites where gold prospectors had
stopped over on their way to the Klondike gold fields. A
red fox dashed across the road in front of the bus and
disappeared toward Squaw Range to the west. About 9:45
P.M. it was still daylight, and we crossed into the
Yukon Territory and soon could see the dribble of headwaters of the "Tat" gradually being fed and mothered by
glacial waters from the Squaw Range.

Near sunset we reached the turnoff point at Dalton Post
and were greeted by a sign: "The public is warned that
grizzly bears are abundant in this area and must be considered dangerous." With a heightened sense of adventure, we left Haines Highway and turned south on a game
trail along Silver Creek for five miles; the trail
became impassable and we walked the last few hundred
yards to our campsite along Silver Creek. As darkness
descended, we were welcomed by a cheerful campfire and
food. Under a bright northern cross, we pitched tents at
the confluence of the creek and the "Tat."

We were at a site where Dalton and Glave stood nearly a
century earlier facing a valley and its river that would
cut through the massive St. Elias range and empty into
the Gulf of Alaska 150 miles downstream. Edward Glave
wrote a series of articles concerning this expedition
that were published in 1890 in *Frank Leslie's Illus-
trated Newspaper*. Glave, Dalton, and their Indian
guides, Shank and Koona Ack Sai, started their expedition from this location in the Yukon headwaters. They
tracked over wilderness before finally reaching Dry Bay.
With little geographic knowledge, the party thought they
were exploring the Alsek when they were actually on the
Tatshenshini. Glave photographed and described the settlements of Neska Ta Heen and Klukshu that were inhabited by the Gunena, Stick and Nua Quas tribes of
Indians, which have long since vanished from the river
valley.

The next morning we were up early to begin our journey
down the river. A few yards downstream from the confluence of the creek and the "Tat," spawning sockeye salmon
flopped in Silver Creek, a giant bald eagle perched on a
pile of driftwood at waters edge, an Alaskan malamute
romped through the camp, shaking and scampering off with
someone's shoe. After a lumberjack breakfast we packed
our gear into waterproof bags and latched things onto
four neoprene rafts. We donned lifejackets and pushed
off into Silver Creek, which quickly joined the "Tat."
The river widened as creeks rushed in from melting gla-

ciers miles away, then clouds rolled in as aspen shim-
mered in the morning breeze. Later in the day, we
approached Kudwat Creek to camp at the base of Pyramid
Mountain, as mist and rain closed in. We beached the
rafts and pitched tents amidst giant bear tracks in the
sand.

In the morning, fog, mist, and drizzling rain were our
companions as we headed farther downstream. Detour Creek
poured in from the right, and the river became deeper
but more narrow as we entered a valley, headed toward
the St. Elias range. Soon we were in cold, spirited
rapids—splashed, chilled, and wet. The river was now
spilling through forest gorges, winding past beaver cut
trees, on past marshy verdant banks of emerald green
ferns. The current gripped, surged and swayed us.

The Carmine Mountain Range came in full view to the
east. We swept past Low Fog Creek and thought it well
named. The water calmed briefly but was again quickly
spirited. Gazing upward, a pair of bald eagles soared in
the misty rain with magnificent grace and balance. We
skittered downstream with the torrent of sensations, as
Stan, the boatman, expertly dodged and dipped the raft
between boulders — sometimes bow first, sometimes sideways, just missing the rocky outcroppings of a vertical
bluff or piled driftwood. Then with a sharp eye, he
spotted something in a swift eddy downstream.

Quickly he pulled the raft toward the bank to the opposite side. A great grizzly churned and splashed out of
the eddy and with only one glance toward us lumbered wet
and dripping into a cottonwood thicket. We had no doubt
spoiled a sockeye salmon lunch for this kingly beast.

The "Tat" widened as Sediment Creek entered from the
right. We came to a great valley, green with spruce and
aspen, a mile wide and with a vista of peaks on either
side. The river slowed and we beached the craft to hike
along the edge of a flat, shallow creek, and on to a
bear trail up to Baldy Ridge. Jim had been on the ridge
once before and led the party, only steps in front of
us. A giant grizzly raised on its hind legs. Jim fired

into the air and then fired again. The bear wheeled and
lumbered off into the thicket.

We changed directions and ascended a knoll where we
sat, scared and sweating. We were soon relaxed by the
view. Across this great valley we saw the many peaks of
the Carmine Range. At the vegetation line herds of mountain goats grazed peacefully. We looked toward the
northeast and saw the river as a silver ribbon, then
followed its course southward where it disappeared into
a hundred peaks. The late August sun felt hot, and I
took off a jacket, then lay down to absorb this wilderness spectacle.

We hiked back to the river and set out for a campsite,
which would be on a gravel bar at the mouth of Melt
Creek, a rushing tributary that drained glacial waters
from the Carmine Range. A campfire soon warmed a
chilled, wind-whipped sand bar. Our first great display
of the aurora borealis welcomed us to the heart of the
St. Elias Mountains, a range with more peaks over 14,500
feet than any other in North America.

Warm sunshine melted the early day's mist, and we were
soon passing cold, swift, inflowing streams. An eagle
whistled and soared above, and then we spotted its nest;
a brown juvenile eagle peered out inquisitively as our
rafts drifted by. In the distance to the west, Melbourne
Glacier came into view and we first glimpsed the wide
mouth of the Alsek River, which we would join. Soon the
river widened to three miles with ice fields, ridges,
glaciers, and snow covered mountain pinnacles on each
side. We were nearing the Alaskan border.

Later in the day, we beached the rafts and searched for
a suitable creek bed to hike for a summit view southwestward into Alaska. After several tries, we found a
creek and ascended along its edge, amidst salmonberry
with ripe fruit. The creek rushed by as we reached its
ice field source a mile up from the river. On this
field, we shielded ourselves behind great boulders as an
avalanche of rocks crashed from above. We traversed the
field, rested on a high grassy moraine before crossing a

second field of ice, and then ascended the moraine
before finally reaching the flat grassy summit of an
unnamed mountain ridge. In one direction we gazed into
Alaska with its many towering peaks of the St. Elias and
Fairweather ranges. In the opposite direction we viewed
as many peaks in British Columbia. Around us were blue-
berries, carpets of wild daisies, asters, and colorful
moss. Far below flowed the braided channel of the Alsek
as it cut deeply into the St. Elias range on its way to
the sea.

Our campsite would be a wide sand and gravel bar a few
hundred yards from the Walker Glacier. We reached the
bar as the sun set across the Alsek. The late day was
spectacular as fluffy, drifting clouds and white mountain peaks became sunset fired, taking on hues of pastel
pink, yellow, and blue.

The following day we hiked across a moraine and an ice
field toward Walker Glacier. The day was damp and
chilly, and the drizzle of the night had glazed the ice,
making footing treacherous. Crevasses and ravines
revealed gurgling, roaring streams beneath us. Wind
whipped across the frigid sheet, then quieted as the sun
appeared from a veil of clouds to reflect off the white
peaks that surrounded us. I left the party and walked
alone toward camp. Once off the glacier and past the
moraine below, I walked across wind-swept sand dune—
their rhythmic patterns reaching toward the swift flowing Alsek River. A willow ptarmigan rustled off tamely;
its plumage was already turning white for the oncoming
winter.

As I neared the campsite, I wondered about the soli-
tude, uniqueness, and beauty of these surroundings and
could hardly realize that few fellow men had experienced
this pristine wilderness.

On the eighth day, we set out for the site of our last
two nights of camping near Alsek Bay. A few miles downstream the mountain curtain opened again, revealing a
site that appeared not unlike Glave's 1890 description
of the Stick Indian settlement of Kluskshu. We entered

this broad valley and rested on its wide beach to view
Mt. Fairweather rising in the distance, then rafted on
downstream. By mid afternoon we had reached our destination, a broad sand dune at the tip of a peninsula. We
were situated in a deep bowl, rimmed by towering, snow-
capped mountains crowned by the 15,300-foot monarch, Mt.
Fairweather. As soon as we reached the beach, we heard
thunderous roar and an echo from the mountains around
the Alsek Bay. We walked to a high dune to view the bay
and the thunder source; there the miles-long tonguelike
tip of the Alsek Glacier lapped at the bay. With a
bionic rhythm, giant pieces of glacier calved off,
crashing into the bay, setting off a roar and then
echoes from the mountains. With each calving, the bay
was churned, but then quieted as the pieces of glacier
became icebergs and slowly moved into the bay and toward
the river.

I pitched a tent on a protected side of a dune and
walked a few hundred yards toward the bay. Wild gerani-
ums were in full bloom, yet in the distance there were
ridges and mountains covered with ice and snow. I
climbed onto a giant boulder for a better view of a mirror pool that reflected Mt. Fairweather. As I sat there,
a magpie flew into a nearby tamarisk tree to squawk in
protest of my trespassing into its late afternoon habitat. My sense must have been similar to Edward Glaves
when he was at this site in 1890. He wrote: "There were
quite recent tracks of large bears around our camp, and
a few eagles angry at our unusual intrusion hovered and
screamed overhead. A flock of gulls who had penetrated
to these wild regions for nesting added a mournful din
to the senses. There is such an incessant display of
scenic wild grandeur that it becomes tiresome; we can no
longer appreciate it; its awe-inspiring influence no
longer appeals to our hardened senses."

The following morning the Sobek crew rowed the rafts
into the mouth of Alsek Bay to retrieve us near our
campsite. We waited anxiously at the edge of the bay,
and soon the rafts became visible as dots amidst tower-

ing icebergs and floating chunks of ice. In the morning,
sunshine, melodious flute music suddenly sounded from
across the bay then echoed with silvered clarity from
the mountains. An oarsman was serenading us with music
from *The Nutcracker Suite*! Alsek Bay remained amidst the
floating bergs of ice chunks, each crystalline mass taking on its own bizarre shape before making its way down
the choked bay toward the Alsek River.

Our last hours on the river were spent rafting toward
Dry Bay on the Gulf of Alaska. The river was swift flowing but clogged with ice. A homesteader rushed from his
cabin to the water's edge to wave a greeting. A salmon-
fishing bald eagle, perched on a pile of driftwood, was
aggravated by a dipping and diving seagull. Tongass Forest rose as a backdrop to the west. In the distance we
saw two small planes that awaited us, then two more
planes flew by, dipped their wings, and landed on a barren strip. L.A.B. Flying Service would fly us back to
Juneau.

We took off toward Mt. Fairweather and almost brushed
it before turning toward the southeast. I sat by the
veteran pilot, Layton A. Bennett, who also owned the
airline. Bennett had been a bush pilot in Alaska for
thirty-seven years, yet seemed enthralled with the snowy
mountain scenery below. Our small plane droned on toward
Juneau as expanses of crystalline peaks reached up from
a wholly untouched, unpeopled wilderness below.

As I left the majestic mountains, I reflected on the
river, beautiful and untamed; the wildlife, abundant and
free. I wondered and then I knew. Yes, this last fron-
tier *must* be preserved so that future generations might
have the joy of this wilderness encounter. I vowed to
return to Alaska, since this land had caught my being as
it did Robert W. Service. His "Spell of the Yukon" –
written at the turn of the century was equal to my own:

> *No! There's the land. (Have you seen it?)*
> *It's the cussedest land that I know,*
> *from the big, dizzy mountains that screen it*

to the deep, deathlike valleys below.
Some say God was tired when he made it;
some say it's a fine land to shun;
maybe; but there's some as would trade it
for no land on earth – and I'm one.

THE RIVER NILE EXPEDITION
The Waccamaw of Egypt

I had had the pleasure of making two previous trips on the Nile River when I traveled on rather large cruise ships. During those trips I had observed the smaller feluccas, which sailed up and down the river, and decided that I would like to sail from Aswan northward to Luxor on one of those twenty-five-foot open boats. I realized that I would have to sleep on boards placed across the boat in a sleeping bag. I also realized that there would be no bathroom facilities on such a vessel. A further concern was that adequate food and provisions would have to be taken on board in Aswan for such a trip, normally lasting four days. I was told in Aswan that none of my concerns would be a problem.

I contacted two former traveling companions who were accustomed to "roughing it," Page Oberlin and Olga Hirshhorn. They agreed to come on the trip and each recruited a gentleman friend to accompany them.

In London, I went to the foremost Egyptian travel company and asked for the best available felucca and crew of two, who spoke some English and were capable of loading and cooking. I indicated that we were willing to pay a premium price for all this. The London agent said, "Leave it to me," British commercial-speak for "I'll take care of it."

Two months later we met up in Aswan. Pawleys Islander, Page Oberlin, and her friend, Bruce Honeycutt, flew in from Atlanta on their way to Addis Ababba, and Olga Hirshhorn, bringing her friend, Carelton Swift, arrived from Washington on their way to Istanbul. We spent three days at the wonderful old Victorian hotel, The Cataract, in Aswan. We took a day trip by air to visit Abu Simbel and returned to Aswan with great anticipation for our voyage to Luxor on some luxurious felucca.

After two days on the Nile we were making little progress because of the lack of wind and the holes in our sails. With a schedule to meet in Luxor, we decided to hire a van to complete the journey. I felt responsible for some of the misfortune of the trip, but my friends maintain to this day that that voyage remains as one of their most memorable and enjoyble adventures.

I wrote a letter to Dick Crayton back at Pawleys Island describing the first day and a half. I had had every intention of mailing the letter from somewhere along the way, but it got to be so long that I ended up keeping it until I got back to Pawleys Island and gave it to him personally.

Dear Dick,

I am sitting here on a palm leaf on the bank of the Nile River, just north of Kmo Ombro in Egypt, waiting for Horus and his young assistant, Tut. When they return we will continue our voyage up this river towards Luxor.

I have just chased away a crocodile. You know how our alligators there on the Waccamaw River have that smiling face. Well, these crocodiles grin too, especially when I pitch them macaroni, but they have sharper teeth than I ever saw on an alligator. Horus has told us that we shouldn't feed them, but as you know, I could never resist a smiling reptile.

You know Page Oberlin, our mutual friend from Pawleys. She's here with me, along with three other people. There's Olga Hirshhorn and Carelton Swift from Washington and Bruce Honeycutt, Page's friend from Atlanta. Page says we're doing the "Voyage of the Obelisk." That's something she's made up, but I suppose it's true in a way. You know obelisks—those tall, phallic, pointed stone pillars? We're following the same route along which these ancient stones were shipped after being cut from a big granite quarry just south of Aswan, which we visited three days ago. These obelisks were rafted up the river to Karnak, a temple near Luxor. But that was over three thousand years ago!

Dick, we're sailing toward Luxor in a little boat these Egyptians call a *felucca*—the same type of boat these folks have been using for four thousand years. Our felucca has a compelling Arabic name, *Salta*, but it didn't take us long to figure out that spelled backwards it reads *Atlas*. Olga discovered this when she read it through the mirror of her hand compact. Atlas is that Greek man in mythology who held the world on his shoulders with hardly a grunt. So we call our little sailboat *Atlas*.

Well, my friend, it's about time for Horus and Tut to return. Maybe we can get on up to Edfu before midnight, so I'll close and write you from Luxor. Bye-bye.

P.S. It's an hour later and our skipper and Tut haven't returned yet, so I'll write a few more lines.

I mentioned the skipper. Well, we don't have an ordinary skipper commanding this felucca. We have a Nubian captain named Horus. I admit quickly that a Horus commanding the *Atlas* is not as romantic as it would seem. You see, he says that his name is Andy. Page and the rest of us realized that any decent Nubian wouldn't have such a name as Andy, so we call him Horus because he has only one eye, just like the famous son of the Egyptian gods, Isis and Osiris. We try very hard to admire and respect him when he is standing there at the stern in his grey tattered night gown outfit. But more often than not, we see him sprawled out asleep across the stern.

Preliminaries to this odyssey seemed to go on forever. First, Olga appeared at our meeting point in a pink hivacious state, all broken out and swollen. Thankfully this was limited to her face. She gazed into the mirror of her compact and moaned, "Oh Carelton, how Picasso-like!" Carelton fed her an antihistamine pill and said, "Picasso, hell. You look more like Hathor with the shellfish hives." Olga looked back into the mirror and whispered to me, "I haven't had the hives since 1978 and that was the morning Joe lost five million dollars on that sorry Toreador Royalty stock." She gently patted her face, snapped the compact shut, and said, "Luxor, Luxor."

Page plans to leave us in Luxor and go on to Addis Ababba. I suspect to buy more sets of those dangling silver earrings she wears. Trying to arrange this trip in Aswan, she left her air ticket with the agent there and was having a terrible time trying to get it back. She and Bruce appeared late at our embarkation point, and she announced, "I'm not going on anybody's felucca, to anybody's Luxor, with a one-eyed Nubian, until that awful travel agent brings back my airline ticket." She gazed at Bruce's sunburned bald head, then looked him in the eye and added, "I also want some Nubian bean dip on board." This is a spicy concoction, very popular in Egypt. Like any other good southern boy from Atlanta, Bruce went in search of a deli.

Finally, with our duffel bags, airline tickets, bean dip and hives we boarded a motor launch to be taken up the Nile a mile or so to the awaiting felucca. Within minutes we had our first glimpse of the boat lying at anchor between two imposing cruise ships: *The Nile Star* and the *Cleopatra*. There was the *Atlas*, and from what had at one time probably been a gleaming white hull sprang a full sail. Full except for three large holes. The motor launch tied up alongside, and we five pilgrims sat in the November sun admiring our dubious craft and its skipper. We observed provisions being taken aboard by a younger Nubian, this Tut whom I mentioned. In the bow of the boat, Tut stowed several see-through plastic bags. We could easily see that we would be fed several cucumbers, eight or ten large squash, some small onions, potatoes, two dozen eggs, six cartons of yoghurt, and a large box of Egyptian macaroni. There were vegetables that not even Page, who is an authority on such things, could identify. We felt reassured when we saw *two* kerosene stoves and *two* large aluminum boiling pots being added to the stores. Our skipper appeared and disappeared several times, but finally in the late morning, we left the motor launch and went aboard the laden *Atlas*.

Olga stood and proudly waved to the affluent passengers aboard the *Cleopatra*, anchored next to us. But alas, attempting to get under way, Horus sailed us directly into its stern. We looked the other way as the *Cleopatra*'s bilge pipe seemed to urinate on our boat. But never mind, the wind finally pushed us into the ancient river and for minutes we sailed northward up the Nile. I say minutes because the river's eastern shore soon greeted us again. In perfect Nubian English, Horus said, "Forgot bread. Tut go five minutes for bag full." Thirty minutes later Tut reappeared with two plastic bags of large, flattened biscuit-like objects and a quart jar of jam, to boot. We cast out once more and headed up the river.

Another obstacle greeted us in the early afternoon. Just beyond Kitchner Island the Egyptian Coast Guard waved us to shore and Horus disappeared again, but this time he took our passports. When he finally returned, Carelton reminded us that Ulysses also had difficulty in getting away from Troy.

We cast off for the third time, sailed northward, and finally were out of sight of Aswan. Olga stood on our makeshift boarded deck, faced up river, patted her face, and announced, "I'm better now. This Nile voyage is good for my hives. I wonder if Cleopatra got swollen while sailing on this river." Her intellectual companion answered, "If she didn't, I'll bet you a pyramid it wasn't Anthony's fault." We all settled in and there was silence except for the breeze whistling by our great sail and, of course, through its holes. Horus stretched himself across the boards in the stern and slept like a mummified cat. Young Tut was in command, tacking the boat onward, to and fro in the late afternoon.

None of us had ever heard anything exactly like all of the late afternoon sounds coming from the shore, particularly the loudspeakers from the villages along the river's bank. These were Muslim holy men chanting their call to prayer to Allah from the minarets. We fondly imagined that they were extolling the river gods on our behalf. Minutes later the sun dropped behind the palms on the Nile's western bank, a chill set in, and, rather apprehensively, we were confronted with our first night on this mysterious river.

As darkness descended, Horus's snoring ceased as if it had come to the end of a coda in some unfinished dissonant symphony. He arose and in passable English asked two simple questions: "Do you have flashlight?" and "Do you eat macaroni?" Page answered for us, "Yes, we adore macaroni, but where is *your* flashlight?" There was silence for a moment as Horus lit the kerosene stove. Then he answered, "Have no flashlight. I am poor."

Now Dick, even you wouldn't go out at night on the Waccamaw without a light. Here we were on this Nile River, on a cold November night, dodging cruise ships, with only my little flashlight to shine against the tattered sail. I sat holding the light against that sail as the wind died down. Then we were adrift. Adrift as we sat on the makeshift deck eating our macaroni and goat cheese. Adrift on the cold Nile and at the mercy of some Egyptian gods and at the mercy of Horus and Tut. The forced witty conversation of my fellow pilgrims did nothing to distract me from thoughts of a possible watery doom. After the macaroni, Carelton rigged my flashlight, and we sat in a circle as he read aloud *Travels in Egypt*, Flaubert's account of his voyage of a hundred years before. The other pilgrims hardly listened except when Carelton read the part about the author making out with a prostitute across a broken column in the Temple of Edfu, and even then there was only a subdued snigger from Olga. We were all clearly worn out and apprehensive after only one day on the Nile. Carelton switched off the flashlight and gave it back to me as we made a pretense of bedding down in our sleeping bags. The *Atlas* drifted ever so gently on the dark Nile as our skipper slept. The Egyptian gods did have mercy on us, for some time around midnight we felt a thud. We had run aground against the river's eastern bank. There was a commotion as young Tut jumped up and seconds later had the felucca tied to a root on the river's bank. Our skipper hardly stirred. He simply seized a portion of the blanket covering Bruce's head, and soon he was snoring again. We pilgrims sat up, marvelling at the clear star-studded sky with the Southern Cross, a new moon, Jupiter to the east, and Venus setting in the west. Then, like South Carolina setting hens, we rearranged our nests for possible slumber. Nobody asked me for a sleeping pill.

We did manage to sleep some last night after reaching the safety of the shore, but at about 5 o'clock a cacophony of sounds awoke most of us. Dick, you know how in the early morning, there on the Waccamaw, we hear the bull frogs and maybe a hoot owl or clapper rail, and the occasional horn of a New Jersey yacht? Well, here in Egypt, it was a lot more noisy. We wiped the dew from our heads and listened in amazement. There were more of those holy men praying through their loudspeakers, and there were roosters crowing, donkeys braying, and frogs croaking. There was the faint whistle of a distant locomotive and the sound of the river lapping against the boat. With Horus's snoring in the background, it all sounded like a disorganized musical fugue.

The first rays of the sun were the signal for our skipper to awaken. He stumbled across to the bow where he lit a kerosene stove, boiled water from the river, and made tea strong enough to walk out of the pot. Emerging from our damp cocoons, we admired the sunrise and watched with amusement the silhouette of an old man riding a donkey, trotting along like a wind-up toy. A flock of glossy ibis flew low over the river, circled, and were soon out of sight over the palm trees.

Well, Dick, I should have turned this into two letters, but I realized that Mabel there at the U.S. Post Office would blow a fuse if you got *two* letters that had been mailed with Middle Eastern stamps, so I'll just continue.

Anyway, a little later that first morning, the wind stiffened a bit and the *Atlas* was again tacking generally northward while we anticipated our first breakfast on the Nile. The breakfast proved to be memorable—memorable because there was none. We had eagerly anticipated Nubian boiled eggs, but each time we tacked and the boat heeled, Tut's kerosene stove tipped over and the pan of eggs spilled out on to the deck. The third time this happened the young man gave up, and the menu was changed to quince jam and the biscuit-like bread. But even that didn't materialize since the jam jar broke as Tut attempted to get its contrary lid off. I had brought some medication to prevent us getting sick, so we took an extra tablet and sailed on towards Kmo Ombro.

I must tell you a little bit about this town because it's an important stop on this pilgrimage. I mentioned the local variety of grinning crocodile. Well, they have inhabited the area around Kmo Ombro for thousands of years. They seem to like the place and for good reason. Since Ptolemaic times, it has been a juncture of routes to gold mines over on the Red Sea and the overland routes to Nubia to the south. You can guess what this meant. Lots of travellers were available for the crocodiles to eat. A question of supply and demand. But instead of running from these reptiles, as we would, these Egyptians got smart and erected a temple in Kmo Ombro in honor of crocodiles in general and a big one called Sobek in particular.

Sobek was worshipped as a god and provided with a harem of girl crocodiles to grin at. He was wined and dined so much that he eventually recip-
rocated and protected everybody from the hazards of the river. When old
Sobek finally died of over-indulgence and cirrhosis at the age of sixty-four
the town officials mummified his body, just like Ramses II. To this day, he's
right there in the temple to be worshipped and presented with offerings.

By the time we had been on our felucca for over twenty-four hours, we
had more or less settled in. We watched all that was going on along the
Nile's bank. I saw a donkey carrying a load of sugar cane that you couldn't
fit into the back of your pick-up. Right behind the donkey were four
women walking along with big water pitchers balanced on top of their
heads, and one was leading a water buffalo, to boot. Two dirty-faced kids
followed, begging for money, yelling Baksheesh, baksheesh!

After our aborted breakfast, Horus had gone back to sleep. Eventually,
late in the morning, he woke up again, stretched, and walked to the bow.
He stood like an old statue, with his long nightshirt outfit waving in the
breeze. He rewrapped his head and yawned. The young Nubian yelled
something and pointed. We glimpsed in the distance the two great minarets
of Kmo Ombro's temple on the Nile's bank. We all stood up on the
boarded deck and in a group moved towards the bow. Our silhouettes
must have looked a bit like the sculpture of the Burgers of Calais as we
leaned forward to see the temple we had eagerly anticipated.

When we reached the bank, our faithful Tut sprang ashore like a gazelle
and moored the felucca to the base of the fallen palm tree. With our back-
packs, we walked on a narrow path towards the temple. We had decided to
give Sobek an offering, for we had survived one night on this ancient river,
survived one night of Horus, Tut, and their felucca. We entered the temple
and found Sobek's resting place and the mummy. We all thanked him. Page
and Olga asked for protection on the river, and Bruce and Carelton each
made an offering of left-over macaroni.

With a sense of reassurance we returned to the *Atlas*, roused Horus, and
in no time cast off and were sailing up the Nile. Tut tried to light the
kerosene stove to boil some you-know-what, but, once again, it tipped
over. Page had brought along a can of tuna fish. She stood up, waved it in

the air, and chanted, "Luxor, Luxor!"

Well, Dick, I'm really going to close now. I'll write another letter from Luxor. I'll tell you what has happened, and I'll tell you more about that one-eyed Nubian.

Bye bye,

Lee

GALAPAGOS ISLANDS
WHERE I MET "DOT"

I knew that it would be difficult, but I had to fly to Miami to change planes. I'd made connections in this air terminal on occasion when I flew in and out of St. Vincent and St. Lucia in the Windward Islands while doing volunteer medical work, so I knew what to expect. In this terminal, where the Spanish language is standard, there was the usual chaos. It reminded me of the air terminals in Cairo, Istanbul, and Moscow. When I booked with Lindblad Expeditions to go to the Galapagos Islands, I had no alternative but to be routed through Miami.

American Airlines clerks had over-sold the flight to Guayaquil, Ecuador, by *fifty* seats. We sat for two hours while disgruntled passengers unloaded, along with their luggage, and other passengers boarded. We flew westward and with my usual luck, there were crying babies in front of me, a "card shuffler" behind, and a woman who talked continually in Spanish beside me. I sat fanning myself and vowed that from now on I would travel by ocean liner.

Arriving in Gayaquil at midnight, two hours late, we had to be up at daybreak for the six hundred-mile flight to Baltra Island in the Galapagos. Flying low over the landing site I could see the *Polaris*, Lindblad's gleaming white ship, lying at anchor in the bay. I knew that my travel problems would soon be over, at least until the flight back to Miami.

On the launch, the *Zodiac*, going to the anchored ship, I thought of Charles Darwin and his visit in 1835, when he was circling the globe formulating his theory of evolution. Darwin remained in these islands only long enough to be convinced that his theory was correct.

As I climbed from the launch to the *Polaris*, I wondered, "I'm on the equator, and it isn't hot." The assigned guide, Monique Van Dousselaire, explained that the Humbolt Current sweeps along the Galapagos Islands cooling them. Monique, a microbiologist from Antwerp University in Belgium, who made her home in those islands, did research for Equador and worked part-time for Lindblad. She spoke authoritatively in a broad French accent, explaining that during the next ten days we would visit the twelve major islands in the volcanic chain, some days crossing the equator four times.

The next morning we sailed south of Baltra to the eastern coast of Santa Cruz Island. The ship docked at Venecia Inlet and, like chicks following the mother hen, we followed Monique onto the *Zodiac* and waded ashore where we walked around hundreds of marine iguanas, all appearing to be asleep. Sally lightfoot crabs crawled over and through them, coexisting peacefully. These were not ordinary crabs; some were a foot in diameter. Nobody seemed to know where their name came from. They reminded me of Clemson University football fans, dressed in bright orange with white.

Monique led us down a footpath to a blue footed boobie rookery, and here we observed these large birds—the size of Canadian geese—in their mating rituals. They paid no attention to us as they continued courting. The female stood and watched the male, standing on one blue foot and then the other, then clapping its beak against hers. The female squawked, then turned away to be greeted by the next male.

As I stood focusing my camera on the boobies, a Galapagos mockingbird lit on the camera to inspect the lens. Farther down the pathway, we saw the Darwin finch, an insignificant-appearing bird that Darwin studied while formulating his theory of evolution. I wouldn't have taken a second look.

That afternoon we sailed several miles to the south to Florena Island. There we viewed the great flock of flamingos on an inlet muddy lake where they prodded into the mud and walked aimlessly, paying no heed to us. At sunset the *Polaris* anchored at Hood Island, and we followed Monique on shore to see the sleeping sea lions on the sandy beach. They seemed lifeless except for the occasional male who was alert, barking, and acting as a sentinel. Near Gardner Bay, and many other places in the Galapagos, we observed the carcasses of marine iguanas lying about. Monique explained that the recent El Niño warm current had killed the sea life these iguanas feed on, and, as a result, these reptiles had starved—half of the iguana of the Galapagos had perished.

The next morning we crossed the equator for the first time, sailing toward the northern tip of the Galapagos' largest island, Isabella. There we watched the complicated mating ritual of the waved albatross. The display between male and female sometimes went on for hours. It was even more intriguing to see these heavy birds trying to take off. They ran, gained speed, and virtually fell off the high cliff where the wind current pushed them upward. Monique said that their method of landing was perilous, and this caused many of their injuries and deaths. Perhaps this is why they fly for months over the oceans, coming to the ground only to mate.

We sailed on around Isabella again crossing the equator to James Island where we boarded glass-bottomed boats to view an abundance of colorful fish swimming in and around underwater grottos and beds of lava. On land the sea lions were awake and played in the shallow pools near Puerto Egas. I finally saw the Galapagos penguins, which were much smaller than expected, like some shorebird. They walked in a straight line on a ledge just above the water.

Coming from Pawleys Island where the double crested cormorant is so abundant, I was anxious to see the flightless cormorant. We saw one on Tower Island, appearing much as our cormorant, but making no attempts to fly, even as we walked within a foot of it. It seemed oblivious to our presence.

On Bartolome Island we saw the great flocks of frigatebirds, the male resting on the ground with its red neck pouch blown-up like a balloon. The females flew overhead, perhaps trying to select a partner. The males all looked the same to me, and I wondered how the female could make a choice. Here we saw a male masked booby who had "captured" a Frigatebird chick, preened and cuddled it, not allowing its real mother to get near.

I had expected to see many giant tortoises in the wild, but alas, there were none. We saw these in the Galapagos National Park and Research Center and were told that they are rarely seen in the island's highlands.

All the action on this Lindblad cruise was not with the boobies, frigatebirds and iguanas. There were lighter moments on the *Polaris*, where most of the fifty passengers gathered at the bar prior to dinner. It was there that I met Mrs. Dorothy Solomon, a New Yorker and rumored wife of one of the financial Solomon brothers. She was alone on the cruise; "hubby" was back in New York, or somewhere, doing money. On the evening we met she was dressed in emerald green chiffon, designer high heels, and had the aroma of a Parisian *parfumerie*. She ordered a second Manhattan, and we talked—the usual small talk. She asked me what I "did" when not on a cruise. She answered, "Wow," when I said that I was a South Carolina shepherd. I said, "Yeah, I have a big flock in the foothills east of the Piedmont Mountains." She sipped slowly, leaving a trace of lipstick on the glass, then asked about their fur. I said, "No, Mrs. Solomon, sheep don't have fur. They have wool."

For an instant there was quietness, except for the chatting going on about us. Then she said, "Just call me Dottie."

The next evening we met again. I said, "Dottie, what do you do when not cruising?"

She answered, "I collect Giacometti."

Since shepherds are not supposed to know about such things, I asked, "What's that?"

She replied, "Oh, dawling, that's the Swiss artist who did those elongated things."

Realizing that I was getting into deeper water, I quickly changed the subject, "What did you think of the blue footed boobies? And the marine iguanas?"

She said, "Oh, dawling, I'm not here to see those scaly things nor the Sally something crabs. I'm here for the equator sun. They say it's adorable for the complexion. You will always find me on the deck soaking up the sun." She took another sip and said, "But I did see one of those pink birds with the long neck fly over the boat, a flamingo, I think. The skinny thing flew over when we were anchored at Florina. Then, yesterday I saw something flying over that looked like it had swallowed a red balloon . . ."

We were nearing the end of the cruise and met for a final time for a drink. She ordered a margarita and I had a Budweiser. She asked me to come to Quogue, Long Island, to visit. She said that she had never entertained a shepherd. She then asked me to call her "Dot."

TREKKING IN NEPAL WITH ROSE AND GIOVANNI

*W*e met on the plane between London and New Delhi. In a short period of time I had learned much about Rose and Giovanni. She was in her early thirties, and Giovanni was fifty-eight. She was Irish and he was Italian. They ran an antique shop in West Kensington—they were on their honeymoon! We had booked the trek out of Pokhara, Nepal, through the same travel agent in London. There was a stop in New Delhi and in Katmandu. I had some misgivings about trekking with other people but realized that trekking alone with only a guide and porter would not be an ideal situation. So, I took my chances and got Rose and Giovanni.

In New Delhi, once over the jet lag, I went out on my own, refusing the long drive to Agra and the Taj Mahal with these travelling companions. It was impossible to get a first class railway ticket to Agra on such short notice, so I settled for Delhi.

I took a taxi to old Delhi and, hiring a rickshaw pulled by a pitiful little man with hardly a muscle, at once found myself in a jam of humanity. He peddled up an incline through masses of people stretching for miles, with frantic chaos and a cacophony of sounds. It became obvious that procreation was in vogue in India. There were automobile horns blowing, bells from bicycles ringing, and shouting from the snarl of people. A lone policeman tried to keep order with only a whistle and a bamboo stick. This was familiar chaos to Indians. The incline became steeper, and my rickshaw driver was overcome with exhaustion. I paid him a few rupees and tried to get out of the avalanche of people. I took the first alleyway I could find and immediately found myself in the midst of the Delhi silver brokerage market. A young official stood on the steps calling out prices. Men sat on pads and yelled back at him, not unlike Wall Street in New York. Nearby workmen pounded silver, flattening it. All this confusion took place amidst vendors cooking strange things with sickening aromas. I had experienced the Delhi silver stock market.

Overcome with a surfeit of humanity, I walked toward an open field to get a breath of air. Busses were parked on the periphery, and I realized that I was near some great Hindu shrine at the Red Fort where pilgrims had come to worship. Emaciated people sat in huddles; some boiled water for tea while others cooked rice over makeshift fires. Others wiped the rear ends of small children after they had defecated on the ground nearby. Although on a pilgrimage, they all appeared forlorn, sad, and hungry. This was old Delhi.

I could have taken the long ride to Agra and watched the Taj Mahal at sunset. Rose and Giovanni were having this pleasure. Instead, I had the Red Fort and a shrine. I had old Delhi.

Two days later, I joined my travelling companions on the flight to Katmandu where we had two days before leaving on the trek. Of course, I heard about the magnificence of the Taj. I had little to say about old Delhi.

I decided to spend the first day in the valley around Katmandu and took a car and driver southward to Patan, called "the most Buddhist city in Nepal." We crossed the Bagmati River. The driver parked the car so that I might observe a typical Buddhist cremation on the river bank. The

Nepali make a commercial venture out of death, as I observed that day. Near the *ghat*, the steps down to the river, a merchant had set up his business to sell wood for the burning process. At the time, flames on the *ghat* were consuming a body, as the merchant squatted near his pile of tree branches. Men friends and family of the deceased bought wood and tended the fire as it belched smoke. They seemed unconcerned that the feet stuck out and would probably be left at the end of the day. Just below the *ghat* people bathed in the river. The only sounds were from the rhythmic beating of clothes being washed nearby and the crackling of burning wood. They all seemed oblivious to death and cremation.

We drove the short distance to the center of Patan and parked near Dunbar Square. Every town seemed to have a Dunbar Square, and I learned that this name was not derived from some Englishman, but was a word meaning "palace." We were at the palace square. This was a weekday, and nobody was around except an occasional monk. Temples—the Krishna Mandir, the Shiva Temple, the Ganesh Temple, and the imposing, four-hundred-year-old Taleju Temple, surrounded me. An old toothless man sat on a pad by its entrance. He sold little packets of shelled nuts—I couldn't resist.

I went into the courtyard and was awed by a four-story pagoda. By its entrance were two statues of river gods. According to the monk attendant, they were dedicated to the Rivers Ganges and Jumna. I found a seat on some steps opposite this pagoda and sat for an hour trying to decipher the various decorative motifs. Finally, I gave up, photographed them, and walked out. The toothless salesman awaited me and motioned that I come with him. I followed him down a narrow street, up some steps and into a primitive dwelling. He took from a shelf a six-inch bronze image of some god holding a flaming lamp. The god's headdress appeared as a male peacock adorned with strings of beads. I judged the image to be from the early seventeenth century and offered five dollars. He took it.

I spent the remainder of the day visiting the great number of pagodas and temples of Patan—the temple dedicated to Shiva, Kumbeshwar, the Bhimsen Temple, and the temple of a thousand Buddhas, the Mahabouddha. The Royal Palace was under restoration, but the Austrian architect in charge allowed me a peep inside. This was enough to convince me that I had to return to Patan. I left the city with my little bronze god tucked safely in a pocket.[1]

I couldn't pronounce it, but I wanted to see the Buddhist temple of Swayambhnath in the nearby town of Bhaktapur, so the car and driver were engaged for the following morning. We parked near another Dunbar Square, and I walked down Pig Alley by the pie shops and across a footbridge over a stream to the base of a hill, where the temple could be viewed through a steady, unforgiving rain. It was somewhat reminiscent of the Sacre Coeur in Paris, but without the painters. I started the climb up, then realized why this place was sometimes called the Monkey Temple. These acrobatic animals had learned how to slide down the handrail and snatch bags from the pilgrims and visitors, vanishing into the undergrowth below. At the top and under the watchful eye of Buddha on the central stupa I viewed Katmandu to the west and the valley in every direction. Here, even smallpox had a goddess, Hariti, who stood overlooking visitors. Two Indian-style temples stood on either side of Swayambhunath. The rain, falling in sheets, forced me back down the hill where I ducked into a café and had curried rice, dal, and tea.

The rain had not ceased when I arrived back in Katmandu, but I was determined to get a glimpse of the city. At the Royal Palace I found myself in something called the Nasal Chowk, a courtyard leading to the nine-story Basantapur Tower, which I climbed for the view. I was the only visitor, so I sat down and dried out, then returned to the courtyard. I refreshed myself for the short walk to yet another Dunbar Square where my guidebook listed forty-eight sites to be visited, including eleven courtyards—or *chowks*. After New Delhi, Old Delhi, Patan, and Swayambhunath—and a ten-day trek coming up—was I ready for eleven chowks? Was I ready for Giovanni and Rose?

We met early the next morning and soon were on the light plane, a STOL, on our way westward between Katmandu and Pokara. To our

---

[1] The British Museum identified it as an early sixteenth-century image of the Nepali god, Bhairab.

north we could view the Annapurnas and Machhapuchhare Mountain ranges, snow covered and spectacular. The plane landed at a primitive airport near Pokhara, where we were required to obtain a trekking permit. As in most third world countries, three people were involved in a task that one could have easily done. But they did it with smiles on their faces—one of the many good characteristics I remember about the Nepali people.

Outside the terminal our five porters awaited, along with two guides and a cook. My porter introduced herself as Nani. This tiny woman was from the nearby village of Ghandruk and was of the Thakoli people. Many years in the sun had wrinkled her, and she appeared ageless, wearing long dangling earrings and two gold rings in her nose. On her forehead was a *tika*, a red spot made from some paste, indicating she was married.

The guide introduced himself as Dawa, which indicated that he was born on Tuesday, a Sherpa tradition of being named for the day of the week when born. He wore a colorful *topi*, a characteristic hat worn by most men in Nepal. I was surprised that we had a Sherpa guide, but in his broken English he explained that he was doing this during one of his rest periods—a time when he was not going to some great altitude. At three thousand meters, our altitude would be no challenge for him.

I felt somewhat embarrassed when Nani took my things, rearranged them, and hoisted them onto her back, along with a folded tent and some of her own possessions. We were off. The extra porters walked behind carrying the cooking stove, eating utensils, an extra tent, medical equipment, food, and water. We spread out and walked westward toward Ghandruk going by a smaller village, Chandrakot. Dawa gave me the honor of setting the pace, telling us that we would walk four miles on this afternoon.

Giovanni and Rose walked far behind, but not far enough that I could not hear the Italian singing. For the next week Giovanni would serenade us with arias, even the soprano arias from *La Bohème* and *Tosca*, between Italian love songs. Like a male mockingbird, Giovanni sang for his new bride. It was not unpleasant singing, but I could have easily done without it, preferring to hear the sounds of the mountains, the birds and the streams, or the clank of the bells from a heard of goats.

We trekked through the village of Hengja where we stopped to rest on a *chautara*, a stone platform built around a large tree. Dawa treated us to a Coca-Cola from the local store. We walked for another hour, then stopped for the evening. The porters pitched the tents while the cook, Prakash, built a fire and prepared supper—*dal*, a bean soup, *gurr*, a potato dish, and mutton stew. After supper Nani danced and sang around the campfire. I was suspicious that she had been fortified with hashish. As the evening wore on she became more and more animated, and Dawa joined her for the dancing as another porter pounded some primitive tambourine. Finally, we retreated to our tents for sleep. I dozed off but was awakened by the sound of Giovanni snoring. But I forgave him. Giovanni was on his honeymoon.

From this date onward I did not write in my diary but memories still persist. I remember a wedding procession which passed, walking southward between two remote villages. We observed the young man being carried toward his bride. He looked serene, dressed in a colorful *longhi* wrap around. He held an orange colored umbrella. His all-male troupe followed, each carrying or playing small bells, flutes, or percussion instruments. One carried a colorful prayer wheel. This contrasted with the pink and red rhododendrons, which bloomed on either side of the road like a stage set.

I remember other meals prepared by Prakash, especially his curried sautéed chicken cooked with yellow rice, okra, and long green beans cut into tiny strips. I remember a breakfast of paper-thin omelets strewn with slices of chilies, cilantro and onions. I remember his "French" toast prepared in a manner that would make a Parisian chef envious.

Nani appeared each morning fresh at daybreak. She was up early and helped Prakash find wood for the fire. I awoke the newlyweds most mornings. Giovanni always stretched like and old cat and said in his broken English, "Where am I?"

On our last day trekking we turned southwestward along a mountainous pathway in full bloom with red rhododendrons, then up an incline for the next hour or so, across a grassy moraine, and into a small village with a monument dedicated to six Gurkhas from the region who had been killed during World War II. Dawa read the inscription as children from the village gathered to look at us. In the afternoon we stopped at "Bhati," a teashop, in a village that had a factory selling Yak cheese. I encouraged Giovanni to buy some, convincing him that it was good for the voice. He obliged. Giovanni and Rose fell far behind, but I could still hear a distant aria. This singing helped me to recall the lines written by William Wordsworth two hundred years ago:

> *Oh blithe spirit!*
> *I hear thee and rejoice.*
> *Oh cuckoo! Shall I call the bird?*
> *Or but a wandering voice?*

We camped a few miles north of Pokhara in the darkness of the early evening. We had a new name for Giovanni. We called him "Cuckoo," and I taught Nani to say "Cuckoo." That evening she dedicated a dance to him. It was her last evening, and she danced on and on. I wrote out the poem so that Dawa could quote Wordsworth. On that last morning, I was up early, having been roused by the temple bells of the nearby village. Dawa got up, yawned, and said that we were on Pun Hill, renowned for its views of Nepal. Through a pine thicket I watched the sun rising and reflecting off the snows of the Annapurna Mountain range. A herd of goats walked in single file toward the north. I could hear the tinkle of bells. Soon we would be back in "civilization," the world of airports, jets, schedules, stockmarkets, and three-pieced suits. I savored the peace, the view, the memories of the past ten days, and the smiling faces of the Nepali. I waited for the others to awaken for breakfast. I waited for one last auria from Giovanni.

THE ROAD TO MANDALAY—THE IRRAWADDY RIVER

Come you back to Mandalay,
where the old Flotilla lay:
Can't you 'ear their paddles chinkin'
from Rangoon to Mandalay,
On the road to Mandalay
Where the flyin'—fishes play,
An' the dawn comes up like thunder outer
China 'crost the Bay!
—Rudyard Kipling

I accepted an invitation to go to the Edinburgh Festival as a guest of Peter McMillin who lived there. At the time, I had no idea that this trip would lead me to Burma and to the "Road to Mandalay."

Peter and I attended several events; the most memorable being the Tattoo performed on the grounds of the old castle by the Royal Scots Guards. As expected in Scotland, this took place in the pouring rain. On the last evening we attended a performance of Eugene O'Neill's *The Ice Man Cometh*. Seated beside us were Paul Strachen and his young Spanish wife, Rosa, and at intermission we chatted. As we left the theatre he handed me his card and said that he was organizing tours of Burma, suggesting I might be interested. Indeed I was interested! I had read that this was "Visit Myanmar" year and the time to go.[2]

After returning to London, I called him at his home in Sterling, a suburb of Edinburgh. I learned that Paul had grown up in Burma, as his father had been a hydroelectric engineer for the Burmese government. He had become an authority on this country, learned its history, spoke the language, and written books on Burma. He didn't approve of some of the things the military government had done, but recognized

---

[2.] Burma is now known as Myanmar.

positive aspects of this form of rule and has had successful dealings with the government. He told me that he had purchased the rights of the Irrawaddy Flotilla Company, founded in 1865, and fifty years later had six hundred fifty vessels on the Irrawaddy, becoming the world's largest privately owned fleet. This company was now reduced to only a name, as the bulk of this fleet was sunk in an act of defiance when Japanese troops invaded Burma in 1942. Current negotiations for him to raise and restore one of these flotilla vessels near Prome had proceeded well with the Government of Myanmar. In November, he would be taking *RV Pandow* on the Irrawaddy River for its maiden cruise. I agreed to join twenty-five others for this voyage.

I flew from London to Bangkok where I joined a Myanmar Air flight to Rangoon. Ko Yu, a representative of Paul's company, met me at the air terminal for the drive to the ultra modern Inya Lake Hotel. I would have preferred the old Victorian-era Savoy Hotel, which had reopened, but Paul did not recommend it. On the drive through Rangoon it was apparent that the city was a contrast of old and new. Giant cranes lifted steel to the top of tall buildings that were under construction. Beside these buildings were dilapidated houses whose occupants, a half-century ago, had experienced the wrath of Japanese occupation. There were few traffic lights, but white-gloved policemen directed the onslaught of bicycles and an occasional car. Rarely was the military in evidence. Ko Yu spoke perfect English and did not search for words. He was an architectural student at the University of Rangoon, but the school had been closed in the aftermath of a recent demonstration against the military. Ko Yu had been one of the student leaders, although his father was a colonel in the army. He had a brother and sister who were physicians—he told me that they kept quiet about the country's leadership.

I had arrived two days earlier than the remainder of the group and Ko Yu agreed to meet me the following morning for a tour of Rangoon. We first stopped to visit the Shwedagon Pagoda, situated on Singuttura Hill near the heart of the city. We started to climb this hill, and I sat down half way up to rest. A fortuneteller came along and Ko Yu negotiated with him about what he would charge to tell my fortune while I sat looking at the pilgrims climbing up toward the pagoda. The elderly prophet said that I would live to be eighty-six years old, I paid less attention when he said that I had two wives and had fathered eight children. Ko Yu handed him a dollar.

As we continued to climb, Ko Yu explained that this Buddhist temple or *stupa* was twenty-five hundred years old and was the depository of eight hairs from the head of the Buddha. Pilgrims came here from all over Burma to pay their respects. We walked by bazaars near the *stupa*'s entrances, which had an assortment of things—lotus blossoms, incense, paper flowers, kites and candles—to be purchased by these pilgrims. We walked on around the golden-domed stupa, stopping at some of the planetary birth posts where pilgrims sat meditating, as monks dressed in long maroon robes, called *antaravaskas*, walked among them. Ko Yu told me about the *Hti* high on top of the *stupa*'s pinnacle. This "weather vane" surmounts the golden dome, where its gold and silver bells are studded with rubies, sapphires, and topaz. The orb above is encrusted with diamonds, crowned with one whose weight is seventy-six carat. We walked on by *zayats* and *tazaungs*, small pavilions and resting places redolent of incense and lotus blossoms. As we proceeded back down the steps Ko Yu quoted from Somerset Maugham, saying that this author likened this pagoda to "sudden hope in the dark night of the soul."

We stopped at Scott's Market, a large bazaar that reminded me of the great bazaars of Istanbul and Cairo—except that in Rangoon, native jade was available at affordable prices. Ko Yu took me back through a labyrinth to find yellow silk, which I purchased to take back to London.[3]

On the way to the hotel, we drove down University Avenue, passing the guarded home of the world's most famous "house prisoner," Aung San Suu Kyi. Ko Yu had few positive comments about her and said that she was not the answer to the country's political problems.

On the following morning the group met in the dining room of the hotel for breakfast and soon we were on a flight to Mandalay. Just south

---

[3.] Ko Yu grew up in Georgetown, Washington where he had gone to private school, while his father was an ADC at the Burmese Embassy and is now finishing his architectural studies at the University of Arizona.

of Mandalay we first glimpsed the wide Irrawaddy River and the *RV Pandaw* lying at anchor. We boarded the flat-bottomed ship, which had originally been constructed in Clyde, Scotland, years ago. Its sixteen staterooms had been renovated, and we had the good fortune to be on this maiden voyage in an atmosphere of pre-war steamers, which had been used by a succession of Princes of Wales and Viceroys of India. The handsome Burmese crew greeted us for tea in the stateroom adorned with teak and brass. The atmosphere and character of the old Viceregal flagship had been revived.

Later in the morning, as myriads of children gathered along the banks and stood gawking, we met on the open deck for Paul Strachen's lecture on this great river. Here is a summary of what he said:

> The Irrawaddy River, as vital to Burma as the Nile is to Egypt, has its headwaters northward in Tibet from the Mali Nmai River. It flows southward for fifteen hundred miles. First it foams, swirls and defiles past Bhamio, then Mandalay and just southward receives the Chindwin River where it widens to three or four miles. It then empties into the delta at the Bay of Bengal near Rangoon, two hundred miles south. At many places the Irrawaddy is only three feet deep and its bed is constantly changing. Along its banks are villages, each with multiple gold-domed Buddhist pagodas, which are lit at night with strings of small white lights, like Christmas decorations. Sometimes these *stupa*s outnumber the houses in these villages.

The following morning, before commencing the river voyage, we went into Mandalay, a city of a two million and 200,000 monks. It was surprising to learn that this city is Victorian, having been constructed by King Mindon in the 1850s. He moved his court here and most of the elaborately carved teak buildings from the former capital of Amarapura. His kingdom was to be short-lived as the British annexed the city along with Upper Burma, converting the Royal Palace to Fort Bufferin in the 1880s.

We drove by the palace, which was under reconstruction to repair damage by Allied bombing during World War II. Its former splendor was still in evidence. On the Royal Palace's northeast corner our vans were parked so that we might climb Mandalay Hill to view the city. We walked by the impressive Shweyattaw Pagoda, then past the kitschy Kyaukdawgyi Pagoda to the hill's top from whence we had a splendid view of the city, the moated Royal Palace and the Shan Plateau to the west. Our faithful Ko Yu was there and explained that after several attempts by the British to recapture this fortified hill during World War II, the Nepali Gurkhas were called in and did the job.

In the evening we drove back into the city for a Chinese meal. It was said to be the most authentic Chinese food away from China. No Burmese native was seen that evening as the city had been taken over by the Chinese who had bought Burmese citizenship—recycled identities of deceased Burmese. Mandalay had become a Chinese city—they owned it.

During the course of the next ten days we traveled down the Irrawaddy River with the sights to captivate a Westerner's imagination. At Ava the boat encountered a sand bar and we were forced to spend the night stuck in the mud. I got up early the next morning and at daybreak sat on the open deck and watched the line of young women carrying bricks balanced on their heads from a brick factory to a waiting boat. They moved like ants, winding their way toward the vessel, always smiling and appearing embarrassed. Some carried babies on their hips—back and forth, back and forth. At dusk they were still carrying bricks—fourteen balanced on their heads. Ko Yu said their pay would be equivalent to $1.50 per day. Between Ava and Bagan we passed lines of boats with rotor paddles raising sand to be sifted for gold. There were lines of barges loaded with teak wood—floating villages several hundred yards long, on their way to docks in Rangoon. We passed small fishing vessels, each flying a Buddhist flag but rarely saw a fish being caught.

On the eastern shore of the Irrawaddy River we stopped at Bagan, better known as Pagan, to see one of the most remarkable archaeological sights in Southeastern Asia. Ko Yu and I left the group and went on our own to the top of Ananda Pagoda where we sat at dusk viewing the twenty square miles of abandoned pagodas—three thousand pagodas and temples in ruins, all a thousand years old. It seems that the place was abandoned after the invasion of the Mongol emperor Kublai Kahn in the thirteenth century. The earthquake of 1975 completed the destruction. In the late afternoon this sight was eerie as we sat quietly and looked out over hundreds and hundreds of terracotta colored brick structures, standing like tombstones, stark and ghostly. It was difficult to imagine that a thousand years ago this place was teeming with humanity. Now there are only western tourists.

The *RV Pandaw* sailed on southward the following morning. At Pokokku, while we waited for the local dancers from the "opera" to board, I tried to buy a Buddhist flag from a small boat that had tied alongside. I tried to communicate via sign language and was invited aboard, the owner thinking, to my consternation, that I wanted a cruise on the river. We sailed off across the Irrawaddy while I tried to relax. I took out a pen and drew a picture of the flag. I bought it for a few *kyat* and we sailed back to the *RV Pandaw* just in time for the opera. The troop performed *Zat* and *Pwe* involving music, dance and acrobatics. (The colorful flag is now in my collection on Pawleys Island.)

We visited an archeological site near the little village of Hmawza. Here I bought candy to give to the many children who had gathered to look at us and to touch us. Delicately some touched, then withdrew and giggled. Each had dabs of white paint on their faces, in designs made from sandalwood paste and placed there for their complexion. One little boy caught my attention. He appeared about four years old and stood apart from the others, sucking a thumb. He wore a red baseball cap, bright crimson plastic boots and a T-shirt, naked below. The shirt was inscribed, "Duke University Blue Devils." I took his photograph.

On Sunday morning I walked around the town of Aunglan. There I met a physician and his handsome family. They invited me into their primitive home, insisted that I have a seat, then served me warm Pepsi Cola. The doctor showed me black and white photographs of his aristo-cratic-looking grandparents. I gave them the only thing I had on me, a ball point pen. They admired it and seemed pleased.

On Monday we sailed toward Prome for most of the day. I sat on the deck and talked with Ko Yu about Burma's religion, its Buddhism. As most boys in Burma, he had been a monk as a child, and he talked of his initiation day, *shinbyu*, a day set by astrologers that he remembered as the most important day of his life. He recalled the silks his family had dressed him in, the neighborhood parade and the family feast afterwards. But most vividly he remembered having his hair cut and his head shaved and putting on the crimson robe that evening. He was a novice and went off to the monastery the following day. This crimson robe would change to white for three months. Like most Burmese youths, this monastic life didn't last—in two years he had taken off the *ultarasanga*, the robe. But Ko Yu had a calmness and gentleness which was instilled into him as a monk, and this would serve him well for the remainder of this life.

In every village we observed these expressionless young monks going from house to house with their lacquer alms bowls, begging then bowing as they received food offerings. There is a phrase in Burma, *thapeik hmauk*, which means, "turning the alms bowl upside down." These monks have periodically done this in defiance against the military rule—they have gone on hunger strikes. Presently there is an uneasy truce between the authorities and the monks which we noticed at the monastery north of Prome, where military commanders and their wives were hosting a noon meal for a thousand monks. One could sense tension in the air. But these military leaders realized that the monastery is the focal point in these villages, that the monks are the respected community leaders, that they are healers, counselors and teachers. Without the monastery and the monk, there would be chaos.

I left the *RV Pandow* in Prome and took a long bus ride back to Rangoon where I flew to Pnom-Penh in Cambodia. I tolerated this depressing city for two days before I could get a flight to Siem Reap, near Angkor Wat. I was met at the small airport by an English-speaking guide and car and spent two more days visiting this great temple of the Khmer rulers. Here I saw no other people except an occasional monk.

What I remember most about Cambodia is Pnom-Penh, with

myriads of human beings with one or another limb missing, filling the streets—victims of land mine explosions. But also the solitary beauty of the thousand-year-old Angkor Wat, which had been discovered in the late nineteenth century, buried in the jungle. Once this was home to a million people, but now it is inhabited only by squawking parrots and monkeys. On the way back to Siem Reap we stopped at a market place where the driver bought dried snake, a Cambodian delicacy which he purchased for his father's birthday.

The following year I went back to Burma and joined the *RV Pandaw II* for a cruise up the Chinwin River. From Burma I went on to Sri Lanka. But that's another story which deserves telling . . . someday.

AN AUTUMN VOYAGE ALONG TURKEY'S ANCIENT CARIAN COAST

*O*ur Turkish schooner, *Kemal Reis*, riding the early October breeze like a narrow eucalyptus leaf, sailed eastward between the Turkish mainland and the Greek island of Kos.

Flying fish welcomed us into the mouth of the Bay of Gokova, while rays of the late afternoon sun glanced off the gleaming stern, mirroring nautical reflections that have been cast in these Aegean waters for more than four thousand years. This was a voyage to a niche of the ancient world steeped in history. After the fall of Troy this coastline saw the Greek migrations—first the Aeolians and later the Ionians, who came to explore and to build cities. In due course it saw some of the splendor of Imperial Rome.

Now here in southwest Turkey all that remains are the encrusted, half-buried shells of these ancient places scattered along a rugged coast-line, defined by headlands, bays, and myriad islets and islands. We five friends, four Americans and a German, had chartered a *gulet*, a fine boat of a type built for many years here, just east of Bodrum. For two weeks our home would be the *Kemal Reis,* a modern schooner but not entirely unlike the Greek boats that ploughed these waters twenty-five hundred years ago. Admittedly, no Greek had a twelve-litre turbo-charged Caterpillar engine to augment the three sails, but vessels then would have been of this size, this shape, and constructed of similar Aegean pine wood. The Greeks, of course, did not have ten double cabins with bathrooms and showers either.

Kaptan Ugur, with an unpronounceable surname, was in command of the *Kemal Reis,* which was named in honor of his father, a Bodrum sea captain who ferried daily passengers to Kos. With trimmed raven-black hair and mustache, Captain Ugur attended the wheel dressed in white Bermuda shorts and armless blue and white striped shirt. When he spoke in broken English he conveyed an impression that left no doubt as to who was in command. Eighteen-year-old Ilyas, the mate, was on his last voyage before being conscripted into the Turkish army. That first afternoon he arranged tea on the afterdeck, but "tea" turned out to be thick Turkish coffee served with *baklava,* flaky nut pastry soaked with honey. Only the faint-hearted ask for coffee Americana or Nescafe as the Turks call it. When we boarded, Ali the cook was already in the galley preparing dinner, peeling and slicing aubergines and cutting the strings from emerald green string beans with the precision of an Istanbul surgeon. Ali's kitchen is no greasy spoon. The oil in the galley is from the olive and in its virginal, first-press edition. His basil is not dried. It is pinched from a live plant growing in a container in the galley. There is a superstition in Turkey that a basil plant brings good luck to a boat.

We travellers were fortunate to come to Turkey's coast in the autumn, just before these schooners enter their winter cocoons. In the autumn the sun still shines warmly but the nights are cool enough for prolonged sleeping. Remote bays and coves appear lonely and the ancient marble ruins are climbed only by goats and a very few lucky people.

The *Kemal Reis* slid into a secluded bay off Orak Island. Kaptan Ugur quickly changed his Bermuda shorts for a red and blue diving suit, armed himself with a spear gun and went snorkelling for octopus, attended by Ilyas rowing a dinghy. From the wheelhouse Ali watched with binoculars for indications of a catch, while we treated ourselves to a first swim in the translucent Aegean. After about an hour there were signals from Ilyas that the prized octopus had been caught. Ali made ready a skillet with olive oil, garlic, aromatic herbs and spices, and changed the menu from lamb *sis kebab* to sauteed octopus.

Before boarding the *Kemal Reis* for our two-week adventure, we had spent the morning in Bodrum, its home port. Bodrum is this city's modern name, but to the romantic it is still Halicarnassus, that opulent Carian city of the Persian Empire, which was founded over three thousand years ago and which stood until it was destroyed by the eastward advancing armies of Alexander the Great. Halicarnassus, the Greek colony which could boast that Herodotus, the father of history, was born within its confines and which was the site of one of the Wonders of the Ancient World. When listing these wonders, I may forget the great library at Alexandria or the Temple of Zeus at Olympia, but I never seem to forget the Mausoleum of Halicarnassus. This ancient monument rose some fifteen stories high to honor King Mausolus, the Persian satrap-governor of Caria who ruled here about 350 BC. This extraordinary tomb's patron builder, Artemisia II, was the wife *and* sister of King Mausolus. Without this monument the English language would lack the word "mausoleum."

Halicarnassus took its place in the annals of ancient history not only for the interest of King Mausolus and his wife-sister, but for what might be called the "Mausolus Family Act," which played to a full house for decades in the glorious days of the city. The five brothers and sisters of this family ruled as governors of the whole of Caria. Upon the death of King Mausolus, his replacement was his queen, who like her namesake, Artemisia I, made an indelible mark on naval history here in the Bay of Halicarnassus when, under her directives, the Carian military cleverly captured the entire navy of Rhodes. Artemisia II sailed with it back to Rhodes to flaunt her victory while her masons at home were erecting the tomb dedicated to her deceased husband. After Artemisia died, her younger sister, Ada of Alinda, became the reigning monarch and married her brother, Idrieus. Paradoxically, they assisted Alexander the Great in the destruction of their own family city. Ada even offered to adopt the young invader. Then the last member of the family, younger brother Pixadoros, came on stage, but it was too late. From his older brother's tomb, Pixadoros could have stood and looked out over a virtually ruined and flattened city. The curtain had fallen on the family act and the theater of Halicarnassus had closed. But that memorable tomb stood for over a thousand years—too big even for Alexander the Great's army to destroy. That could only be done by a fourteenth-century earthquake. Eventually most of the fallen marble blocks and columns of the tomb were carted away under the auspices of the Knights of St. John to build here in Halicarnassus one of the most formidable of the crusader bastions, St. Peter's Castle.

In Bodrum we had two hours before setting sail in which to find and explore the site of Mausoleus's tomb. On the way there we walked through the bazaar — an alley-way crowded with brass, spices, and carpets. We bargained for a pair of carpet-like sandals with curled-up leather toes which, no doubt, a local would never consider wearing. We walked along the waterfront lined with colorful *gulets* and then up a narrow incline toward the minaret of a mosque and on to *Turgutereis Caddasi*, a street straight out of the Middle Ages. Among the closely-huddled stone and brick shops was the Tamair coffee house where, in mid-morning, men sat in a smoke-filled room playing dominoes and watching a televised soccer football match. An old, unshaven man dressed in baggy black trousers and a smart, black-billed cap leaned against the doorway of the coffee shop with a long string of amber worry beads in his hands. Across the little street, a hardly noticeable sign on a white stone wall read, *Mausolos Muzesi*. This marked the entrance to the remains of what was once one of the Wonders of the Ancient World.

The attendant hardly looked at us as we each paid the 1000 Turkish lira (about 25¢). He was too busy waving his arms and chattering to a friend who sat nearby. We walked into the enclosure and to our right gazed down some twenty feet into a rectangular cavern. We went down the steps into its pit, disturbing several unfriendly gray cats, a red rooster and three hens, who evidently lived here in the midst of Ionic capitals, great marble blocks and drums of fluted columns. One other tourist joined us as we approached a weathered and faded sign pointing toward a deeper recessed pit. It read in Turkish and English, "*Mavsolos Un Mezar*" — "Mausolo's Tomb Chamber." As we looked into the eroded and empty pit, another gray cat scampered out of its carpet of weeds.

We were silent leaving the site. The attendant was still talking and gesturing and across the street the old man still leaned against the coffee house clutching his worry beads. I thought of the legend that Artemisia drank red wine laced with her husband's ashes. Had she seen what her husband's tomb is like today, she might have preferred the bitter-sweet tea of the oleander.

That evening, as we awaited our meal, Ali brought us chilled glasses of Tryka white wine and shortly afterwards announced "*sadir*," a word we soon learned meant "supper." That first supper aboard the *Kemal Reis* was as memorable as the next ten. Ali provided a first course of cur-ried creamed vegetable soup followed by sauteed octopus, aubergines and tomatoes simmered in oil and fresh basil, green beans, and *coban salatasi*, a salad of cucumber, sweet pepper, onion and tomato in a yoghurt and fresh mint sauce. The dessert was simple: succulent pome-granates.

Adjourning to the foredeck, we were greeted by the Milky Way spread like sea foam above us and punctuated by an occasional shooting star. Jupiter rose on the eastern horizon and with good binoculars we could just see the planet's four little moons. Afterwards, in comfortable cabins, we were nudged into sleep by the rhythmic beat of the halyard against the mast.

The following morning, continuing eastward, we sailed by the vil-lage of Oren into Gokova Bay and stopped to swim in the shadow of ancient Keramos. Later, we anchored in the shelter of Cape Akbu, and were pleased and not surprised that another *gulet* had found this seclusion for the night's anchorage. Next day we crossed the bay to Sedir Island, which Kaptan Ugur first circled and then approached in stately manner, much as Cleopatra's Egyptian boat must have done when she came to this charming, secluded island to pay court to Mark Antony. Here she wooed him on her own sand for, according to legend, she had shipped Sahara sand here on barges. As we did, she and the Roman general may well have sat in one of the rows of the ruined Greek amphitheatre — ruined even in Cleopatra's day. We contemplated the uprooted marble stage floor and olive trees growing between the stone seats. Before Ilyas rowed us back to our boat, we swam in the picturesque cove and then sat for a few minutes basking in the sun on Cleopatra's sand.

In the late afternoon we tied up at the village of Karaca Sogut alongside a yacht flying a German flag and two other *gulets*, whose crews welcomed us as we disembarked. This is a vacation village and, with the summer season over, was abandoned except for a coffee house, where the cheerful owner challenged us to a game of backgammon. He swiftly beat our most accomplished player and we learned that backgammon is the Turkish national pastime. On our walk back along narrow streets bedecked with bougainvillaea and hibiscus, we gathered wild flowers for the dining table and ripe pomegranates hanging from trees along the empty streets. After dinner the boats' crews sat in close groups on the boardwalk, singing to the accompaniment of a strange-sounding percussion instrument. Their singing became louder and more pulsatingly tribal as they drank *raki*, a native spirit, which is distilled from aniseed but is oddly reminiscent of Tennessee moonshine whiskey.

The following morning we were met by a pre-arranged taxi, which would take us the fifty miles across Dachta Peninsula for a day's visit to Dalyan and the site of Caunus on the northern border of ancient Lycia. From Seyut Bay we were driven on a steep winding road into the pine-scented hills past rocky outcroppings, which looked like the mountains in Japanese scroll paintings, and past rows and rows of pastel-blue square bee hives. The road flattened out gradually and we drove through acacia trees and eucalyptus groves. An old woman dressed in black was busy in the early morning sun shaking her olive tree and we passed three school-boys, dressed in neat blue cotton suits and neckties, who waved and shouted greetings. We still had about an hour's drive to reach Dalyan. At the town wharf we paid a few lira to lease a caique for the river journey down the Dalyan delta to Caunus. While boarding we could already see Dalyan's legendary Lycian rock tombs cut into the cliff facing the delta. Our efficient boatman, Yalmiz, an architecture student in his spare time, sped us along the river and then more slowly through tall reed groves, where we flushed purple kingfishers and interrupted the feeding of the ubiquitous great blue herons. Ibis flew overhead as we floated past the gates of a fishery that supplies grey mullet to the town. The boat followed a sinuous path through an even taller thicket of bullrushes before we finally reached the derelict remains of Caunus.

Yalmiz escorted us up the hill, past the circular foundation of a Roman temple, to a Greek amphitheater tucked into the slope of a hillside. We moved on to the impressive miniature Caracalla-like baths and then to the remains of a Byzantine church. Within an hour we had been ushered through three of the ancient cultures which had flourished here. Returning to the uppermost half-circle of the old theater, we looked out over the nothingness of ancient grandeur, then beyond to the vast expanse of reed beds in the delta, once the site of a thriving bay filled with ships. Beneath these reeds, perhaps, lay the fossilized shadows of ships from Crete. According to Herodotus, the early Caunians traced their roots to this land of King Minos.

Back in Dalyan we climbed the rock cliff to view more closely the two horizontal rows of Lycian tombs, which were carved like pinkish-yellow cameos into the limestone rock facings. We ascended a narrow path past beds of wild herbs, asphodel and tamarisk trees to come within feet of the facades of these burial places sculpted in the Ionic style.

Before driving back to Karaca Sogut we joined Yalmiz at his favorite *lokanta*, a Turkish cafe, where in the early afternoon by the waterside we ate a simple lunch of *coban salatasi* with soft white cheese and crusty bread. As an out-of-tune marching band played in the distance, we toasted Yalmiz with a glass of Efes beer and said our good-byes.

Towards the end of our first week we cruised westward along the southern coast of the Bay of Gokova adjacent to the Datcha Peninsula, or Triopium, as it was known to the Greeks. This peninsula, with its rugged hills and cliffs, juts out like a gnarled finger separating the Aegean from the Mediterranean.

We were nearing the peninsula's westward reaches and heading towards Knidos on a windy overcast day and were reminded of the apostle Peter's arrival here on a similar stormy day as he was being ferried to Rome as a prisoner. The vessel transporting him was delayed here and then went on to be wrecked somewhere westward.

We were more fortunate. Near Takir Point, on the peninsula's tip, two sails were hoisted to give stability as we cruised under Takir lighthouse perched precariously above. The *Kemal Reis* churned southward into the Mediterranean, then east into an old seaway that at one time was one of the busiest water thoroughfares in the world. Suddenly the sun broke through and the sea calmed. A pair of dolphins, loping up and down like carousel animals in front of our boat, welcomed us to Cape Kiro and into the great harbor. There above us lay the time-ravaged ruins. Knidos, once renowned for its sculpture, its medical school and its wine industry, was home to seventy thousand people. Today, only a custodian and three *lokanta* owners live here.

Ilyas rowed us ashore and tied up at a great rectangular block that lay at the edge of the harbor, a few feet below the ancient Greek Amphitheater from our mooring stone. Near the theater, Ahmet, the official custodian, dressed in a faded black uniform and cap, waved eagerly from the porch of his little white-washed stone house. He joined us at the *lokanta* while we fortified ourselves with Turkish Coffee and then motioned us proudly toward the great hill of ruins.

We started the long ascent and only then could we begin to comprehend the extravagant extent of the remains of Knidos. Up and up the zig-zag slope we trudged, meeting only two other tourists and a flock of black goats clambering over white marble blocks of architectual components. We stopped at an ancient sundial, supposedly erected by Eudoxus, a native of Knidos, who designed the first observatory. Higher on the hillside we reached the remarkable circular temple foundation, which was excavated by the archaeologist Iris Love and an American team in the 1960s and where the sculpted figure of Aphrodite once stood. Miss Love was enterprising and controversial. She proceeded from there to the British Museum to sort through Newton's finds, among which she discovered a marble female head which she maintained belonged to Praxiteles's Aphrodite housed, headless, in the Louvre. This claim was never substantiated and the head still lies in the dark basement of the British Museum.

A quarter of the mile higher up we could see the perfectly preserved Hellenistic city wall on the hill's crest extending like the long, low back fin of a dragon. Looking back we could see the grid plan of the terraced narrow streets below, laid out like an inclined checkerboard. To the west lay the silted naval and military harbor and to the south the one-time island that completes the crescent of Knidos. Resting on the foundation stone of the Temple of Aphrodite, we thought about Knidos at its zenith, when the colony's city council was progressive enough to commission from the Athenian sculptor, Praxiteles, a nude statue of their patron goddess, Aphrodite. It was no ordinary Greek female figure. Even Pliny, the authority on everything, called it "the finest statue in the world." Praxiteles's goddess was based on his shapely courtesan mistress, Phryne. It is recorded that she made a point (or perhaps two points) with an Athenian judge when she appeared in a court case and displayed her bare breasts. This nude sculpted goddess put Knidos on the tourist map.

Dismissing thoughts of Aphrodite, we scrambled down toward the amphitheater, past innumerable vertically excavated shafts of pottery shards — the kitchen dumps unearthed by Iris Love's team. By the remains of the sanctuary of Demeter, we stopped to view the basin of the Great Harbor, where in the late afternoon shadows, our white *Kemal Reis* bobbed, toy-like. It seemed that Knidos would have a crowd tonight, for another *gulet* had sailed in. Now we were a flotilla of two.

That evening we treated our crew to a supper of red mullet in the *lokanta*. It was a special occasion as Selim, the proprietor, was entertaining his three grandchildren, who had arrived from Dachta. Several fish-loving cats joined the family feast, but they went unnoticed by the old patriarch, who was busy sawing sour oriental chords on his battered violin.

On the final day of our Utopian voyage we were treated to one last special surprise by Kaptan Ugur. Near Bodrum we anchored just off volcanic Black Island and were rowed to one of its several gaping cave openings. We swam far into the warmth of a thermal stream, into an ebony-black watery catacomb, before returning to daylight and to the world.

The next morning in Bodrum a van awaited under the gangplank to take us back to Izmir for our return home. We reluctantly disembarked and then embraced and said goodbye to our Kaptan, to Ilyus and to Ali. They responded with an old Turkish farewell, "*Gule, gule,*" which means, "Go with a smile." We went with smiles, with waves and with a vow to return the following year to sail farther south along the ancient Lycian coast aboard the *Kemal Reis.*

BEHIND THE IRON CURTAIN

*J*ohn Nelson, the maestro and music director of the Indianapolis Symphony, was invited to come to East Germany to become the first American conductor to lead the Leipzig Gewandhaus Orchestra, one of the most historic and renowned symphonies in Europe. I could not resist John's invitation to visit during his stay.

West Berlin

I flew from London to West Berlin in late January 1987 and found that Berlin had not fully recovered from the war. The city appeared forlorn, dismal, and depressingly buried in deep snow, which had turned grey from coal smoke and soot. The city had been leveled from bombing and was built back in the German "modern" style of architecture—boxes set side by side. The Hotel Knot where I stayed was one such box. My room was on the fifth floor, where I looked out through gauze-like curtains toward the Berlin Wall a mile away. The small room was sparsely furnished. It lacked warmth.

This late Saturday afternoon I walked a mile to the opera house to purchase a ticket to hear "Il Trovatore." The ticket office was closed until the evening. I went back to the hotel and donned jogging attire and ran for three miles on the icy sidewalks. That evening I returned to the opera house and for $15 purchased their best ticket. Both inside and out, the opera house looked like a gymnasium, but the fine quality of the performance compensated. The audience was handsome and better dressed that the usual opera goers at London's Royal Opera House. As expected, the Germans took their opera seriously.

I had only the following morning to visit West Berlin, and joined a small tour bus that came by the hotel. The Reichstag on this cold Sunday morning was memorable, with schoolboys playing soccer on its vast lawn of trampled snow. All was quiet except for the thump of the football and the yelling of the children. I stood in front of the gallery and remembered how Hitler had declared that he was Germany's Chancellor here in 1933. Through the archway and to the east I could see the shivering East German guards walking aimlessly.

The bus drove on to the Brandenberg Gate and again I recalled how Hitler had gone through these gates with the pomp of Emperor Augustus or Emperor Julius Caesar. But today nobody went through—it was on the line, its opening was fenced, it was a part of the Berlin Wall. The bus drove on to Potsdam Plaza, which at one time had been a busy, thriving and joyful central locale in Berlin, but now it was only a vacant and forlorn place. We left the bus and climbed to a platform for a view into East Berlin. Wind whipped across a snowy no-man's land dotted by periodic towers with peeping, cold GDR soldiers. Below us were the graves of East Germans who had been killed while trying to escape to the West.

We went on to Charlottenberg Palace, then visited the Egyptian Museum across the street. The prized bust of Nefertiti seemed not to have been affected by all this commotion of war. After thirty-five hundred years her face was still placid.

East Berlin

Back at the hotel I collected my bags, but was told that I could not get a taxi to the East German entry point—it was forbidden. I walked the mile to Fredrickstrasse Station on the underground and took a train that weaved its way through a labyrinth to the East. Alighting there, I purchased a visa and was inspected by several dismal unsmiling women, each reinspecting my visa, each being sure that I had purchased enough East German currency, from Western dollars. I exited the station and now faced chilling wind, blowing snow, and a long taxi queue. No taxi came. I talked with a Peruvian embassy official who stood in the line in front of me. She suggested that I should take the underground on to my hotel, then left her place in line to give directions. Presently a young German tapped me on the shoulder and said in perfect English, "Do you desire a taxi?"

In his Russian car, he identified himself as Dieter Beck and indicated that he was "moonlighting" on the weekends as an illegal taxi driver, trying to get enough western currency to purchase a television set at the "Interstore." He took me to the ultra modern Palace Hotel, gave me a telephone number and suggested that I call if I needed assistance—or a taxi. I gave him five dollars.

By now it was late and I had just enough time to get to the opera house around the corner where Mozart's *Figaro* was being performed by the East German State Opera Company. The opera was beautifully presented except for some of the singing. East Germany's best singers were in America and Britain earning their pay in dollars and pounds— their opera back home suffered vocally. But the restored opera house was a Baroque jewel and the audience matched, with ladies in long dresses and men in black ties. They looked better than their counterparts in West Berlin or London.

The next morning I ventured out to a "shopping center" where I saw long queues at each shop which had anything of significance to sell. One such shop had a "sale" of unpainted 8" x 10" wooden picture frames. I stopped and watched, as curious shoppers stood three-deep to inspect the twelve-dollar frames. Three young clerks waited, while not a frame was sold. In the afternoon I visited the Pergamon Museum to see the Greek Altar of Zeus, the Market Gate of Miletus and the Lion Gate and Processional Way to ancient Babylon. These treasures were worth the trip to East Berlin and its depressing madness.

Early in the evening I called Dieter Beck to come to the hotel and invited him to dinner, if he would take us to some local restaurant. He obliged and we drove to three gloomy places before one would accept us. Dieter explained that the government owned all the restaurants and they did not welcome diners. We finally found an eating place and were crowded into a table of young soldiers where we dined on pig's feet and kraut, washed down with beer. The café was thick with smoke and the smell of grease while western music played through the loud speakers.

On the way back to the hotel, Dieter told me of his plight. He had been a public relations official for East Berlin's Opera Komike and had been offered a similar position in West Berlin. On his way to the west in a diplomatic car, he was stopped by police and then served a two-year prison sentence. One of his main objectives had been to visit his teenaged daughter in West Berlin. Now he was working at various jobs—anything to obtain western currency for another planned escape. At midnight, as a final gesture, he took me to the railroad station to purchase a ticket for the trip to Leipzig, saying that tomorrow I would stand in line for hours to purchase such a ticket. At the station we walked through and around hundreds of young Africans lying on the cold concrete, awaiting a train to Moscow.

Leipzig

The following day I boarded the "Leipzig Express" for the four-hour ride through flat, monotonous countryside, snow-covered and desolate, and through villages seemingly abandoned. The cry of the whistle matched my feelings as I reflected on the last four days. The train sped through Luckenwalde and Wittenberg and crossed the Elbe. I was lulled to sleep, then awoke as we approached Europe's largest railroad station, twenty-six tracks in the heart of Leipzig. Around the corner, I checked into the Astoria Hotel, a thirty-story modern hotel with every convenience, including prostitutes. In the early evening, across the street, I met John and Anita Nelson in their hotel and we had dinner. What a breath of fresh air!

In the morning Anita and I took a taxi to the concert hall where John was rehearsing in the Gewandhaus Orchestra for a French program—Ravel, Lalo, and John Nelson specialty, Berlioz, his "Symphony Fantastique." After rehearsal we went to St. Thomas Church where John knelt beside the grave of Bach. He kissed the snow at the foot of the monument.

The following evening I attended John's concert with the Gewandhaus, along with eighteen hundred others, who packed into the hall. The evening went well and John returned for five curtain calls—and an invitation to return the following year.

In the morning, my alarm clock sounded and at daybreak I was at the train station for a trip to Dresden. Inside the great Victorian-era terminal the wind whipped through, blowing coal smoke and carbon monoxide inhaled by East German and Russian soldiers, peasants, businessmen and travelers. Wearing an old Russian fur hat and putting on a depressed expression, nobody gazed at me. I looked more like Dr. Zhivago than any of them. Finally, we cheated the winter cold and packed into the warm train for a ride southeastward, through Meissen, Grimme and Markleeburg, each buried in snow.

Dresden

In Dresden I walked to the front of the station and joined the long line awaiting the non-existent taxi. Standing in the deep snow I squirmed, stood on one leg and then the other, took deep breaths and hugged myself. My time for a taxi came an hour later. We crossed the frozen Elbe River—the skeletons of bombed buildings stood in the snow like old tombstones. The taxi driver left me at the Albertinium Museum, but a sign indicated that it was closed on Friday. I walked high above the Elba to the Porcelain Gallery. It too was closed. I stopped at an East German version of cafeteria and ate Ukrainian soup, then walked on to The Semper Gallery where I saw a Leonardo, Correggio's "La Notte," several Canalettos, and Giorgione's "Sleeping Venus," enough visual treats to reward me for a long difficult day—which was not over.

It was now 4:00 P.M. and I held a railway ticket to return to Leipzig an hour later. I asked a gallery official to call a taxi, but she indicated that this was not possible. So I walked hurriedly the two miles back along a path made in the snow, to the station and found no Leipzig train listed on the notice board. I was told at the information desk that there were no more trains going there on this day. I searched for, and found, an English-speaking businessman who told me to come with him on the 5:15 to Grimme where I could change trains and go on to Leipzig. During the wait, I watched passengers standing in long lines to buy bread and salami-like sausages, which they washed down with diluted orange drink. Then I boarded the train and made my way back to Leipzig.

The following morning I had breakfast with John and Anita before boarding a train for East Berlin. Officials from my hotel had arranged for a taxi to meet me at the station to take me from East to West Berlin and the air terminal, at the cost of sixty marks. The taxi driver recognized me—I had told the hotel clerk that I would be wearing a black fur hat, a red scarf and carrying a grey bag. In a Mercedes, the only one I had seen in the East, we sped toward checkpoint Charlie. The guards quickly looked under the hood, under the back seat and in the trunk. They didn't notice the person in the fur hat.

Before getting the bags from the trunk, the taxi driver presented me with a bill for 120 marks. I pleaded because I only had seventy marks left, then told him I could give a personal check, showing my nearly empty billfold. He seemed not to know what a personal check was, so I handed him the checkbook. He took his glasses off and held the blank checks close to his eyes, then nodded that this would be acceptable. I wrote a check and he unlocked the trunk.

The week's tribulations were not over. At the British Air counter I fumbled for my ticket back to London. It was missing. While the boarding announcement was being made, I quickly purchased another ticket for two hundred seventy-five pounds, equivalent to four hundred fifty dollars, using my American Express card. At the security checkpoint, the guard asked for eight marks for the airport tax. Now I only had two marks left, a relatively worthless amount. Then I remembered that I had two pounds change in a shaving kit. This would buy an underground ticket from Heathrow air terminal to Victoria. I would be left with twenty pence.

As the airplane taxied down the runway, I felt secure and clever. I had survived one week behind the Iron Curtain.

FLORENCE, THE CITY OF STONE

*T*he Christie Fine Art School in London was over and my appetite was whetted to learn more about the Tuscan Renaissance. The best place in Europe for such study was the British Institute of Florence where the lectures were in English. The idea of living in Florence also appealed to me. I had visited Rome and Florence previously, and I preferred Florence. Rome seemed too large, impersonal, and noisy. It has been said that all roads led to Rome, but as far as I was concerned, they also led out again and northward toward Florence. This city reminded me of someone's old dimly lit drawing room holding "Cabinets of Curiosities," Renaissance furniture and painted cassones in palazzos reached by narrow cobblestone streets.

But how was I to get into this school? Their classes were filled with students years younger than me and there was a waiting list. I received their application and it needed two endorsements. In London, I knew the former ambassador to Italy, Sir Ronald Arculus and he was on the board of Directors of the British Institute. Sir Ronald had introduced me to this school and gave me a letter of endorsement. The other came from Robert Cumming, head of the Christie Fine Art School. The application was submitted and, to my surprise, I was accepted for a two-month course.

The school's secretary called and asked if I would like to be a paying guest at the residence of an English-speaking widow of an Italian diplomat. I accepted this offer of housing when I learned that another British Institute student would also be staying there.

I arrived in Florence late in the afternoon and took a taxi to Piazza Donatello and met Contessa Maria Vittorie Grozzi. Having little to say, she showed me to a room that overlooked the square. On the desk there was a typewritten list of the "house rules" in English. These rules included such things as the hours when the water would be heated for a bath, instructions about double-locking the front door, the time of breakfast and the evening meal. There was a warning about the loudness of radio playing. Smoking was not mentioned. The Contessa kept a cigarette dangling from her lips at all times. I dined alone that evening since the other guest was not due to arrive until the following day.

The next day, a cold rainy February morning, I took a crowded bus from Piazza Donatello to fashionable Via Tornabuoni and walked past Guccis, past the Palazzo Strozzi, by Ferragamo and across from St. Triana I walked into the British Institute's premises in the thirteenth-century Palazzo Spini-Feroni. On the piano nobile, the high ceiling lecture hall engulfed me, but I took a seat in the old drawing room of Geri degli Spini, with twenty-three others: twenty-one young ladies, two young men, and me. I felt at home, as this was the ratio I had experienced at Christie's in London.

For the next eight weeks I was exposed to erudite lectures on Dante and Machivelli given in a gruff monotone by old Count Neri Capponi, a well-known Florence legal mind. When he lectured on the political conflicts between the fourteenth-century Guelphs and Ghibellines and sided with the latter, it became apparent that his direct ancestor had been Niccolo Capponi, who headed the Tuscan republic during the sixteenth-century. But the old count proved to be a most congenial Florentine when I got to know him better. His gruffness had melted. I dozed through Maria Fossi-Todorow's stony cold lectures on Brunelleschi, as this elderly doyenne's mind was as faded as her 1950 black and white slides of the Duomo. But the lectures by Marcello Bellini on Renaissance architecture and Susan Maddox's presentations on Benvenuto Cellini were as polished as the pearls on the goldsmith's salt cellar.

Terena Thompson, the secretary at the British Institute, didn't get rosettes in her purse for housing me with Contessa Grozzi. The old contessa ruled her domain on the Piazza Donatello with an iron fist. This was a residence where she sat all day in a dimly lit drawing room—it was without illumination because she sat cemented to a wine stained, overstuffed, mohair chair with the room's wooden shutters closed. Smoke billowed from her wrinkled mouth and from a pointed nose that had long ceased to smell. The contessa blew cigarette smoke toward a black and white television set while she was immersed in a flicker of Italian and Spanish soap operas and the television replied with mundane images aimed at her dwindling neural synapses. But she was alert enough to know the instant I left my room, for within a cigarette cough she was there to rearrange my desk and remind me that dinner was at eight o'clock. I tolerated this strange Florentine hostess only because of a fellow British Institute student, Andros Nicolaides, the Cypriot ambassador to Italy who had come to Florence to polish his Italian language. With cajolery, Andros was able to lighten the time we spent at dinner with this old lady, but I could not force myself to join in the banter. The only blessing I received there was the lasting friendship made with Ambassador Nicolaides, who later became Ambassador to the United States and eventually was my guest in South Carolina. After two weeks with

Contessa Grozzi, I leased my own residence closer to the British Institute.
There was much time in which to wander around the stony environs
of Florence—to walk along the ancient city wall, which had been
designed by Michelangelo, and up to the unfrequented Church of St.
Miniato al Monte on a hill overlooking the city. I joined friends for picnics in the Bobli Gardens behind the Pitti Palazzo or on the grassy lawn
of Fort Belvedere. I attended mass at St. Maria Novella, where under
Masaccio's fresco of the Virgin and St. John the Evangelist, I worshipped with only a dozen other people, while an old Dominican friar
played an electric organ. There was no choir here on ordinary Sundays—
it only sang on special occasions. More often I attended mass nearer my
residence at the Church of Santa Croce, where aloof Franciscan fathers
conducted a more formal and somber service. It seemed strange to walk
into this sanctuary and to immediately be confronted by tombs containing the bones of Michelangelo on the right and Galileo on the left, while
walking on tomb markers for Black Death victims. Regardless of the
weather outside, in this old damp church layers of clothes were needed
to keep warm. Usually I went early and took a seat adjacent to
Donatello's gilded limestone carving, "The Annunciation," and from
here I could see Giotto's frescoes of the apostles behind the altar. The
warmth of Donatello and Giotto was a stark contrast to the coldness of
the Franciscans, who seemed not to enjoy the mass or the surroundings.
Even the sparse elderly congregation seemed too cold and unconcerned
to express any joyful emotion. But then I had to remind myself that
these were Florentines, who by their nature did not show emotion over
church matters when it came to worship.

The Italian language was not a problem. I understood and could
speak a few words of Italian, but nobody ever knew this. I had no desire
to know what the Italians were chattering about although I had some
idea, as I observed their waving arms and watched their gestures. Had I
known exactly what they were saying it probably would have detracted
from the Puccini-like settings. No longer would it have been opera. No
longer would it have been *Gianni Schicchi.*

A highlight of this stay in Florence involved the visits of American and English friends, particularly Dr. Richard Howland, who had just retired from Smithsonian Institution. Dick was a scholar of the classics and had friends in Florence. He was as familiar with Florence as his own living room in Washington and we had pleasure roaming about—to the Bargello, the Pitti Palazzo and the Ufizzi and Academie, and to off-the-beaten-track places such as Michelangelo's Museum. I hosted a party in his honor for his old friends, my new friends, and British Institute faculty and students. I won't forget that evening, as the electricity failed while guests were arriving. We lit the old stairway with candles—and guests never knew that this had not been intended. Dick stood in my residence and by candlelight, chatted in three or four languages to guests, going easily from English to Greek to Italian. Dick was 80 years old! Sir Harold Acton, the English expatriate was one of the guests. This elderly aesthete invited us to his estate, La Pietra, two days later for lunch. But that's another story!

During my final week at the British Institute I gave the weekly Wednesday evening "Cultural Lecture." I called it "Arcadia, Mistress of Nineteenth-Century American Painters." This lecture evolved as I learned that Europeans generally had little knowledge about this period of American painting. As far as most were concerned, American art started with Jackson Pollock. Prior to him they knew little. Knowing that I was to give this lecture, I had gathered eighty-five colored trans-parencies of American nineteenth-century paintings from museums across this country. All of these painters had spent formative years of study in Italy. They included Washington Allston, Alfred Bierstadt, George Inness, Thomas Whithridge, Samuel Coleman, and Thomas Cole, who incidentally had painted the foremost panoramic view of Flo-rence during the nineteenth-century. There were thirty painters repre-sented in the lecture. For completeness, I added a few slides of works by Winslow Homer and Thomas Eakins, although they had not visited Italy. To my gratification, the hall was filled to capacity that evening. Later I accepted an invitation to give the same lecture to the Italian Cul-tural Institute in London.

My two-month stay in Florence had been memorable. But I was to return twice more, once to participate in an archaeology excavation beneath the Piazza della Signoria, and another time to organize and host "Eine Kleine Nachtmusik" to commemorate a Rossini anniversary. Utilizing music students from the academe, I presented a program at the Pallazo Perugi featuring Rossini—and Gershwin. Later that evening a black tie audience from Florence and Siena sipped champagne. I did speak some Italian later that evening!

Time like an ever rolling stream,

Bears all its sons away.

They fly forgotten,

As a dream dies at the opening of the day.

— Derived from Psalm 90